D0467474

Rebooting Justice

Rebooting Justice

MORE TECHNOLOGY, FEWER LAWYERS,

AND THE FUTURE OF LAW

Benjamin H. Barton & Stephanos Bibas

ENCOUNTER BOOKS

New York   London

First American edition published in 2017 by Encounter Books, an activity of Encounter for Culture and Education, Inc., a nonprofit, tax exempt corporation. Encounter Books website address: www.encounterbooks.com

Manufactured in the United States and printed on acid-free paper. The paper used in this publication meets the minimum requirements of ANSI/NISO Z39.48-1992 (R 1997) (*Permanence of Paper*).

FIRST AMERICAN EDITION

LIBRARY OF CONGRESS CATALOGING-IN-PUBLICATION DATA
Names: Barton, Benjamin H., 1969– author. | Bibas, Stephanos, author.
Title: Rebooting justice : more technology, fewer lawyers, and the future of law / by Benjamin H. Barton and Stephanos Bibas.
Description: New York : Encounter Books, 2017. |
Includes bibliographical references and index.
Identifiers: LCCN 2016058767 (print) | LCCN 2016059671 (ebook) |
ISBN 9781594039331 (hardback) | ISBN 9781594039348 (Ebook)
Subjects: LCSH: Justice, Administration of—United States. |
Law reform—United States. | Legal services—United States. |
Technology and law—United States. | BISAC: LAW / Courts. |
LAW / Criminal Law / General. | LAW / Civil Law. | LAW / Legal Services.
Classification: LCC KF384 .B374 2017 (print) | LCC KF384 (ebook) |
DDC 347.73—dc23
LC record available at https://lccn.loc.gov/2016058767

Contents

CHAPTER 1

Introduction

Fans of the podcast *Serial* will recall the story of this high school murder: On January 13, 1999, Baltimore teenager Hae Min Lee disappeared after high school and was later found strangled and buried in a park. The next year, her ex-boyfriend Adnan Syed was convicted of her kidnapping and murder and sentenced to life imprisonment. There was no physical evidence linking Adnan to Hae's murder, so at trial the State built its case on three main kinds of evidence: First, Adnan's acquaintance Jay testified that Adnan had told him in advance that he was going to kill Hae and that, after the killing, Jay had helped Adnan to bury Hae's body. Second, the State introduced cellphone call and location records that suggested that Adnan and Jay may have been together midafternoon on January 13 and that, the same evening, the cellphone was near the park where Hae was buried. Third, there was character evidence, some of which suggested that Adnan was angry about the breakup and was the kind of person who could have killed his ex-girlfriend. Also, Adnan offered no evidence to support an alibi or that he had tried to page Hae after she disappeared.[1]

But, as *Serial* fans will also recall, the State's case suffered from serious weaknesses. First, Jay had plenty of incentives to blame someone else to minimize his own punishment. Jay was a marijuana dealer who had had previous run-ins with the law. He repeatedly admitted, to police and to the jury, that he had lied about various facts to avoid blame or minimize punishment. By his own admission, he was involved in burying Hae's body, which made him at least an accessory to murder and warranted suspicion that he was the killer. As Jay admitted, the police detectives threatened to charge him with Hae's murder unless he implicated Adnan in the killing. Conversely, prosecutors offered him an extremely favorable plea bargain, under which he received only a suspended sentence and served no jail time. They also took the highly unusual step of getting him a specially selected private defense lawyer, perhaps to further his cooperation. And Jay kept changing details of his story, weakening its credibility.

Second, the cellphone call records conflicted with Jay's own time-line. Jay admitted Adnan had lent him his car and cellphone for much of the day, so the presence of the phone near the grave site might implicate Jay rather than Adnan. And the details of the midafternoon call do not line up with the testimony of the woman who received that call: She vaguely remembers a call close to the *evening*, and testified that it happened while Adnan was at a job that he did not get until two weeks later. Third, the character evidence was conflicting, no one had accused Adnan of any remotely similar crimes before, and character evidence alone hardly suffices to prove a crime beyond a reasonable doubt. The same is true of Adnan's lack of proof of an alibi or of trying to page Hae after her disappearance.

There was thus plenty of ammunition for a good defense attorney to use to create reasonable doubt. The lack of physical evidence often matters greatly to jurors used to *CSI* and similar crime shows. Jay was an admitted liar and drug dealer who had repeatedly changed his story to make it fit the police and prosecution's version of events. Character evidence is flimsy, and a good defense lawyer could easily have turned the cellphone records against the prosecution to highlight the implausibility of its timeline.

Adnan's family and friends from his mosque banded together to hire Cristina Gutierrez, who, as a former public defender, had a reputation as a ferocious advocate. Unfortunately, Gutierrez performed terribly. She suffered from multiple sclerosis, and she repeatedly squeezed Adnan's family for money without doing enough to prepare in return. Gutierrez's investigation was shoddy, and she failed to use alibi witness Asia McClain, who specifically remembered a long conversation with Adnan during the time when Adnan was supposedly strangling Hae. At trial, she was disorganized, had not mastered the facts, offered no expert witnesses or theory of the case, and was so aggressive that she made Jay seem reasonable.

Adnan may or may not have committed the murder, but we can have no confidence in his conviction because Gutierrez failed to put up a vigorous fight. Yet, to this day, he remains in prison. Today, a decade and a half later, the criminal justice system must wrestle again with whether to reopen Adnan's conviction to make up for his shoddy defense.

Adnan's case was not alone. About a dozen of Gutierrez's other clients said they had paid her, and sometimes she had come back to them asking for more, but she had not filed their pleadings in court. Gutierrez stopped communicating with her clients and has also been accused of seeking publicity and failing to pass along plea-bargain offers.

Gutierrez's dishonesty and uncommunicativeness were predictable and preventable. When she applied to become a lawyer, the Maryland bar authorities were warned that she had been convicted of shoplifting and apparently had lied about her surname to the police to hide that conviction. She had also omitted the conviction from her law school and job applications, yet Maryland's highest court admitted her to the bar. As the dissenting judge put it, "Given this young woman's prior record, how can we *know* that her demonstrated qualities of dishonesty, untruthfulness, and lack of candor will not again rise to the surface?"[2] A year after Adnan's conviction, after multiple clients had filed complaints with Maryland's Attorney Grievance Commission, the Commission found that client money that Gutierrez should have safeguarded in a trust account was simply gone. Gutierrez agreed to her own disbarment rather than fighting the charges.[3] The bar authorities failed in their mission to ensure justice by ensuring high-caliber lawyering.

Adnan's case is extreme, but not unusual. Appointed criminal defense lawyers are often wildly overburdened and so plead their clients guilty as quickly as they can. Right now, somewhere in America, an innocent criminal defendant faces very serious criminal charges with almost no hope of a vigorous defense.

Readers with even a passing familiarity with the U.S. Constitution may find this fact puzzling. America is a nation founded on justice and the rule of law. We declared independence from England in part because King George III had repeatedly interfered with colonists' legal rights and "the Administration of Justice." Our Constitution is a legal as well as a political charter of liberties and limits on power, and the Pledge of Allegiance ends by affirming that our nation stands for "liberty and justice for all." Carved on the east face of the Supreme Court building in Washington is the inscription "Justice, the Guardian of Liberty." For more than five centuries, the statue of Lady Justice has been depicted blindfolded, to guarantee equal justice to rich and poor alike. Since 1963, *Gideon v. Wainright* has guaranteed a free lawyer to any felony defendant who cannot afford to pay for one. But, all over the country, *Gideon*'s promise of justice for all is undercut by poorly funded indigent defense systems and overloaded defense counsel. *Gideon* is among America's most famous and beloved Supreme Court cases, and rightfully so. It is virtually impossible to represent oneself properly on felony charges in an American court. Nevertheless, *Gideon* and the cases that have followed it have hardly eliminated fundamental unfairness in America's criminal courts. Moreover, appointed criminal defense lawyers and legal aid are only for the truly poor—people below or close to the poverty line. But middle-class people are at least as likely to face legal problems, and to face them alone.

The situation in America's civil courts may be worse. Mothers seeking child support, tenants fighting eviction, and laid-off workers claiming unemployment or disability benefits usually cannot afford lawyers. They routinely endure long delays and great difficulty navigating courts by themselves before they can receive justice. In many courts, *pro se* (without a lawyer) litigants face substantial challenges: confusing procedures, complicated laws, and hostile judges and clerks. In a 2010 American Bar Association survey of state court judges, 94% stated that unrepresented parties fail to present necessary evidence; 89% said they suffer from procedural errors; 85% said they fail to effectively examine witnesses; and 81% noted that they are unable to object to improper evidence offered by an opponent. A simple Google search for "*pro se* divorce nightmare" lists story after story of litigants proceeding *pro se* and encountering every sort of obstacle: hostile clerks, confusing procedures, bad paperwork, weird legal terminology, and angry judges. *Pro se* litigants are at a deep disadvantage when they must face off against represented opponents. A divorce case is naturally upsetting; feeling railroaded by an opposing lawyer and the judge compounds the stress and anguish of going through a divorce.

Both civil and criminal courts in America rely heavily upon lawyers to process cases. In criminal court, most defendants have lawyers (overburdened and underpaid, but lawyers familiar with the process nonetheless). In civil courts, the number of *pro se* matters (cases where one or both of the litigants does not have a lawyer) is staggering and on the rise.[4] In Maine, 75% of family matters involve at least one *pro se* party, 88% of tenants are unrepresented in eviction actions, and 80% of all litigants in protective order cases are *pro se*. In New York City evictions, 88% of tenants are unrepresented and 98% of landlords are represented. In Washington, DC, 98% of tenants are *pro se* and 93% of landlords have lawyers.

In Milwaukee, 70% of family-law litigants resolve marital status, custody, and child-support issues without counsel each year. In Philadelphia, 89% of child custody litigants lack the assistance of counsel in proceedings that determine who will parent their children. In California, 80% of family law cases involve at least one party proceeding *pro se*.

The rate of *pro se* litigation was not always so high. In the 1970s, unrepresented parties were rare, appearing in fewer than 10% to 20% of cases. Between then and now, we have seen a dramatic and accelerating increase. The Chief Justice of the California Supreme Court cited a 35% rise in the number of *pro se* litigants in 2009 alone. The number of *pro se* bankruptcy petitions grew 187% from 2006 to 2011, more than twice the overall rate for bankruptcies.[5]

In 2014, the World Justice Project ("WJP") ranked ninety-nine countries on access to civil justice and access to criminal justice. America finished twenty-seventh in civil justice (between Chile and Botswana) and twenty-second on criminal justice (between France and Botswana again).[6] Nor is the WJP some international body that was created to embarrass the United States; it was founded by the American Bar Association and is headquartered in America.

Former Harvard President Derek Bok famously noted that "[t]here is far too much law for those who can afford it and far too little for those who cannot."[7] Our laws and procedures are too complex, and legal advice too expensive, for poor and even middle-class Americans to get help and vindicate their rights. Criminal defendants facing jail time may receive an appointed lawyer who is juggling hundreds of cases, lacks a private investigator or other support, and immediately urges them to plead guilty. Civil litigants are worse off; usually, they get no help at all navigating the maze of technical procedures and rules. The same is true of those seeking legal advice, for instance in planning a will or negotiating an employment contract.

There is a paradox here. America has more lawyers than any country in the world, and law schools are graduating more new lawyers than there are jobs. Yet legal education and legal advice are horrifically expensive. Even a small firm's legal help costs $150, $200, or more per hour. And in our adversarial system, having a good lawyer on your side matters a lot. But not many people can afford even a few hours' help at those rates, and this problem extends beyond the poor to reach most Americans. If you need to get a divorce, file for bankruptcy, or defend yourself against a charge of driving under the influence, you will quickly learn how expensive legal help is.

This is not a well-functioning market: Lawyers and judges have written the rules in ways that make them expensive to navigate, sometimes out of a laudable desire for perfect fairness and sometimes to protect lawyers' turf from competition. Bar authorities keep nonlawyers such as paralegals from offering more affordable competition, yet they rarely prevent incompetent or dishonest lawyers like Cristina Gutierrez from harming their clients or punish them for doing so. Lawyerization carries significant costs: It slows and complicates matters, and it tilts the playing field toward the side with the better lawyer. The three problems just mentioned—cost, funding, and complexity—are intertwined.

Bar associations and most legal scholars tell a much simpler story, and propose a much simpler solution. In their version, *Gideon* and the cases that expanded it are all part of the twentieth-century march of progress toward more law, more lawyers, more procedures, and thus more justice. The solution to the problem is thus more *Gideon*: more funding for the government-funded lawyers we already have (like public defenders and legal aid societies) and expansion of *Gideon* to more areas, notably into civil cases.

That picture of progress is far too rosy. Half a century after *Gideon*, there is still too little money and too few lawyers for all criminal cases, let alone civil ones. (Spending taxpayer money to hire lawyers for criminal defendants is not terribly popular.) For instance, New Orleans public defender Rick Teissier had to handle 418 defendants, including many serious felonies, in just seven months, leading a judge to quip: "[n]ot even a lawyer with an S on his chest could effectively handle this docket." But, while other professions such as medicine are finding innovative ways to drive down costs by using technology, paraprofessionals like nurse practitioners, and self-help advice, lawyers resist innovation or loosening their monopoly.

Access to justice matters. It is important for a nation founded on the rule of law. But lawyers and elaborate procedures are means to justice, not ends in and of themselves. Lawyers often help to promote justice, and they are important for the most complex, high-stakes cases such as defending those charged with felonies. Felony defense counsel need reasonable workloads, compensation, and support to do their jobs well. But lawyers can also get in the way of justice—by, for instance, delaying a mother's ability to collect child support from a deadbeat dad. And lawyers come at a very high price. Budgets are tight, and it is not at all obvious why spare funds should go to elaborate civil litigation as opposed to housing, policing, education, healthcare, or roads.

For years, we have been stuck in a *Groundhog Day* loop of bickering. Liberals argue that access to justice is a travesty, and demand that courts or legislatures spend more money on individual lawyers for individual cases. They loudly proclaim that anything less makes a mockery of justice for all. Conservatives respond that government cannot afford to pay for even the system we have now, let alone additional lawyers. They also argue that if the government were smaller and less obtrusive, access to justice needs would shrink regardless. This argument, and the proposed solutions on both sides of the aisle, has gotten us nowhere.

There is, however, a third way. The answer is to simplify and change the process itself. In the civil and criminal courts where ordinary Americans appear the most, we should simplify complex procedures and assume that parties will not be represented, rather than the other way around. Just a shift in the baseline expectation to assuming *pro se* status would make an enormous difference.

We cannot untie the Gordian knot by adding more strands of rope; we need to cut it, to simplify it. This book is a sober second look at the "more lawyers, more justice" creed. The real world of legal problems looks like an emergency room, with too many patients and too little time and money. We need to do triage, to narrow our ambitions, to focus on the cases that are the most complex, most serious, and most meritorious. Where lawyers are truly indispensable—primarily in felony defense—we need to focus our funding, to make lawyers meaningful in practice. That means paying defense lawyers about as well as prosecutors, hiring enough of them so their caseloads are comparable to prosecutors' caseloads, and providing them with investigative and forensic support like what prosecutors enjoy through police departments and crime labs.

Where the stakes are lower or the issues are simpler, Americans need simpler, cheaper alternatives to giving everyone a free lawyer. The good news is that there are a bevy of options, and many of them are becoming available just in time. In particular, new technologies and approaches to dispute resolution offer us the opportunity to streamline and simplify, to the benefit of everyone (except possibly lawyers). For many simple civil and even minor criminal cases, we could reform the process to let technology do the work, funneling parties through stepped, online dispute resolution starting at computerized mediation, passing through human, non-lawyer mediation, and proceeding into our current system only after making every effort to end the case cheaply and quickly.

Legal services organizations can ration free lawyers for the fraction of cases that are the most complex or for the clients least equipped to handle even simplified procedures, such as the mentally ill or the illiterate. Law schools could offer shorter, cheaper ways to qualify as a lawyer. Licensing rules could let trained paralegals, social workers, and accountants handle routine, specialized work just as physician assistants and nurse practitioners do. We could simplify court procedures and rules of evidence and ask clerks and judges to assist *pro se* litigants and do more of the work themselves so they rely on the parties' lawyers less.

In short, the legal system needs to go on a diet, to make it slimmer, faster, cheaper, and thus fairer. And lawyers need to get out of the way and let cheaper alternatives flourish.

Some will argue that these changes are unrealistic, or that the current complexity of law and procedure is necessary to guarantee correct results. But the current system is broken and courts have repeatedly tried to fix it by adding more rights to lawyers, though legislatures repeatedly fail to fund these rights. At a certain point, it is foolish to make the supposedly perfect the enemy of the good. Moreover, simplification is more democratic, empowers the citizenry rather than judges and lawyers, and fits our country's history and design. For the first century of this country's existence, a literate citizen could represent himself in court effectively. We have drifted so far from those roots that some regard simplification as impossible and argue that the only answer is to find more lawyers to handle more cases. To the contrary, the only realistic answer is to lessen the need for lawyers.

Part I of this book explains the contours of our access-to-justice crisis. Chapter 2 describes the issue in criminal courts. Criminal defense is, and always has been, radically underfunded in comparison to prosecution and police resources. This underfunding drives larger caseloads, fewer investigatory resources, and much lower salaries. The upshot? Systematic ineffective assistance of counsel is prevalent all over the country. It would be an easy problem to solve if it were a few bad apples. Instead, the system itself forces appointed defense lawyers to plea out as many cases as they can as quickly as possible, often with little investigation and less legal work. Underfunding breeds overwork, and together they lead to poor defense lawyering. The reality is much darker than *Gideon*'s shining ideal.

Chapter 3 describes the history of the right to appointed counsel in criminal cases, from colonial times to the present. In the eighteenth and nineteenth centuries, there was no constitutional right to appointed counsel, but criminal procedure was much more straightforward and a literate citizen could represent himself in court relatively easily. In the twentieth century, criminal procedure became more complicated and having a lawyer changed from a luxury to a necessity. Courts responded by creating and then expanding a right to appointed counsel. This right started with death penalty cases and then spread to felonies in federal courts, then to state court felonies in *Gideon*, and eventually to any misdemeanor threatening even a day in jail. This expansion was *not* accompanied by a strong right to effective counsel. Courts have been very hesitant to second-guess even facially deficient lawyering or to order any particular level of funding or to limit caseloads. The predictable result? Defendants have a right to a lawyer but no particular level of service.

Chapter 4 lays out the problem in civil courts. Legal aid funding has been in steady decline since the 1990s, and is down 63% from its high point in the 1980s. Because of limited funding, legal aid organizations turn away more than half of the eligible persons seeking help. *Pro bono* (charity, free legal help) has grown, but cannot possibly meet the overwhelming need. And legal aid and *pro bono* are only for the very poor; there is no help for the middle class. If a middle-class person needs a divorce or change in child custody, or must probate a will, she will need to pay a lawyer for help or proceed *pro se*. Despite a glut of law graduates and unemployed lawyers, hourly rates remain stubbornly high (averaging $190 an hour even for solo practitioners), and even the simplest legal tasks are likely to cost thousands of dollars. Predictably, this has led a number of Americans to "lump it" (live with their legal problems) or proceed in court without a lawyer. But many American courts are not set up to handle *pro se* cases, and some are outright hostile. The end result is that in the country with the most lawyers per capita, a huge chunk of the population cannot afford to access the courts for the most basic of legal problems like divorce, child custody, and property disputes.

Chapter 5 addresses the history of the poor and middle class in civil courts. As with criminal law, civil-court procedures and the underlying laws in the eighteenth and nineteenth centuries were simple enough that literate Americans could represent themselves. For example, in the mid-nineteenth century, a number of states allowed any citizen to appear in court. From the 1880s on, civil courts came to be lawyer-dominated and it was harder for the poor. Charitable legal aid societies were formed to help the "deserving poor" and were eventually converted into government programs, but they have never come close to meeting the needs of the poor, let alone the middle class. Other solutions—*pro bono*, increased legal aid funding, court appointments, and a proposed civil *Gideon* right—have all failed. Despite the good intentions of everyone involved, access to civil justice continues to erode.

Chapter 6 explains the political economy of our current mess. If everyone agrees that we have a problem, why has it kept getting worse? Part of the answer is the time and expense of legal education, and part is our adversarial system's expectation that each side will hire a capable lawyer for itself. Part of the answer is legislative indifference to funding free civil and criminal lawyers. Part of it is natural judicial hesitation to order any particular level of funding or to expand *Gideon* into civil cases. Part of it is that high defense lawyer caseloads and low funding are key ingredients in America's shift to a plea-driven system. If we spent more on criminal defense, there would be more investigation, more motions, and more trials. In a nation of rising caseloads and fixed judicial resources, that would worsen the backlog of cases.

Part II turns to how America might start to fix this mess. The message of Part I sounds gloomy, even fatalistic. Progressive social engineering to provide more lawyers seems doomed to fail. But we must stop confusing lawyers with justice. The prospects for improving access to justice are much better if we are willing to think outside the box, beyond giving each person a full-service lawyer for free. For years, civil *Gideon* advocates have argued for transplanting the broken *Gideon* system from criminal courts into civil courts. In Part II, we argue that is exactly backwards—the nascent *pro se* court reforms of civil justice should be transplanted into our broken criminal courts.

Chapter 7 critiques the old ways of addressing these problems, what we call the "more lawyers, more justice" fallacy. It begins with the failed movement for a civil equivalent of *Gideon*. The Supreme Court has twice rejected civil *Gideon*, most recently in *Turner v. Rogers*, a 9–0 decision (on which both authors worked on the winning side). *Turner* signals the death of civil *Gideon* for the foreseeable future. Civil *Gideon* is not only unrealistic but unworkable. *Gideon* has largely failed in criminal courts and would work even worse in civil courts. Creating such a right would make lawsuits slower and more complex, tilting them against unrepresented litigants on the other side. The evidence that lawyers are necessary in all cases is surprisingly weak, particularly for simpler disputes. Time and money are limited, and lawyers are too expensive. Plus, courts are much worse at social reform than at doing justice in individual cases.

Similarly, we need to break out of the political and legal arguments that have crippled *Gideon*'s great promise on the criminal side. America will never be able to offer every criminal defendant facing any amount of jail time a criminal defense equal to what the wealthy can afford. But we can focus our efforts on the cases that so desperately need our attention and care: serious felonies.

Chapters 8–11 describe the new approaches that have been most successful. *Pro se* court reform, technology, and a loosening of restrictions on legal practice are transforming some courts from a hidebound anti-*pro se* attitude into simpler, fairer places where litigants can succeed with or without a lawyer's assistance. While there are few reasons to be optimistic about the failed approaches of the past, there are many reasons for optimism today. But we must not let vested interests—judges, clerks, and lawyers—get in the way.

Chapter 8 discusses technological innovations. Private, nonprofit, and government computerization of legal services have already transformed the market, and we are in the very nascent stages of this revolution. It will be a long time before computers can replicate human legal reasoning fully. But computers can already outperform humans on many routine legal tasks and, as data collection and computing power improve, computers will be able to do more and more. Legal publishers can provide interactive websites and fillable forms for routine transactions. Hotlines, chat rooms, and message boards can answer discrete questions without requiring full-service representation. And interactive websites promise faster, cheaper adjudication without having to gather everyone in the same room at the same time. Internet merchants such as eBay have already proven that online dispute resolution can work cheaply and smoothly.

Chapter 9 discusses *pro se* court reform. There are plenty of ways to simplify procedures, forms, and rules so non-lawyers can represent themselves *pro se*, and many of the most promising reforms have already started. Court clerks should actively assist *pro se* litigants. Some courts have hired dedicated *pro se* clerks. America should even expand small claims courts, which often ban lawyers in order to keep proceedings simple and fast enough for non-lawyers. This chapter also argues that we should change the judicial role in some American courts. We can learn from the American system of administrative law judges and from European courts. We can adapt the inquisitorial system, in which court officials actively investigate the facts and probe the evidence instead of relying on the parties' lawyers. That approach can cut through distracting procedural games to focus on the facts and issues at the heart of a case. Though inquisitorial judging sounds like an exotic foreign transplant, American administrative agencies already use similar methods to adjudicate unemployment and Social Security disability claims, and so do small claims courts. In fact, many Americans may be *more* familiar with inquisitorial systems thanks to Judge Judy, Judge John Brown, and their many imitators.

Chapter 10 describes how we can generate cheaper lawyers and paralegals. Legal education is at an inflection point and, for the first time since the 1950s, the possibility of a cheaper, shorter, and more flexible route into practice might be a reality. Right now, students must invest three years and more than $150,000 to qualify as public defenders. Yet, many argue that the current third year of law school is largely superfluous. In many other countries, paralegals, social workers, and notaries provide a range of legal services. Some states have started to experiment with licensing non-lawyers to practice law outside of court. These "limited license legal technician" programs should be expanded. And America must relax its rules against unauthorized practice of law to open the door to these paraprofessionals, much as the medical profession now allows nurse practitioners and physician assistants to provide simple care.

Chapter 11 describes how some of these approaches can be imported to criminal court, and where they should not. America needs to do triage, and felony cases deserve the most funding and attention: They carry the heaviest punishments, the worst collateral consequences (such as deportation), and the most stigma. They also have the most complicated procedures, such as jury trials and related motions, which require lawyers to navigate them. We envision a grand bargain, in which public defenders would spend much more time up front investigating, negotiating, and defending felonies. They would also have substantially more support, ranging from private investigators to forensic and medical experts. Their salaries, caseloads, and support should be comparable to those of prosecutors, and their performance standards need more teeth.

By comparison, minor criminal matters should be handled in a manner that does not require lawyers at all, by the state or the defendant. Simpler cases need cheaper solutions. That is the other half of the grand bargain: cutting lawyers elsewhere to save more for felony defense. The government should not have to provide free lawyers for minor misdemeanors that carry no serious collateral consequences, and states should experiment with simpler, cheaper ways to try these cases. Prosecutors would have incentives to send less serious cases to these faster courts, reserving felony charges for more serious cases that deserved them.

Chapter 12 concludes the book on both a hopeful and cautionary note. In the face of these problems, reformers may be paralyzed by pessimism, or forget the past and be doomed to repeat it. Efforts to expand *Gideon*'s dream have repeatedly failed. But Chapter 12's conclusion argues that these failures can pave a new road to success. Advances in law, medicine, and technology point toward a very different model, one that is simpler, cheaper, more flexible, and less regulated. The current crisis poses a danger, but also an opportunity to loosen lawyers' monopoly and increase overall access to justice.

Technology also requires a note of caution, however: Technological advances have also made our legal system's burgeoning complexity possible. Courts, regulators, and legislatures have seemingly endless resources to add layers of additional complexity to our already overweening substantive law. This chapter recognizes that procedural complexity is easier to achieve and more popular, so our book focuses on those solutions.

Part I
=
The Problem

CHAPTER 2

The Reality of Criminal Justice
for Poor Defendants

Because of his defense lawyer's incompetence and sloth, Jimmy Ray Bromgard served fourteen years in prison for a child rape that he could not have committed. At about 4 a.m. on March 20, 1987, an intruder broke into a home in Billings, Montana, and raped an eight-year-old girl. The intruder stole a purse and a jacket and fled back out the window. The police arrived, and after questioning the eight-year-old, drew a composite sketch of the perpetrator. One of the officers thought the sketch looked like Bromgard. The police brought Bromgard in and the eight-year-old victim picked him out of a lineup, but she was not sure it was him. She placed her certainty at "60%, 65% sure." Again at trial, she reiterated that she was "not too sure" about her identification. Bromgard claimed he was innocent and that he had been asleep at home when the crime occurred.

At trial, the state also presented forensic evidence against Bromgard. The semen found on the victim's underpants could not be typed using then-existing technology, but the state's expert claimed that hairs found on the victim's bed sheets could be. He testified that there was less than a 1-in-10,000 chance that the hairs were not Bromgard's. Unfortunately for Bromgard, this testimony was demonstrably wrong. There has never been a statistically reliable process for comparing hair samples. At best, the numbers were educated guesses; at worst, sheer fabrication. A later peer-review committee of forensic scientists termed the statistical evidence junk science and urged the Montana Attorney General to audit the expert's other cases.

There was thus much ammunition for a defense lawyer. Unfortunately, Bromgard was appointed John Adams, a local defense lawyer who worked on contract for Yellowstone County, Montana. Nicknamed "Jailhouse John Adams," he was paid an annual retainer to take appointed cases, regardless of how many he took or how many hours he worked. Unsurprisingly, Adams was not particularly diligent. He had already been found ineffective by a federal court in other cases and was known to miss court appointments while playing cards in a local bar.

Consistent with his reputation, Adams did almost nothing for Bromgard. He met with him once before trial. He hired no investigators or forensic experts. This meant that the prosecution's expert testimony identifying Bromgard as the rapist to a 1-in-10,000 certainty went virtually unchallenged. Adams did no investigation himself. He filed no pretrial motions challenging the witness identification or the expert's testimony. He did not prepare Bromgard to testify at trial. He did not present an opening argument. He even failed to file an appeal after Bromgard was found guilty and sentenced to 40 years in prison. And yet the Montana courts repeatedly found Bromgard's representation effective.

In 2002, Bromgard was exonerated by DNA evidence after serving fourteen years in prison for a crime he did not commit. The semen on the girl's underwear could not possibly have been Bromgard's.

Sadly and amazingly, Jimmy Ray Bromgard's story is not unique. Even in the most serious of cases, where a defendant faces the death penalty, court-appointed defense counsel can be jaw-droppingly awful. Justice Ruth Bader Ginsburg put it nicely: "I have yet to see a death case, among the dozens coming to the Supreme Court on eve of execution [stay] petitions, in which the defendant was well represented at trial. . . . People who are well represented at trial do not get the death penalty." Appellate courts have found that defense lawyers who were drunk or asleep or ignorant of the law or disbarred or mentally ill were adequate to satisfy the Constitution's guarantee of effective counsel.[1]

This is not a problem limited to the relatively small group of criminal defendants who face the death penalty. To the contrary, the sorry state of criminal defense has a broad effect at all levels of American society. This is partially because criminal law has metastasized to the point where, as federal judge Alex Kozinski has put it, "You're probably a federal criminal" already.[2] It is also partially because few citizens worry too much about the state of criminal defense until they are the ones who need defending.

Take, for example, a case much more common and less weighty than a child-rape or capital-murder trial, and one much more likely to affect the middle class: a charge of driving under the influence (DUI). Before you discount a DUI charge as relatively insignificant, consider that in most states a DUI charge carries a mandatory fine, jail time, public service, *and* the loss of driving privileges for a year. In some states, it could also result in the seizure of your car. And also remember that, depending on your body weight and blood alcohol level, as few as two beers could put you over the legal limit.

Imagine that you are a pharmaceutical sales representative. On a Friday night, you take a group of doctors and nurses out for drinks and a brief sales presentation. On your way home, a police car pulls you over. The officer asks if you know why she pulled you over. You do not. She mentions that you failed to use your turn signal when you changed lanes. You are pretty sure you did use your turn signal and start to argue. The officer interrupts and asks if you have been drinking. You mention that you have been out for drinks, but did not have more than a glass or two of wine. The officer asks you to step out of the car and then asks you to perform the three standardized field sobriety tests: the walk-and-turn test, the one-legged stand test, and the horizontal-gaze nystagmus. Five years ago, you hurt your right knee running, and you try to tell the officer that you may not be able to perform the tests. The officer asks you not to interrupt and to listen to the instructions. At the end of the tests, the officer announces that you failed and asks you to take a Breathalyzer, which comes in above the legal limit. She then books you for DUI and carts you to the hospital for a blood test.

Because you were arrested on a Friday evening, you may have to spend the weekend in jail, awaiting a bail hearing on Monday morning. If convicted, you will not only risk imprisonment but will also lose your driver's license for one year. For a pharmaceutical sales rep, that is career suicide.

Fortunately for you, there are several potential defenses: If the officer lacked reasonable suspicion to pull you over (if you did in fact use your turn signal, for example), you can have the charge thrown out.

Many squad cars have video recordings, but copies are available only if properly requested. If the officer administered the field sobriety tests incorrectly, or if your knee made performance impossible, you may also have a chance. You could also argue that the Breathalyzer was inaccurate (a surprisingly common occurrence).[3] Even the results of a hospital blood test can be debunked, because they usually occur at a time lag from the driving itself.

Even a routine case, then, involves complicated moving parts and high stakes for the defendant's liberty versus society's safety. Unfortunately for you, presenting any of these defenses is highly technical and expensive, and well beyond the ability of almost any *pro se* defendant. Hiring a lawyer to defend a DUI case is not cheap. In Knoxville, Tennessee, the typical charge just for the first step of the process (the preliminary hearing) is between $2,000 and $10,000. A representation from first appearance to a jury trial can run into six figures. People are willing to pay these prices because the ramifications of a DUI are so weighty. An appointed lawyer is a possibility, but most middle-class individuals earn too much to qualify. Many states set the eligibility limit at 25% above the federal poverty line, so in 2016 a single person would need to earn less than $14,850 a year to qualify.[4]

Even if you earn that little, good luck getting an appointed lawyer to pursue each of the avenues of possible defense outlined above. First-offense DUI is frequently a misdemeanor, meaning a fee cap of as low as a few hundred dollars, hardly enough to cover more than a few hours of work.

In theory, American criminal justice depends on a contest of equals. In this boxing ring, the defense lawyer is the champion in the defendant's corner. Our adversarial system counts on the defense lawyer to challenge the prosecution's case vigorously, to test whether a defendant is guilty and what punishment he deserves. Criminal defense lawyers are supposed to ensure the accuracy and fairness of lineups, police interrogations, guilty pleas, trials, sentencings, and appeals. To defend well, a defense lawyer must meet with his client multiple times to build trust and draw out the whole story as well as leads on potential alibi and character witnesses. If his client is held in jail, he must repeatedly wait in line and clear security pat-downs and scans in order to visit him. He must then track down potential defense witnesses, spend time talking with them, and locate everything from medical records to forensic experts. He must become familiar with the entire case and consider possible defenses and alternative explanations, as well as factors that might warrant a reduced or alternative sentence. He must negotiate over a possible plea bargain, stand ready to try the case if needed, and advocate at sentencing and on appeal, which requires researching and writing a substantial appellate brief. All of these steps take time—weeks or days, not just hours—but harried defense attorneys rarely have time to spare.

The reality falls far short of this ideal. As this chapter explains, criminal caseloads are too great, and funding too scarce, for defense lawyers to match the prosecution. Defense lawyers are paid significantly less than prosecutors, making it hard to attract talent, and they lack the prosecution's police investigators, crime labs, and other support. They must also juggle hundreds of cases at a time, making it impossible to investigate, analyze, and vigorously defend each one. Each jury trial requires dozens if not hundreds of hours for pretrial preparation, motions, witness interviews, jury selection, jury instructions, and rehearsing direct- and cross-examination as well as opening statements and closing arguments. Instead, defense lawyers plea bargain most cases quickly, sometimes right after meeting their clients for the first time. In practice, they can do little to test guilt.

There is another casualty: the jury trial. Anyone with a passing familiarity with the U.S. Constitution and Bill of Rights knows that the Framers counted on the jury to be the ultimate bulwark against government power. Instead, the jury trial has been virtually sidelined by rampant plea bargaining in a criminal system that could not possibly try even 10% of the cases filed.

Each year, American police make 13 million arrests. Half a million are for serious violent felonies like murder, rape, robbery, and aggravated assault. Arrests for serious property crimes (like burglary and theft), drug crimes, driving under the influence, and non-aggravated assaults number about a million and a half each. The indigent defense system is poorly equipped to devote individualized attention to this constant barrage of cases for two related reasons: underfunding and overwork, which together breed poor performance.[5]

Underfunding

Half a century ago, *Gideon* promised equal justice to rich and poor alike, but *Gideon*'s promise remains chronically underfunded. At least once a decade, a new report comes out decrying the state of *Gideon*'s promise and noting the problem has only gotten worse since the last report. In the early 1970s, just a decade after *Gideon*, money and manpower shortages had "seriously crippled" effective representation, including the extension of appointed counsel to misdemeanor cases. In the 1980s, funding for indigent defense remained "grossly inadequate." By the 1990s, "[t]he long-term neglect and underfunding of indigent defense ha[d] created a crisis of extraordinary proportions in many states throughout the country." In the early 2000s, the ABA marked *Gideon*'s fortieth anniversary with a report lamenting "that a significant funding crisis persists today." A 2009 report noted that, because indigent defense costs keep rising and the economy remains weak, "Funding shortages are guaranteed to worsen." And in 2013, a report marking *Gideon*'s fiftieth anniversary found that the result of these funding shortages was "staggeringly low rates of compensation for assigned counsel across the nation." While some states have raised funding or taken over responsibility from counties, sometimes funding increases have not even kept up with inflation, let alone caseloads.[6]

While federal and state governments have large criminal justice budgets, totaling $179 billion annually in 2007, most of that money goes to police, prosecutors, crime labs, prisons, and the like. Only 2% of that total supports indigent criminal defense. The amount spent on indigent defense each year, $3.5 billion, sounds like a lot, but that total must cover more than a million felony cases and at least as many serious misdemeanors each year. That means each case averages a total of perhaps one workday of a defense lawyer's time, with little support for private investigators, forensic science experts, and the like, let alone for the days and weeks needed to go to trial. State and county defense budgets are more likely to be cut than other parts of the criminal justice system and much less likely to keep up with inflation and rising criminal caseloads.[7]

Across the country, indigent defense receives far less money than prosecution each year. In Tennessee, for example, the $130 million-plus spent on prosecution is more than double the $57 million for indigent defense; in California, the disparity is more than $300 million each year and growing. In some places, defense funding depends on unreliable sources such as traffic tickets, fines, or court fees, which may not keep up with rising caseloads.[8]

The chronic funding squeeze hurts defendants in a number of ways. First, it means that there are fewer defense lawyers to handle the same number of cases charged by prosecutors. Across the country, there are many more prosecutors than public defenders. In a rural New Jersey county, for instance, the prosecutor's office has twice as many lawyers and seven times as many investigators. In New Orleans, the ratio is almost three prosecutors per public defender. And in Houston, the district attorney's office budget is twice as large as that for indigent defense.[9]

Second, underfunding squeezes compensation. Some appointed lawyers are public defenders, who are salaried, full-time employees specializing in criminal defense. Idealism draws talented and public-spirited young lawyers to public defense, but financial pressures as well as crushing caseloads burn them out and make it hard for them to stay. Public defenders' salaries average in the mid-five figures, starting around $50,000, less than a third of the starting salary at the biggest law firms. Many public defenders still owe big student loan debts from college and law school and struggle to make ends meet. In the words of a public defender, "If you want to raise a family, buy a house and a car, that's not going to happen." Lawyers may thus avoid taking these jobs in the first place, or must leave them after a few years. They may even have to moonlight, holding a second job to make ends meet. The salary squeeze makes it hard to attract and retain talent and cultivate expertise. Excessive turnover means public defenders may have less experience and expertise than their prosecutor opponents.[10]

Other appointed defense lawyers are called "assigned counsel," meaning that they work as solo practitioners or in small private law firms but accept some court-appointed cases for a fee. Some lawyers, especially young ones, volunteer for these cases to gain experience or fill spare time; others are dragooned by courts that need warm bodies, even if they do not ordinarily do criminal work. These lawyers have to cover their office rent, utilities, secretaries, computerized research, and the like. In part to cover these overhead expenses (which average $80 per hour), private lawyers charge private clients close to $200 per hour or more.[11]

Assigned counsel, by contrast, earn only a fraction of that for court-appointed cases: Hourly rates for felony defense average less than $65, and rates for misdemeanors are often closer to $50. Moreover, hourly compensation is often capped around a few thousand dollars for felonies and several hundred dollars for misdemeanors (as little as $180 in New Mexico), meaning there is often no additional pay for investing more than ten or twenty hours.[12]

Some counties try to save money by using a third option, contract attorneys. The county contracts with a law firm, often the lowest bidder, to accept some or all court appointments in exchange for a flat fee per case or for the entire caseload. In other words, lawyers are paid per contract or per case, not per hour.

For both assigned counsel working under a fee cap and contract attorneys paid a flat fee regardless of what they do, the natural incentive is to invest little work and plead cases out swiftly. Conscientious lawyers strive in good faith to represent their clients zealously, but they are forced to juggle enough cases to pay their secretaries and office rent and put food on their tables. Preparing a case and proceeding to trial is almost never cost-effective, so it remains rare. For attorneys who carry both court-appointed and privately retained cases, minimizing work on appointed cases leaves more time for more lucrative private cases. Thus, studies of assigned-counsel systems find that low pay drives away qualified defense lawyers and discourages effective preparation.[13]

Contract attorneys face an inherent conflict of interest, encouraging them to do the bare minimum needed to earn their flat fees and scrape a profit from their low-bid contracts. The winning bidders are not the most zealous defenders, but the ones who put in the least work. Trial courts may like and favor such low bidders, because they make their clients plead guilty fast and thus spare the courts work. Empirical studies confirm that contract attorneys file fewer motions, seek less expert assistance, are less likely to take cases to trial, more often have their clients plead guilty immediately, and provide worse representation overall.[14]

Take, for example, a poor misdemeanor defendant in Chicago. His lawyer can earn only $30 per hour of out-of-court time up to a maximum of $150. If the lawyer persuades his client to plead guilty immediately, he stays under the cap. But if he investigates the case and prepares for trial, there is zero additional compensation beyond five hours' work. Few lawyers will try cases for free instead of jumping at whatever plea is offered.

Or take a first-degree felony defendant in New Mexico, where assigned lawyers earn a flat $700 for the entire case (even less for less serious felonies). If the lawyer persuades the client to plead guilty immediately or before much investigation, the lawyer can cover several hundred dollars' overhead and turn a profit. If instead he spends dozens of hours investigating, interviewing witnesses, negotiating, and preparing seriously for trial, he earns zero additional pay. In short, low hourly rates, flat fees, and fee caps discourage hard work and zealous representation.[15]

Let us be clear that we are blaming the system, not the defense lawyers. None of the criticisms discussed here depends on imputing greed or selfishness to well-meaning public servants. Regardless of their laudable motivations and intentions, the problem is baked into the system's underfunding and overwork.

Third, underfunding hits not only defense lawyers but also their support staff. Because of custom, practice, and the rules of ethics, lawyers are not supposed to testify in their own cases. That means that prosecutors and defense lawyers must rely on others to interview witnesses, visit crime scenes, or conduct scientific tests if they want that evidence to be usable in court. This is rarely a problem for prosecutors because they build their cases on police detective work, with follow-up by in-house investigators, coroners, doctors, and forensic experts. Prosecutors likewise can rely upon larger staffs of paralegals and secretaries, and better libraries and technology.

Defense lawyers can rarely match the prosecution team. They have few if any in-house investigators to check possible alibis and no crime labs to analyze drugs or bullets. In Houston, for example, the district attorney's office has funding for thirty investigators compared with zero for the defense. Across the country, funding for interpreters and medical and scientific experts is paltry, and courts are reluctant to authorize such expenses. Nevada judges have punished defense attorneys who request expert funding, and an Indiana judge even admitted that he had stopped assigning cases to a lawyer because he had filed too many motions, visited his jailed clients too often, and sought too much in reimbursements. Clark County, Washington closed down a contract attorney office for seeking too much money, and Montana officials have likewise threatened to terminate attorneys' contracts for seeking modifications or too many psychological evaluations. Contract attorneys, who usually have to pay experts out of their own flat contractual fees, are often unwilling to cut into their already meager compensation. Defense lawyers' libraries and computers may also be inadequate and outdated. Even bare necessities such as desks, bookcases, telephones, and private interview rooms may be in short supply, as they were in San Francisco and Prince George's County, Maryland.[16]

Underfunding also means that the law on the books may not match the reality on the ground. The failure to provide adequate funding for needed expert witnesses is one example. Another is the failure to provide free lawyers in misdemeanor cases. The U.S. Supreme Court has held that misdemeanor defendants have a right to court-appointed counsel in any case in which they ultimately receive actual jail time or even a suspended sentence. Even though states are bound to follow these rules, sometimes they do not. So, for instance, the Chief Justice of the South Carolina Supreme Court openly criticized the requirement of lawyers for suspended sentences as "misguided, . . . so I will tell you straight up we [are] not adhering to [that requirement] in every situation." Some Michigan courts do not even offer counsel in misdemeanor cases. In many other situations, judges and prosecutors routinely bargain with unrepresented defendants, do not tell them their rights to counsel, and get them to waive (give up) their right to appointed counsel.[17]

Excessive Caseloads

The twin problem of underfunding is overwork. Professional standards recommend that defense attorneys carry a maximum of 150 felony cases, or 400 misdemeanors, per year. Even these benchmarks are contested and seem very high, particularly if lawyers lack private investigators and other support. Assuming time off for two weeks' vacation and government holidays, there are roughly 240 working days a year. The recommended caseloads mean that a lawyer would handle one felony every 1.6 days or almost two misdemeanors a day. Obviously very, very few of those cases could proceed to trial or even receive significant investigation or motions practice.

In reality, however, defense lawyers routinely juggle far more than these recommended caseloads, sometimes hundreds more. Miami's public defenders face annual caseloads of nearly 500 felonies or more than 2,200 misdemeanors, yet that office's budget was recently cut by an eighth. In Chicago, Atlanta, and Utah, annual misdemeanor caseloads exceed 2,000. As noted, even as criminal caseloads keep rising, the number of public defenders lags behind the number of prosecutors, driving up each public defender's caseload.[18]

Underfunding also exacerbates caseloads for assigned counsel. If they are paid low and capped amounts per case, they may have to accept more cases than they can handle well in order to make a living.[19]

Contract attorneys have it worst of all. Some contracts require the winning bidder to accept however many cases are filed, often for the same overall flat fee. If caseloads jump, they must do far more for the same amount of money by getting rid of cases as fast as possible. One county contracted with a three-person firm to handle about half of its caseload for just over $400,000, amounting to 1,523 felonies plus 3,587 misdemeanors that year. That works out to about $80 per case for all fees and costs. Each case averaged less than one minute of private-investigator time. Of the more than 5,000 cases that year, only 12 went to trial—less than one quarter of one percent. Two of the lawyers split the felonies, meaning each disposed of about 761 felony cases that year, almost all by guilty plea. A single associate handled all 3,587 misdemeanors, nearly 300 per month, by pleading them all out at the first court appearance. When the misdemeanor associate was given a felony case, she saw a strong argument for suppressing the evidence from a warrantless search. But after she asked for more time to develop her client's strong argument, she was fired for refusing to flush the case with a guilty plea.[20]

Like underfunding, overwork has long persisted and grown despite calls for change. In 1973, average caseloads already exceeded the professional standards just mentioned. They spiked in the 1980s and 1990s and remained excessive over the last two decades. The problem is a chronic one.[21]

Instead of thoroughly investigating, discussing, negotiating, and contesting guilt, busy defense lawyers dispose of cases as fast as they can. They rarely file motions or objections, let alone go to trial. They often meet their clients for the first time in courthouse holding cells and hurriedly converse for a few moments before having the client plead guilty and be sentenced. This common practice is known as "meet 'em, greet 'em, and plead 'em" (or just "meet 'em and plead 'em"). Thus, an Atlanta public defender may receive up to forty-five new cases at an arraignment, meet them all while they are chained together in a courthouse cell, and have many of them plead guilty and be sentenced right there.

Of New Orleans defender Rick Teissier's 418 cases over seven months, dozens of which were serious felonies, he pleaded out nearly a third of them at arraignment, the first formal hearing on the criminal charge. A recent Florida study found that 70% of misdemeanor defendants pleaded guilty at arraignment; one third of them did so without a lawyer. These arraignments lasted, on average, for less than three minutes. A lawyer who has just met his client in a courthouse hallway or holding cell can do little to explore possible defenses or mitigating circumstances. He simply pushes the case along like another widget on the plea-bargaining assembly line.[22]

In many places, lawyers often are not appointed immediately or are too busy to meet with their clients right away, so their clients may languish in jail for months. By that time, a jailed defendant charged with loitering, prostitution, or public intoxication may already have served more time than the typical sentence for a minor charge. As a result, defendants plead guilty in exchange for time served, rather than fight it out.[23]

Ineffectiveness

Partly as a result of overfunding and overwork, appointed defense lawyers sometimes perform poorly. Lawyers who are overwhelmed with cases often do little or no investigation, consult no experts, file no motions, and settle for whatever plea and sentence the prosecutor chooses to offer initially. Flooded with cases, they also grow cynical and burn out.

But the effectiveness problem extends beyond lack of time and overwork. Appointed defense counsel receive paltry pay and endure poor working conditions, making it hard to attract talent and retain seasoned veterans. There are basically three types of lawyers who are willing to endure these conditions. First, some lawyers become public defenders out of a sense of mission or ideological commitment to the cause, which can inspire them to brave adversity and fight hard. Many young idealists eventually burn out, but in the meantime they bring energy to their mission. Second, some young lawyers take court appointments or public defender jobs long enough to try some cases, make names for themselves, and gain marketable experience. But once they have trial experience, they are more likely to use it on behalf of more lucrative paying clients. They may continue to take a few court appointments to fill spare time, but seldom specialize in them.[24] Third are the leftover lawyers at the bottom of the market. Lawyers whom few private clients would hire may wind up with court-appointed cases instead, regardless of the stakes. There are few checks to ensure minimal talent and performance.

In this third category, there are many stories of defense lawyers who nap during parts of trials, alcoholics who are arrested for driving while intoxicated on their way to court, and defense lawyers who are mentally ill or use cocaine or amphetamines during trial. Yet courts sometimes do not replace these lawyers, remove them from appointment lists, or overturn resulting convictions. On the contrary, some judges discount these evident impairments, let these lawyers continue, and even praise their work. Judy Haney, for example, faced the death penalty for murdering her abusive husband. Though the stakes could not have been higher, the judge held her lawyer in contempt for showing up to trial visibly drunk at 9:30 a.m., *and then let him finish out the trial the next day.* If even napping, drunk, or drugged lawyers may pass muster, then garden-variety incompetence hardly raises eyebrows. The standard of competence is shockingly low and in hindsight convictions seem to have been inevitable, so there is no harm, no foul. As the vice president of the Georgia Trial Lawyers Association put it, "You put a mirror under the court-appointed lawyer's nose, and if the mirror clouds up, that's adequate counsel."[25]

Even in capital cases, defendants fighting for their lives may be stuck with defense lawyers who do not take the most basic steps for their clients. They may not find alibi witnesses, medical records that corroborate a self-defense claim, or evidence that a client is mentally retarded or schizophrenic. Some defense lawyers may do nothing for their clients and even undermine their cases. At James Messer's capital trial, his lawyer gave no opening statement, barely cross-examined the prosecution's witnesses, presented no defense witnesses or evidence, made no objections, failed to develop obvious mitigating evidence, and repeatedly suggested that his own client deserved to die. As a result, Messer was executed. Other capital defense lawyers have referred to *their own clients* using racial slurs such as "nigger," "wet back," and "little old nigger boy."[26]

The bottom line is grim. You get what you pay for, and we as a society are politically unwilling to pay for much. Limited defense funding cannot keep up with rising caseloads, let alone attract and retain enough good, experienced defense lawyers and support. America spends plenty to arrest and prosecute criminal cases, but will not level the playing field with equal funding for the defense. Other factors include the complexity of our legal system, the cost of support and overhead, and the substantial time needed to investigate and tailor each client's defense. Underfunding breeds overwork, and together they lead to poor defense lawyering. The reality is much darker than *Gideon*'s shining ideal.

CHAPTER 3

How We Got Here:
Criminal Defense

To understand where America is going, we have to understand where we have been. This chapter offers a brief history of criminal procedure and the right to an appointed lawyer. We start with the story of *Powell v. Alabama,* the case that launched modern constitutional criminal procedure when the United States Supreme Court used the Bill of Rights to the Constitution to overturn a state court criminal conviction for the first time. It was also one of the first cases in which the Court sought to manage what passed for justice in the Jim Crow–era South.

The story of *Powell v. Alabama* takes us back to a dark time in American history.[1] In 1931, ordinary Americans were so desperately poor that they would jump onto a freight train in one town and "hobo" their way to the next in search of work or food. South of the Mason-Dixon line, Jim Crow still ruled. The Ku Klux Klan was everywhere, and lynchings, cross burnings, and other atrocities were a way of life. And yet, with the Depression in full swing, there was little appetite for reining in the American South.

On March 25, 1931, a freight train left Chattanooga for Memphis along the Southern Railroad Line, the oldest east-to-west train route in the South. To avoid the Cumberland Plateau, the line runs south through Alabama from Tennessee before turning north again to Memphis. A few dozen youths, black and white, hopped aboard the long freight train in an open gondola car, hoboing their way to Memphis. Unsurprisingly, the racial mixing was volatile. Barely outside of Chattanooga, on the far side of the Lookout Mountain tunnel, a fight broke out. A white teenager stepped on the hand of Haywood Patterson, a black teenager traveling with his friends. According to Patterson, the white teen refused to apologize and said, "This is a white man's train. All you nigger bastards unload." When Patterson and his friends refused, the white and black youths began hitting each other and throwing stones. The black teens eventually got the better of it and threw the white teens off the train. The victory proved beyond costly, however. The white boys walked on to the next town and told the stationmaster that a gang of blacks was beating up whites on the train and that they wanted to press charges.

The stationmaster sent word ahead to Paint Rock, Alabama, and a lynch mob/posse assembled with ropes and guns. They stopped the train and dragged all the riders off. They found nine black teenagers, but also two young white women wearing men's caps and overalls. A serious situation turned very dangerous. In the Jim Crow-era South, blacks and whites were legally required to live separately, and black men and white women were *never* to be seen together. At first, the women chatted with several bystanders, but about twenty minutes later they told a deputy that the blacks had gang-raped them, offering little detail.

The black teens were fortunate to escape with their lives. They were bound and driven to the jail in nearby Scottsboro, Alabama. A lynch mob gathered in the night, and frenzied news coverage began calling for blood. Soon, the media dubbed them "the Scottsboro Boys." To stave off the lynch mob, the sheriff had to move them to a sturdier jail in the next town, threaten to shoot to kill any lynchers, and call out the National Guard.

Officials also promised swift justice, and the public demanded it: Locals complained that it took all of five days to indict the teens. The state sought the death penalty for eight of the nine teens and life imprisonment for the youngest, who was thirteen. At arraignment, the court did not ask the defendants whether they wanted to hire counsel and did not give them time to do so. They had no lawyer to investigate or prepare before trial.

The first of the four trials began on April 6, a mere twelve days after the incident. As usual, blacks were systematically excluded from the jury pool. A mob of five to ten thousand gathered outside the court-house, which had to be protected by National Guardsmen wielding machine guns. The judge appointed as defense counsel Stephen Roddy, a real estate lawyer who had been sent from Chattanooga by some of that town's leading black citizens. Unfortunately, Roddy was an alco-holic who could hardly walk a straight line the morning of the first trial and who protested that he was unprepared and did not know Alabama law. To help him, the judge appointed local lawyer Milo Moody, who was nearly seventy, doddering, and senile. Roddy had less than half an hour with his clients before the trial began and effectively no time to investigate the facts. The appointment of counsel was largely a sham.

Despite inflammatory news coverage and the lynch mob, the court refused to move the trials. The medical evidence of gang rape was weak: While doctors found semen in both women's vaginas, it was non-motile, almost ruling out intercourse in the previous few hours, and the amount found in one of them was far less than a gang rape would have produced. Neither woman was bruised, injured, or hysterical, and their clothes were not torn even though they had supposedly been gang-raped in a rail car full of jagged rocks. One of the two could not even identify which of the defendants had supposedly raped her. Yet the judge all but precluded defense counsel from cross-examining the victims about their history of prostitution and their sexual intercourse with their boy-friends the night before the incident. Neither defense lawyer offered an opening or closing argument, and they called no witnesses besides the defendants. Each trial lasted only a few hours and convicted all defen-dants; all but the youngest one were sentenced to death.

Southerners prided themselves on having let justice take its course as a substitute for lynching. Outsiders saw the trial as a travesty and a legal lynching. The Alabama Supreme Court affirmed the judgment in a brisk 6–1 ruling. The U.S. Supreme Court eventually reversed, and on retrial one of the two women recanted her entire story, but Alabama juries kept convicting the defendants. There were eventually three more retrials. Charges were dropped against four of the defendants, but five were eventually convicted and ended up serving substantial prison sentences.

The outcome of *Powell* seems painfully obvious today, but it pre-sented a terrible dilemma to the U.S. Supreme Court. On the one hand, the trial transcript and circumstances were shocking and unacceptable to jurists. The evidence was shabby, the trial was rushed, the defense lawyers did almost nothing, and the jury was packed with white Southerners who would have convicted the Scottsboro Boys based on appearance alone.

On the other hand, the U.S. Supreme Court had previously refused to overturn state criminal convictions for violating a specific provision of the Bill of Rights. In the nineteenth century, the Supreme Court had treated the Bill of Rights as limiting only the federal government, as suggested by the First Amendment's first word limiting only what "Congress," not state governments, could do. After the Civil War, the Fourteenth Amendment explicitly required states to provide "due process of law," which was later interpreted to forbid at least mob-dominated trials. But even after the Fourteenth Amendment, the Supreme Court had specifically declined to apply the Fifth Amendment's guarantee of a grand jury indictment to state prosecutions, reasoning that the Fourteenth Amendment's Due Process Clause did not list or require states to follow the specific guarantees of the Bill of Rights.[2]

Thus, until *Powell*, the Court had declined to specify any particular constitutional criminal procedure governing state prosecutions. Doing so would have required upsetting decades of precedent and starting to apply the Bill of Rights to the states. So *Powell* was a true "crossing the Rubicon" moment. Would the Court take responsibility for managing the unmanageable? Would it overturn a string of cases and tradition allowing states largely to handle their own business in criminal matters? But if it chose to let *Powell* stand, would it be a silent partner in Jim Crow–era "justice"?

The Court chose the path of justice and overturned the convictions. American criminal procedure and constitutional law have never been the same. *Powell* was the first step in the journey that led us to the system we have today. Our system is unquestionably a radical improvement over 1931-era justice, but it has not come without its own costs and wrong turns.[3]

Today, the constitutional right to criminal defense counsel is far broader than it was two centuries or even half a century ago. On its surface, criminal defense has grown much stronger, progressively marching toward a fair, level playing field. But this simple story of progress overlooks the costs and tradeoffs. While the Supreme Court has repeatedly expanded the right to criminal defense counsel, it has paid much less attention to funding and implementing it. As the right has broadened, it has also grown shallower. The Court began by responding well to high-stakes injustices in complex criminal trials. But as it kept expanding the right down the criminal justice pyramid, it also watered it down. Without legislative cooperation, courts by themselves cannot and will not guarantee defenders the salaries, support, and caseloads they need to represent their clients vigorously and effectively. In practice, poor criminal defendants have a right to a warm body with a law degree and not much more.

The Right to Hire One's Own Defense Lawyer

Until almost three centuries ago, English defendants were forbidden to hire defense counsel in routine felony or treason cases. Defendants usually knew the facts of their own cases, and in defending themselves they would air their version of events. Trials were a bit like shouting matches among the victim, defendant, and witnesses, with few technical rules of law or evidence that would require a lawyer's intervention. But then prosecuting attorneys began handling some prosecutions (in lieu of victims) and relying on dubious evidence by paid informants. Thus, in the mid-eighteenth century, English courts allowed defendants to hire defense lawyers to cross-examine prosecution witnesses and speak for their clients more generally. The goal was to level the playing field against public prosecutors.[4]

The American colonies likewise rejected the older ban on privately retained defense counsel. And after the Revolutionary War, the Bill of Rights ensured that defendants could hire their own lawyers to protect them from government oppression. The Sixth Amendment guarantees every criminal defendant the right "to have the Assistance of Counsel for his defense." This was understood to mean a right to hire one's own lawyer, not to have the government provide one for free.[5] The colonies did not routinely appoint defense counsel.

Over the course of the nineteenth century, the American legal system grew much more professionalized. Professional police forces grew up, investigating crime and turning evidence over to the prosecution.

Public prosecutors displaced more and more victims bringing private prosecutions, and in response defendants who could afford to do so hired defense counsel.

Some states, by statute or practice, appointed defense counsel for capital or even noncapital felonies, though these were often unpaid: New York started doing so by 1810 and California began in 1872. But Massachusetts and Florida, for instance, did not appoint lawyers for noncapital felonies until the second half of the twentieth century.[6]

Cities then started creating public defender offices as either government agencies or nominally private charities, beginning with Los Angeles in 1914. Advocates sympathized with poor defendants and sought to end their exploitation by shyster lawyers. Some early boosters favored public defenders as aggressive advocates for defendants, while others hoped they would be almost the mirror image of prosecutors: "quasi-judicial officers [who] would owe a duty not only to their clients, but also to the state." New York lawyer Mayer Goldman even suggested that public defenders would not "seek to defeat justice by securing the acquittal of a guilty defendant," but would instead "work harmoniously" with public prosecutors to bring out the truth, protecting the innocent from conviction and the guilty from excessive punishment. These conflicting visions reflected ambivalence about whether adversarial combat against the prosecution or a more neutral, inquisitorial system would better serve truth and justice.[7] In the end, public defenders were built and run as traditional, adversarial representatives of defendants' interests, but these competing sales pitches reflect public qualms about criminal defense that persist to this day.

Once prosecutors and defense lawyers ran many criminal cases, courts developed rules of evidence and procedure to regulate trials, making them longer and more complex. (In the eighteenth century, most trials lasted no more than a few hours; in the nineteenth, they could run for days.) Prosecutors and defense counsel also developed plea bargaining. As repeat players, they could forecast likely outcomes after trial, develop going rates, and build the trust needed to strike bargains and short-circuit these new, elaborate procedures. In other words, increasing complexity begat professionalization, which begat more complexity, which in turn begat shortcuts such as plea bargaining to circumvent costly, cumbersome procedures.

Powell v. Alabama Redux

By the twentieth century, trials had grown long and complex. Defendants could no longer just stand up and argue with victims and witnesses about whodunit. Felony jury trials required elaborate pretrial investigations, witness interviews, jury selection, opening statements, direct- and cross-examination, evidentiary objections, closing arguments, jury instructions, sentencing, and post-trial motions and appeals. Yet many defendants were too poor to hire their own lawyers, and these defendants were often the ones who needed help the most. Many parts of America (especially rural areas) did not have public defenders, and even public defender offices could not represent everyone.

Well into the twentieth century, the U.S. Supreme Court avoided interfering with state criminal justice systems. But the racism and legalized lynchings of the Jim Crow–era South prodded the Court to act. In *Powell v. Alabama*, the U.S. Supreme Court reversed the defendants' convictions, holding that Alabama had denied them their right to hire counsel of their choice. Central to the Court's reasoning was the need for legal expertise to navigate complex trial procedures. Without counsel, the due process right to be heard would mean little. "Even the intelligent and educated layman has small and sometimes no skill in the science of law," such as the technical rules of pleading and evidence. Without "the guiding hand of counsel at every step," innocent men risk being convicted based on incompetent, irrelevant, or inadmissible evidence, even if they have strong defenses. That was especially true of the young, illiterate Scottsboro Boys, who were surrounded by a bloodthirsty mob, cut off from their friends and families, and on trial for their lives. Though the issue had been framed as giving defendants time to hire counsel, the Court threw in an aside that opened the door to free lawyers, at least in these extreme circumstances: Courts must appoint lawyers for those who cannot hire them, at least for "incapable" defendants in capital cases.[8]

Powell was an important first step toward protecting poor criminal defendants. Yet its reasoning and focus raised more questions than they answered. For starters, the Scottsboro Boys did have lawyers, and they never sought court-appointed lawyers free of charge. As the dissenters noted, the Court's language about appointed counsel was dictum—that is, irrelevant to deciding this case. The Court should not have addressed the right to counsel, which covers whether a defendant has a lawyer at all. The real issue in *Powell* was what counsel must do to be effective. But the Court in *Powell* all but avoided that question, as it would continue to do later. The right-to-counsel cases make much of the presence of counsel, but little about how to tell if that counsel was effective.

More generally, the real problems in *Powell* were not so much the defense lawyers as the rush from the arrest to the trial, the exclusion of blacks from the jury, the domination by a lynch mob, and the biased judicial interference with cross-examining the victims. But tackling Southern racism head-on would have been too explosive, shaking the foundations of Jim Crow criminal justice. In that respect, the right-to-counsel ruling was a dodge, and the Court largely avoided acknowledging the strong racial biases that had tainted the trial. Nevertheless, it planted the seed of a constitutional right to appointed counsel (albeit a small and limited one) that would flower in coming decades.

Even *Powell* itself is not an unmitigated triumph. The Supreme Court overturned the Scottsboro verdicts one more time in 1935 in *Patterson v. Alabama* and *Norris v. Alabama*, because Alabama systematically excluded blacks from those juries. But Alabama kept retrying the cases, and eventually the Supreme Court let convictions in five different cases stand.[9]

Beyond Capital Cases: From *Betts* to *Gideon*

Not long after *Powell*, the Court clarified that federal criminal defendants had a right to appointed counsel, as did capital (that is, death-penalty) defendants in state court. Criminal cases are full of "intricate, complex, and mysterious" legal rules and prosecuted "by experienced and learned counsel," so federal defendants needed lawyers to level the playing field. For three decades, however, the Court refused to extend this right to state criminal trials. In *Betts v. Brady*, the Court held that a poor defendant has no fundamental right to appointed counsel in all cases. Where there are special circumstances that make a defendant unable to try his own case, states may have to appoint counsel on occasion to satisfy due process of law. But Betts was a mature man of ordinary intelligence with past experience in criminal justice, and he chose a bench (non-jury) trial, which made the procedures more informal and flexible. He had no special need for a lawyer to navigate the procedures.[10]

In later decades, the Court proved increasingly willing to find special circumstances requiring appointed counsel even in routine cases. Reviewing matters case by case in hindsight, the Court could not provide clear guidance to lower courts and legislatures on which cases needed counsel. As Justice Harlan eventually put it, "[t]he Court has come to recognize, in other words, that the mere existence of a serious criminal charge constituted in itself special circumstances requiring the services of counsel at trial." Thus, in 1963 the Court overruled *Betts* in *Gideon v. Wainwright.*[11]

Clarence Gideon was a sometime drifter, gambler, and small-time thief. In 1961, someone broke into a pool hall in Panama City, Florida, and stole coins from the cigarette machine and juke box, as well as some beer and wine. Witness Henry Cook identified Gideon as the burglar, though Cook had a criminal record and may have committed the crime himself. A police officer arrested Gideon with pockets full of change, which he later testified he had won by gambling. Gideon's request for appointed counsel was denied, and he was convicted of breaking and entering with intent to commit a misdemeanor.

The Supreme Court unanimously reversed Gideon's conviction, overruling the special-circumstances requirement to trigger appointment of counsel. Writing for the Court, Justice Black stressed that the Sixth Amendment's right to appointed counsel is fundamental, so states must follow it to ensure due process of law. "[I]n our adversary system of criminal justice," poor criminal defendants need appointed counsel to ensure fair trials. "Governments . . . quite properly spend vast sums of money to establish machinery to try defendants accused of crime," and defendants who can afford it hire "the best lawyers they can get." Thus, for both the prosecution and the defense, "lawyers in criminal courts are necessities, not luxuries." Tellingly, when Gideon was tried a second time, his appointed defense lawyer caught the prosecution's key witness (Cook) in a lie about his criminal record, and the jury quickly acquitted Gideon.

Gideon was rightly hailed as a triumph for justice, a heroic decision vindicating the little guy and ensuring justice for the poor. Anthony Lewis immortalized the case in his stories for the *New York Times* and his prize-winning book *Gideon's Trumpet*, and Henry Fonda later played Clarence Gideon in a movie made for prime-time TV. But one of the most striking facts about *Gideon* is that the Court largely followed developments in the states, reining in a few Southern outliers, rather than leading them. By the 1960s, all but five states routinely appointed counsel for poor felony defendants. Almost two dozen states filed an amicus (friend-of-the-Court) brief supporting Gideon (!), led by Minnesota Attorney General and future Vice President Walter Mondale, while only two other states supported Florida. The very end of Justice Black's opinion cited the former brief, implicitly confirming that *Gideon*'s rule had proven workable in the states. *Gideon*, in short, was a right on which almost everyone could agree.

Stretching *Gideon* to Minor Cases

Gideon left open a plethora of questions, including how serious a crime must be to qualify for appointed counsel, how well an appointed counsel must perform, and what compensation and resources he must have. On the first of these questions, the Court soon extended *Gideon* beyond felony cases to misdemeanors, in *Argersinger v. Hamlin*. The Florida Supreme Court held that the constitutional right to appointed counsel extends only as far as the right to a jury trial, that is, to crimes punishable by more than six months' imprisonment. But the U.S. Supreme Court reversed Jon Argersinger's concealed-weapon conviction and ninety-day jail sentence, extending the right to counsel to all cases in which a court imposes *any* actual imprisonment. The Court argued that even low-stakes cases may be too complex for laymen to handle themselves, and even brief imprisonment can harm defendants' liberty, careers, and reputations. The Court also worried about "assembly line justice," and hoped that appointing lawyers for misdemeanants would give defendants a chance to examine and fight all criminal charges. The majority dismissed concerns about cost, asserting that only a couple of thousand lawyers, about half of one percent of all lawyers, would be needed to handle all non-traffic misdemeanors in the United States. In his separate concurring opinion, however, Justice Powell worried that the right would cost and demand much more, exacerbating court congestion and delay.[12]

Argersinger is dubious for several reasons. First, *Argersinger* is far more radical than *Gideon*. *Gideon* merely codified a right that was already working in a majority of states. But *Argersinger* swept far more broadly, creating a new right that was broader than most states' practices at the time. Given the novelty and breadth of the right, it is unsurprising that the majority's predictions proved to be far too sanguine. Second, the Court relied upon the American Bar Association's recommendations, but of course the ABA's members are the ones who benefit from the Court's full-employment mandate. Third, the right to a jury trial is expressly guaranteed twice in the Constitution, and the Founding Fathers made it central to the Bill of Rights. Yet the Court treated its novel right to counsel as more fundamental than the venerable right to a jury, stretching it much further.

The Court, in *Alabama v. Shelton*, extended *Argersinger* to suspended sentences that later result in imprisonment. But in *Scott v. Illinois* it drew the line at cases imposing imprisonment, not just fines, heeding earlier warnings about cost. Broadening the right to fine-only misdemeanors, it worried, "would create confusion and impose unpredictable, but necessarily substantial, costs on 50 quite diverse States."[13]

The bottom line? The very limited right first announced in *Powell* had grown broad indeed: *All* criminal defendants facing even a day of jail time, plus defendants with suspended sentences that later result in jail time, plus juvenile defendants facing imprisonment, get a free government lawyer if they cannot afford to hire one. Misdemeanors that result only in fines do not require a lawyer.

Minimal Performance Standards

Collectively, *Gideon*, *Argersinger*, and *Shelton* extended the right well beyond capital cases or felonies to millions of misdemeanors, making its reach quite broad. But the Court refused to make it deep. It has imposed only the most minimal standards for how well appointed counsel must perform and what pay, support, and resources they must have in order to assist their clients effectively.

Even though the Scottsboro Boys had lawyers, the circumstances prevented their lawyers from giving "effective aid" in preparing and trying the cases, making their trials fundamentally unfair. More than half a century after *Powell* and more than two decades after *Gideon*, the Supreme Court finally defined "effective aid" as requiring only minimal competence in *Strickland v. Washington*. In so doing, it revealed how little the right ultimately guarantees in practice. The point of the right to counsel is to ensure a fair trial with a just result by testing the prosecution's case. Our adversarial system relies on defense lawyers to play that role, but the Supreme Court has hardly held their feet to the fire.

Unfortunately, *Strickland*'s standard is so complex and murky in practice that it requires lawyers to litigate ineffectiveness after the fact. Under *Strickland*, courts assess ineffective assistance of counsel in retrospect, when reviewing convictions and sentences, and require defendants to bear the burden of proving both (1) deficient performance and (2) prejudice. On *performance*, reviewing courts must be "highly deferential" and strongly presume that any debatable decisions were reasonable tactical choices rather than errors. It treats lawyering as an art, not a science, with few definable rules. Courts do not seek to raise the prevailing bar, but simply to ensure that defense lawyers' performance fell within the "wide range" of reasonable competence. In other words, *Strickland* is supposed to catch outliers but simultaneously makes it hard to define "outliers." Bar standards and checklists are at most guidelines, not rules. In the past decade or so, the Court has paid more attention to bar standards in assessing counsel's failures to investigate mitigating evidence in capital cases or to advise clients pleading guilty that they may face deportation. But these guidelines do not amount to codes for defense lawyering; opinions relying on these guidelines are the exception, not the rule.[14]

By and large, ineffective assistance still depends on fact-specific, case-by-case judgments of effectiveness. The lack of concrete standards impedes teaching defense lawyers how to defend effectively and relieving defendants whose lawyers fail to do so. *Strickland* is all about reviewing individual cases after the fact, not promulgating or codifying rules for future cases ahead of time. Because the point of the right to counsel is to ensure a fair, adversarial trial, *Strickland*'s test of prejudice is whether the trial's result was fair and reliable. Courts will presume prejudice only when the state failed to supply defense counsel altogether or interfered with his performance, or the defense lawyer labored under an actual conflict of interest. Otherwise, defendants must prove, case by case, "a reasonable probability" that the error changed the trial's verdict of guilt or sentence. "Reasonable probability" means "a probability sufficient to undermine confidence in the outcome," in light of all the evidence.

The *Strickland* Court also advised that either prong of the test, performance or prejudice, could come first in a reviewing court's analysis. Unsurprisingly, this has meant that reviewing courts often *start* their analysis with a catalogue of the evidence of the defendant's guilt before finding no prejudice. Once the prejudice issue is settled, courts can briefly ratify the performance of the lawyer or just ignore it altogether. This is one of the reasons why truly horrible lawyering by drunk or sleeping lawyers has been allowed on appeal. The reviewing courts focus on the prosecution's case (evidence of guilt), find no prejudice, and then glide over the defense work, regardless of how bad it was. To paraphrase Justice Scalia, making prejudice the focus of our ineffective assistance of counsel analysis is "akin to dispensing with jury trial because a defendant is obviously guilty."[15] The primary question should not be whether the prosecution presented sufficient evidence of guilt; that is easy to do when an opposing lawyer does no work at all. The focus should be on whether the defense lawyer fulfilled the constitutionally crucial role of *actually providing a defense*.

Strickland's performance standard is too weak, too vague, and far too deferential. The Court in *Strickland* bent over backwards to guard against Monday-morning quarterbacking. The Court reminded us that calculated risks sometimes fail, and admonished that courts should not second-guess counsel's decisions in hindsight. Moreover, defense lawyering is a craft or an art, not a science, so different craftsmen may investigate and try cases very differently. For instance, one defense lawyer will attack a prosecution witness's truthfulness on cross-examination; another will more subtly question his memory or eyesight. One will try to strike a deal to cooperate with the prosecution; another will hang tough in plea bargaining. One defense lawyer will take the risk of having his client testify to an alibi, at the cost of being cross-examined about his prior convictions; a second will put on no witnesses but poke holes in the prosecution's theory to create reasonable doubt. While that is all true and calls for some judicial deference, it makes these tactical judgments hard to second-guess in hindsight.

Unfortunately, the murkiness of *Strickland*'s standard plus the strong presumption of effectiveness make it extremely hard to review convictions case by case. The lack of rules makes it hard to specify what a defense lawyer should have done and so what qualifies as an error rather than a judgment call.

The strong presumption of reasonableness compounds the problem of vagueness, leading courts to imagine reasons why a defense lawyer might have meant to do something that in fact was a dumb mistake. And instead of 20/20 hindsight, reviewing courts fall into the opposite trap: In retrospect, convictions seem inevitable, and it becomes easy to dismiss errors as immaterial to the foreordained result. Psychologists call this perception the "inevitability bias." That perception is particularly strong because most convictions result from guilty pleas, which lack trial transcripts to document counsel's performance and are colored by defendants' admissions of guilt.[16]

Moreover, *Strickland*'s focus on a few bad apples distracts attention from the broader deficits that breed systemically poor representation in the first place. As Chapter 2 explained, the problems of poor defense lawyering are rooted in system-wide underfunding and overwork. By and large, courts cannot and will not fix these deeply flawed structures. They are loath even to specify and enforce maximum caseloads, salaries, and support staff. Those are all systemic foundations of the problem, which bear indirectly on the guilt and conviction of any particular defendant before a court. A few adventurous state courts have tried halting prosecutions in excess of recommended defender caseloads, or ordering their state legislatures to increase defense funding, equalize prosecutors' and defense lawyers' salaries, or at least cover defense lawyers' out-of-pocket expenses. But courts are poorly equipped to manage tax revenues, other funding sources, and budget tradeoffs in a world of scarcity. Though court orders have occasionally led to one-time bumps in indigent defense funding, any gains have been transient; inflation and rising caseloads soon wipe them out.[17]

As a result of all these failings, *Strickland* means little in practice. Defendants routinely challenge their lawyers' performance when they are convicted, and reviewing courts routinely rubber-stamp their convictions and sentences. Courts of appeals, swamped with frivolous ineffectiveness claims, approach each one with a jaundiced eye. As Justice Jackson put it, "It must prejudice the occasional meritorious application to be buried in a flood of worthless ones. He who must search a haystack for a needle is likely to end up with the attitude that the needle is not worth the search."[18] This is particularly so because reversing a conviction would require a whole new trial, often with similar lawyers and resources in similarly strapped and busy circumstances.

Thus, courts wind up reversing only a small percentage of all cases, catching only the most egregious outliers. As Chapter 2 explained, courts sometimes even overlook lawyers' abuse of drugs and alcohol and napping during trials. They rarely overturn less glaring malpractice, let alone mere failure to test the prosecution's case zealously. In short, any "lawyer with a pulse will be deemed effective."[19] *Gideon*'s trumpet is muted.

Powell began from the top of the pyramid of crimes. It envisioned equal justice and a level playing field for the most serious crimes in the most outrageous circumstances: a mob-dominated legalized lynching of young black men accused of raping white women. *Gideon* rightly generalized *Powell* to all felony cases, now that they have become too complex for laymen to navigate on their own. *Gideon* was right both symbolically and practically; it was an important step toward leveling the playing field in felony cases. But simply announcing a right does not make it effective. The Court kept extending this vision of formal, Cadillac justice down the pyramid to more and more misdemeanors, beyond courts' ability or legislatures' willingness to implement it well. And legislatures kept expanding the breadth and depth of criminal laws so as to claim political credit and give prosecutors more tools. As a result, the system grew ever more complex and more reliant on plea bargaining to clear growing dockets. *Argersinger* even envisioned routine constitutional challenges to vagrancy prosecutions, as if even the tiniest and most routine cases were snowflakes to be marveled at in all their hidden complexity. As *Strickland* shows, *Gideon* means far less in practice than it should in theory. The emperor has a few clothes, but his suit is shabby indeed.

CHAPTER 4

Access to Justice in Civil Courts

Every other week during the semester, the University of Tennessee's Homeless Legal Advocacy Project troops out to the Knoxville Area Rescue Ministry, a local homeless shelter. Under the supervision of Professor Ben Barton or another licensed attorney, students try to answer the legal questions of Knoxville's homeless. If the cases are simple enough, the students take them on. The results fall into telltale patterns: patterns not only of typical problems and solutions, but also of basic legal issues that are too complicated to handle without a lawyer but too expensive to handle with one.

Take, for example, divorces. The University of Tennessee Law School's clinics are regularly asked for advice or help in divorcing a spouse. Two groups of homeless people can get divorces relatively easily. If the potential client and spouse are local, have no children and little property, and substantially agree about the divorce, the process is straightforward. The students can go to the Tennessee Supreme Court's website and print out forms "for divorces where both spouses agree on all parts of the divorce, there are no minor or dependent children involved, and the spouses do not have a lot of property."[1] The forms come in English and Spanish. The Tennessee Access to Justice Commission developed the forms and, by order of the Tennessee Supreme Court, every court in the state *must* accept them if properly filled out.

These forms are meant for the poor, but a simple, agreed-upon middle-class divorce could use them as well. Similar forms are available for a fee through LegalZoom and other online forms providers. Middle class couples with simple divorces can also hire a lawyer (who likely just fills in the forms described above) for as little as $500. In short, for the homeless or the middle class, there is not much of an access-to-justice problem for extremely simple divorces.

If the homeless client has suffered abuse in the marriage, it is also fairly easy to seek a divorce. This is because, like many legal aid offices, Legal Aid of East Tennessee gives priority to divorces where one spouse claims abuse. They have to apply some such filter, because the demand for free legal services greatly outstrips the supply of free lawyers. So, unless the client claims abuse, he or she goes on an endless waiting list. This filter is sensible, as Legal Aid's funding is tight and it must decide who needs help right away. Nevertheless, the filter does severely limit the types of divorces Legal Aid handles. Anecdotally, it has another effect: prompting over-claims of abuse. Well-meaning legal aid screeners may tell a potential client, "I'm sorry, we can't take your divorce because we focus on divorces where abuse occurred." The desperate client's natural response is to remember, or even make up, some kind of abuse. So even if the divorce is complicated and disputed, if a person can meet the legal aid income guidelines (125% of the federal poverty line) and claim spousal abuse, he or she can get a free, government-paid lawyer to pursue a divorce.

If the client's income is more than 125% of the poverty line, he or she is altogether out of luck for a free lawyer. That income ceiling is a very stringent requirement. In 2013, it was $14,363 for a one-person household. This means that a full-time worker earning the minimum wage ($15,080 annually at $7.25 per hour) is ineligible for legal aid.

Unfortunately, only a fraction of our clients fall into one of these two categories, and of course most middle-class divorces do not. First, note the irony of requiring divorcees to agree on everything before they can get divorced. Most people seek divorces because they have trouble getting along with their spouses.

Second, a wide range of potential problems can make a divorce contested or complicated. Our clinic has had multiple potential clients where the spouse is in another state or was even deported back to another country. Often, there are children, disputed assets, allegations of abuse, or all of the above. Sometimes the other spouse simply does not want to get divorced at all, or at least not on the client's proposed terms. Homeless people have sometimes lost all track of their former spouses.

Middle-class divorces are even more likely to involve disagreements. Consider two recurring scenarios: disputes over custody and asset distribution. Many divorces include children, and choosing which parent should make educational or medical decisions or how to share physical custody can be extremely challenging. Most courts award custody based on what would be in the "best interests of the child," considering all of the relevant circumstances. Thus, the fights can get particularly nasty, dredging up every deficiency and every bad parenting moment of either spouse. The fights are long, costly, and bitter. They are also very hard to navigate without a lawyer. To handle a full-scale custody dispute properly, a litigant must take discovery of the other side, which requires interviewing witnesses, requesting documents, and submitting lists of questions. He or she must file motions, which often request information or seek to toss the case out or narrow the issues and questioning. And he or she must understand and navigate the rules of evidence, which have complicated requirements for laying a foundation and authenticating documents and the like. A *pro se* litigant cannot do this well. In 2005, small-firm lawyers and solo practitioners charged, on average, $182 an hour. Even at $100 an hour, the costs add up pretty quickly.

These custody problems recur over time. Consider a divorced parent who decides to move for work or family out of town or out of state. The court will reconsider the issue under the best-interests-of-the-child standard. The bitter ex-spouses can once again air each other's faults and alleged bad parenting. The legal fees will cost thousands more. There is also the potential for what poker players call "short-stacking." In tournament poker, there are special strategies for when one player has a lot more chips than another (the "short stack"). Essentially, the richer player can bully the short stack into folding repeatedly by betting a lot. Drawn-out custody battles sometimes recur because one spouse can afford to keep hiring a lawyer and the other cannot. In these circumstances, the costs of the process, not the merits, largely determine who wins and who loses.

Likewise, divorcing spouses often disagree about how to define or divide marital property. Generally, marital property is property acquired during the marriage, except for property inherited or given as a gift to one spouse. But there is always room for dispute: Special rules govern commingling of funds. Spouses earn and jointly spend money during a marriage, confusing matters. And one spouse may even accuse the other of hiding or mischaracterizing assets as non-marital. Finding assets or disputing which assets to include in the division of property is time intensive and very expensive. It starts with the cumbersome discovery process, in which each side demands documents, questions witnesses in depositions, and seeks information from the other side. The process continues with more investigation, and ends with litigation over what property to include and how to divide it. These disputes are governed by a mix of common-law standards, court precedents, and statutes. A *pro se* litigant would thus find it hard even to figure out what law applies, let alone how to litigate the issues properly.

Lumping It

Given the costs and complexity, the potential client may well just have to "lump it"—find some way to agree on the underlying issues, stay married until the divorce becomes uncontested, or simply stay married for good. Why? Because the process is so complicated that it requires a lawyer to navigate, and there are simply no lawyers they can afford. In some cases, that might be salutary: choosing not to sue a neighbor over a property dispute, for example, might save money and improve relations, and unhappy couples are sometimes better off working out their differences instead of divorcing. Many of these problems, however, are more like needed divorces or changes to child custody arrangements. People who cannot afford lawyers to solve these problems suffer real hardships.

There is plenty of evidence of an access-to-justice problem. Two empirical studies suggest that poor and middle-class Americans suffer these problems frequently. The most comprehensive such study is the American Bar Association's 1994 study *Legal Needs and Civil Justice*, which canvassed both low- and moderate-income Americans. ("Low income" meant 125% of the poverty line and below, and "moderate income" meant the middle three-fifths—from 20th to 80th percentile—of households). About half of all households had at least one unmet legal need during 1992 (excluding desires for standalone legal advice), but nearly three-quarters of the low-income households' problems and two-thirds of the moderate-income households' problems were never brought to the civil justice system.

Professor Gillian Hadfield compared this study to studies of legal needs around the world. Americans were about as likely to have a legal need and about as likely to use a lawyer to solve those problems as citizens of other countries, but were far more likely to "lump it." Citizens in England, Wales, Scotland, and Slovakia got advice from non-lawyers much more often, apparently filling the gap.[2] Almost a third of Americans lumped it in the 1994 survey, compared with under 5% in the U.K. and 18% in Slovakia. Hadfield concludes:

> These studies suggest that the U.S. legal system plays a significantly smaller role in providing a key component of what law provides— ordered means of resolving problems and disputes—than either comparable advanced market democracies or countries still in the early stages of establishing the basic institutions of democratic governance and a market economy.[3]

The World Justice Project's (wjp) 2014 version of the Rule of Law index further demonstrates that the United States lags behind other industrialized countries in access to justice. The wjp surveyed or interviewed more than 100,000 citizens and legal experts in ninety-nine countries; it found that the United States fell in the bottom half of the high-income countries on their aggregate measure of the rule of law and was a staggering 25th out of thirty wealthy countries on the civil-justice measure.[4]

Other studies, focusing solely on poor Americans, have found even greater unmet need. The most recent comprehensive study is a 2009 report by the Legal Services Corporation (lsc), which presents three different measures of unmet need.[5]

First, the report found that, because lsc lacked enough money, it had to reject almost a million cases per year—just over half of all eligible clients. These numbers do not include people who were denied services by non-lsc-funded programs and those who did not seek legal help at all. They also do not include potential clients who were ineligible under the stringent poverty guidelines (generally set at 125% of the federal poverty line), that is, middle- and lower-middle-class people. Lastly, the number of clients "served" by LSC programs includes people who received partial or unbundled services or limited advice, such as a five-minute telephone call, a brief chat at a help desk, or a do-it-yourself manual. In Chicago, for example, these "brief services" make up 80% of the clients counted as served.[6]

Second, the report amalgamated data from studies of seven states—Alabama, Georgia, Nevada, New Jersey, Utah, Virginia, and Wisconsin. These studies show that low-income households have as many as three different legal needs a year, and that fewer than one in five of those needs is addressed with the help of a private or legal aid lawyer. Even using a stringent definition of "legal need," a large majority of serious legal problems are not addressed with the help of a lawyer.

Third, LSC compared the number of lawyers providing services to the poor (whether or not they worked for LSC) with the number of private attorneys. Nationally there is one attorney for every 6,415 poor people and one private attorney providing personal legal services for every 429 people in the general population. The number of private attorneys per capita is somewhat misleading, however, since a good number of those lawyers work primarily for corporations and businesses.

Other studies report similar findings. For example, a 2008 study in Washington, DC, found that: (1) 97% of tenants who go to court as defendants in a dispute with their landlords (typically in eviction proceedings) are not represented, (2) 98% of domestic violence victims and respondents are unrepresented, and (3) 98% of respondents were unrepresented in paternity and child-support cases. In Texas, only 20% to 25% of eligible poor litigants are represented in court. That rate actually sounds high given this ratio: There is roughly one legal aid lawyer for every 11,000 income-eligible Texans.[7]

Professor Gillian Hadfield offers an alternative measure of legal services for the poor and middle class.[8] She divided the total amount of money individuals (as opposed to corporations) spent on legal services by the average hourly rate for small firm and solo practitioners and then again by the U.S. population. In 1990, Americans bought an average of 1.6 hours of legal services per person for the year, or 4.15 hours per household. By 2012, the number had declined 30%, to 1.3 hours per person or 3.0 hours per household. Spread out by legal problems rather than households, the numbers are even starker: In 1990, American households were able to use roughly 4 hours of legal time, on average, to address a legal problem. By 2012, that amount had shrunk to 1 hour and 30 minutes. Even if you double these rough averages, they cannot cover most legal problems. Most Americans cannot afford to hire a lawyer, even for serious legal problems like divorce, criminal defense, or foreclosure.[9]

Further evidence is the flood of *pro se* litigation in American courts, frequently over very important and complicated issues.[10] The rate of self-representation has been growing and spreading into more serious legal disputes since at least 1998, and it has accelerated since 2008.[11] A great number of American courts have tipped over to having a majority of the cases feature at least one *pro se* party. Examples include courts that handle evictions, family law, debt collection, and child support.

The Cost of Private Help

So why do people with legal problems, especially middle-class people, forgo hiring private lawyers? Every town has firms that advertise $500 divorces. These teaser rates, however, are only for simple divorces. As a Knoxville private attorney's website explains:

> Attorney's fees will vary based on the individual attorney and the complexity of the divorce. An uncontested divorce with nothing left to work out, no real property, and no minor children will cost anywhere from $150–$1500 depending on the attorney. In a contested divorce, it is more difficult to estimate fees because of the uncertainty of how much work will need to be done on the case. Most attorneys bill by the hour on contested matters and will usually require a retainer up front.[12]

A contested divorce is like a home in the Hamptons: If you have to ask how much it will cost, you probably cannot afford it.

How about a *pro bono* lawyer, a private-firm lawyer volunteering for free as a public service? As noted below, *pro bono* work is fairly limited, especially in family law. Few lawyers have the expertise needed to handle a contested or complicated divorce, and the ones with the expertise are small-firm and solo practitioners struggling to make ends meet. Nor is divorce work particularly fun or sexy, making it a low priority for lawyers volunteering their time.

So maybe file *pro se*? American judges and clerk's offices are notoriously impatient with *pro se* litigants.[13] Clerk's offices are frequently told not to give any legal advice to *pro se* litigants. Many have been told that if they gave legal advice, they could be sued civilly or criminally for engaging in the unauthorized practice of law. Judges are similarly impatient. They much prefer to have lawyers file and process cases correctly than to have confused non-lawyers stumble about.

Take a seemingly simple issue that came up in the Homeless Project. The potential client was a recovering drug addict who had moved down from Cleveland and left his wife behind. After a few years in Knoxville without any contact, he decided to seek a divorce. He started at the local court clerk's office by asking how to divorce someone in Ohio. The clerks refused to say whether to file in Tennessee or Ohio. They refused to explain how to serve a party in Ohio. They certainly did not explain which state's laws would apply in Tennessee or how the laws might work out in a contested divorce. Nor should the clerks have answered all of those questions—they likely had no idea how to answer.

Online forms are not much help in these circumstances. The documents are for simple divorces. They do not apply to bumps in the road, even simple issues like a dispute in custody arrangements or different state locations.

And don't think that this problem is limited to the homeless or the poor. Though Americans often think of access to justice as a problem of poverty, it afflicts the middle class too. Middle-class people have it worse, since they cannot use legal aid and are likelier to have some assets over which they can fight. A typical retainer for a contested divorce is $10,000 up front. Not many Americans can afford justice at that price.

Even in a market glutted with lawyers, it is still quite expensive to pay an individual lawyer to research a legal problem, let alone to pursue litigation or draft a legal document. Thus, both poor and middle-class Americans often must proceed without counsel or "lump it" by living with problems that courts could solve.

Where Are All the Lawyers?

In short, ordinary Americans cannot afford to hire a lawyer even for very serious and complicated problems, the problem is growing worse, and the system is poorly equipped to handle the resulting flood of *pro se* litigants. How can this be? The legal profession continues to grow faster than the population, adding more than 46,000 new law school graduates in 2013. It is puzzling that in the midst of the worst law recession since the Great Depression, access to justice remained deplorable. Where are all of these displaced lawyers and why are they not servicing this need?

First, roughly a quarter of lawyers are not in private practice, working directly for corporations or in government or a law school. Of those in private practice, the most lucrative and sought-after work is in representing or suing corporations. From the 1950s until 2008, large corporate law firms grew steadily in terms of number of lawyers, percentage of the profession, revenues, and profits. Virtually all large-firm work is for corporations or very wealthy individuals.[14]

Even small firms and solo practitioners make the most money by working on contingency or via class action and suing corporations, insurance companies, wealthy individuals, or other deep pockets. This area grew enormously from the 1960s through 1990s, although tort reform has since stalled the growth.[15]

So in the areas of representing or suing corporations, there are too many lawyers chasing the same work. Consider this bizarre fact: A person who slips and falls outside a Walmart has his pick of lawyers, many of whom advertise on television, billboards, and public transport. A person seeking a divorce must reach a speedy agreement with her spouse or burn through much of the family's assets.

But what of the lawyers who cannot make a living working for or suing corporations? Surely they should aim their services at the needy middle class. Here, legal complexity again rears its head. Working by the hour for individual middle-class customers is actually very hard to do profitably. The best evidence is the earnings of solo practitioners, the lawyers who primarily handle the legal needs of small businesses and ordinary Americans. According to IRS filings, in 1967, the average income for a solo practitioner was $10,850 (or $74,806 in 2013 dollars).

In 1988, an average solo practitioner earned $38,393 ($74,735 in 2013 dollars), basically stagnant over a twenty year period. In 2010, solo practitioners earned $46,560 ($49,741 in 2013 dollars). Solo practitioners' annual earnings dropped by almost $25,000 between 1998 and 2010, nearly a 37% decline.

Consider a series of income studies by the Alabama Bar Association, showing a marked decline from 1985 to 2009.[16] The figures below are inflation adjusted to 2009:

17% of Alabama attorneys were making at least $200,000 in 1985 in 2009 dollars, while only 8.7% of Alabama attorneys were making $200,000 in 2009.

54% of Alabama attorneys were making at least $100,000 per year in 1985, as compared to 28% in 2009.

In 1997, 76% of Alabama attorneys were making at least $67,000 per year in 2009 dollars. In 2009, only approximately 49% were making at least $67,000.

In 1997, 40% of Alabama attorneys were making at least $134,000 per year in 2009 dollars. In 2009 20% of Alabama attorneys were making at least that much.

Perhaps most significantly, 23% of Alabama attorneys were making *less than $25,000* in 2009, and 37% were making less than $50,000.

There are several remarkable statistics here. Like the IRS data, the Alabama survey data shows a collapse in small firm and solo practitioner earnings over the last twenty years. There are still lawyers who make a good living, but it is a much smaller percentage of the profession. Almost a quarter of the lawyers surveyed, who had practiced for an average of fifteen to twenty years, earned less than $25,000.

That last statistic also tells you everything you need to know about why lawyer oversupply has not solved the access-to-justice problem. Roughly one quarter of the lawyers surveyed in Alabama in 2010 are earning less practicing law than they could as managers at McDonald's, yet access to justice remains an acute problem in Alabama, as it is everywhere else. This is because it is impossible to lower the hourly or per-transaction fees low enough on individualized, bespoke services to meet the need at an affordable price. Before these lawyers lower their prices further, they will leave the practice altogether. One recent study found that roughly a third of law school graduates since the 1980s are not practicing law. Some of these people found better, non-legal jobs, but most of them left the profession because they could not make a living in the brutally competitive small firm/solo practitioner market.

The problem is partly that these lawyers know only how to handle each case individually. It is possible to use technology and non-lawyer assistants to help with legal forms, but those solutions are of limited help for in-court work or legal research. Part of the problem is procedural complexity: The system is too complicated to permit a low, flat fee for something as variable as a contested divorce or a child-custody battle. The effect of technology on this problem is yet to be determined. Interactive forms and virtual offices might let lawyers lower prices enough to draw in new clients and better serve the middle class, particularly for non-litigation work such as wills and estate planning. Or online forms providers may prove so disruptive that they make the market for small firm and solo practitioners even worse.

So if the market will not solve the problem, what about the government? Legal aid organizations have been government supported for almost fifty years and have done amazing work with their resources, but they are far from meeting the need. First, because of stringent income guidelines, legal aid organizations offer little help to the middle or working class. Second, legal aid funding has been in decline for years. Federal funding for the Legal Services Corporation declined by 63% over the last three decades. State funding has also declined, and low interest rates have cut the funding from IOLTA accounts. (IOLTA, short for interest earned on lawyers' trust accounts, is often funneled to fund legal aid.) The result is a dearth of funding and legal aid lawyers, surely not enough to meet the need.

Perhaps *pro bono* is the answer? Professor Deborah Rhode has been a national leader on encouraging *pro bono*, but is also realistic about its efficacy:

> Precise figures are unavailable because only seven states require the reporting of pro bono work. Moreover, many lawyers have included in their reports activities such as bar association service; favors for friends, clients, and family members; and cases where

fees turn out to be uncollectible. Based on such reports, a lawyer's average pro bono contribution is estimated at less than half a dollar a day and half an hour a week, and much of this assistance does not go to individuals of limited means or to organizations that assist them. Fewer than one in ten lawyers accept referrals from legal aid programs or groups serving low-income communities. Less than half of lawyers in the nation's two hundred most profitable firms have contributed at least twenty hours a year.[17]

Pro bono work is admirable, but cannot begin to meet the need. And again, *pro bono* work is generally for the poor, not the middle class.

The Upshot

This is the paradox of American justice. In a country built on justice for all and the rule of law, we have created a legal system so expensive and unwieldy that most Americans cannot afford it. We spend more on lawyers than any other country, and yet most Americans are priced out of the market.

Instead of rehashing tired, failed arguments about increasing legal aid, civil *Gideon*, or *pro bono*, we need to simplify civil justice itself, using technology to build it around *pro se* litigants rather than lawyers. This neglected approach is both the most likely to occur *and* the best solution. As we shall see, there are courts, entrepreneurs, lawyers, and law schools working together to make our solution a reality. For the first time in years, there are reasons to be optimistic about access to justice, as a combination of computerization, new competition for lawyers, and court reform make access to justice an expanding reality.

CHAPTER 5

How We Got Here:
Civil Law

American civil law and procedure used to be much less complex and formal. Many judges, magistrates, and justices of the peace were not lawyers. Ordinary citizens could appear in court and argue their cases.

Bar admission was informal. How informal? Consider the bar examination story of John Birch of Bloomfield, Illinois. Birch met with his bar examiner, a local attorney named Abraham Lincoln, in Lincoln's hotel room. Lincoln met him at the door in a state of partial undress and then proceeded to examine Birch orally while taking his afternoon bath:

> He asked me in a desultory way the definition of a contract, and two or three fundamental questions, all of which I answered readily, and I thought, correctly. Beyond these meager inquiries . . . he asked nothing more. . . . The whole proceeding was so unusual and queer, if not grotesque, that I was at a loss to determine whether I was really being examined at all. After he had dressed we went downstairs and over to the clerk's office in the courthouse, where he wrote a few lines on a sheet of paper and directed me to report with it to Judge Logan.[1]

When Birch presented the letter, Judge Logan smiled and swore Birch in. The note from Lincoln read: "My Dear Judge—The bearer of this is a young man who thinks he can be a lawyer. Examine him, if you want to. I have done so, and am satisfied. He's a good deal smarter than he looks to be."[2]

From the late nineteenth century on, laws and procedures have grown more formal and complex. Thus, most civil litigants now need lawyers to navigate for them, which has naturally hurt those who cannot afford one. Poor people have probably never fared particularly well in American civil courts, so recent talk of a *pro se* or access-to-justice "crisis" merely recognizes a longstanding problem.

Over the last four decades, however, things have indeed gotten worse. American law has kept growing more complex and more intrusive. And lawyers' hourly rates have kept rising, as the traditional answers to these challenges—increased funding for legal aid, a civil *Gideon* right, more *pro bono* work—have largely failed.

America's history of access to civil justice divides roughly into four eras. First, through most of the eighteenth and nineteenth centuries, American justice was much less formal and the reach of the law was much more limited. The country was largely agrarian and the courts were informal and often run by laymen. A literate American with some help could likely prosecute or defend any civil suit he might find himself in.

In the second era, from the end of the nineteenth century until the 1960s, the legal profession and the courts became more powerful and formalized. America became increasingly industrialized and urbanized, and absorbed a massive wave of immigrants, so we relied increasingly upon the law, lawyers, and legal structures to settle disputes and organize society and the economy. The law's widening scope was coupled with increasing complexity. Discovery (exchanging potential evidence before trial) became the norm in litigation. Statutes and common-law doctrines expanded to cover much more human interaction. The regulatory state grew. All of this meant that ordinary Americans were more likely to need lawyers.

The increased emphasis upon law put the poor, especially immigrants, at a terrible legal disadvantage. While urban charities responded by founding legal aid societies, these organizations were small, charitably funded, and often ineffective.

Third, from the 1960s until the 1980s, there was tremendous growth in both the number of lawyers and lawyer incomes, demonstrating the burgeoning need for legal services. There was also a great flowering of interest and funding for civil lawyers for the poor. The federal government funded legal aid societies to an unprecedented level. Law schools founded clinics. As desegregation and environmental lawsuits succeeded, nonprofit law-reform groups became more prevalent.

Finally, the last three decades have shown the problem with our increasing dependence upon lawyers. The access-to-justice crisis has grown and spread upwards. What has been treated as a problem solely for the poor has become a problem for most Americans, even though there are many more lawyers than ever and many more law school graduates than there are jobs for lawyers.

Why the mismatch between supply and demand? Rules forbidding the unauthorized practice of law keep cheap non-lawyers from the market. Law school is much too expensive and law students now graduate with crippling student debt. Law schools also teach and highlight legal complexity, rather than attempting to streamline legal services and teach a cookie-cutter approach, and for good reason: American law and procedure are extraordinarily complex, making it dangerous to mass-produce services.

We have also seen a collapse of support for the 1960s approach to the legal needs of the poor. Legal aid societies came under attack. Budget cuts plus inflation have chopped their funding in half, and stringent controls regulate the sorts of work they can perform. *Pro bono* programs have become more formalized, but still reach little of the great need. And the Supreme Court has twice rejected civil *Gideon*, probably for good. It is time to try new approaches.

1700–1880: Lay Justice

American law and procedure were much less complicated during the eighteenth and nineteenth centuries, and the rules on lay representation were much looser. In a largely agrarian economy, fewer Americans were likely to find themselves in civil court. If a citizen could read and write, he could probably represent himself competently. Rules against the unauthorized practice of law were rare and never enforced outside of court, so litigants who needed help could consult lawyers or non-lawyers. Even many judges were not lawyers.

This was especially true during the mid-nineteenth-century period of Jacksonian democracy, when governments deprofessionalized the courts and the legal profession as part of a broad-based attack on cultural elites. State governments dismantled many barriers to entry and formal regulation of the legal profession. New Hampshire, Maine, Wisconsin, and Indiana abolished their requirements for appearing in court altogether.[3] In 1800, a set period of preparation for bar admission was required in fourteen of the nineteen states or territories. In 1840, it was required in eleven out of thirty. By 1860, it was required in only nine of thirty-nine.[4] Legislatures sought to reform and codify the common law and eliminate special pleading forms. As a result, courts were often informal and lay people were welcome to plead their own cases.

1880–1965: The Professionalization Project

The growth of cities, the industrial economy, and immigration led to greater reliance on law and the courts to organize our society. Plaintiffs injured by streetcars, railroads, textile mills, and factories filed far more negligence suits in the late nineteenth century, and these suits were more time-consuming and witness-intensive than contract cases and the like.[5] There was a tremendous growth in the number and nature of statutes, regulations, and court-made common-law doctrines. Federal and state bureaucracies were created and grew exponentially.

At the same time, bar associations, judges, and law professors strove to professionalize the legal profession and the courts. Court procedures formalized to the point where only trained and experienced lawyers could operate the rules of evidence or procedure in a typical civil case.

State supreme courts and bar associations became much more engaged in regulating the legal profession. Between 1880 and 1950, they erected more and higher barriers to entering the legal profession. Law schools replaced apprenticeship, and then ABA-approved law schools replaced shorter and cheaper night law schools. A formal, written bar examination run by a central administration under the state supreme court replaced informal judicial interviews. Over time, most courts were run by lawyer-judges and procedures, and the law itself grew much more complicated.

Professionalization and complexity undoubtedly brought benefits to our increasingly populous, urban, industrializing country. But the growth of law came at great cost to immigrants and the poor. They faced a bevy of legal and quasi-legal problems, including loan sharks, unsavory landlords who could evict them without notice, and employers who would refuse to pay wages earned. Upton Sinclair's *The Jungle* memorably chronicled how recent immigrants were bewildered and exploited by meatpacking plants and predatory home sellers and lenders. Between court fees, language and cultural barriers, and the cost of lawyers, there was little justice for the poor.

In response, charities founded legal aid societies in many large cities. The first recorded American legal aid society started in New York City in 1876 as an offshoot of The German Society, a charitable organization focused on assisting German immigrants.[6] In 1890, it was renamed the Legal Aid Society of New York, with an expanded mission to render legal aid to the "worthy" poor. In 1888, the Ethical Society of Chicago started a similar organization.

By 1917, there were forty-one legal aid societies, including a handful of government-sponsored public-defender programs and a few nascent law school clinics. These clinics were not offered for credit or as part of the curriculum, but did let students volunteer to help the poor.

The publication of Reginald Heber Smith's masterwork *Justice and the Poor*, in 1919, sparked increased interest in legal aid. Smith treated the problem not as one of substantive law reform, but one of simplifying procedures and improving access to legal services. That argument was, and still is, controversial in poverty-law circles. It is echoed in the continuing debate over focusing on representing individual clients versus broader constitutional and legislative reforms. *Justice for the Poor* also argued that legal aid was a necessary bulwark against communism and worker revolution. It noted that unfair court procedures might "[t]hrough bitter disillusionment" turn immigrants and others "to the influences of sedition and disorder."[7]

The book is also an exhaustive and fascinating look at the state of the poor in America's courts around 1920. Its description of the inadequacies of state-appointed counsel in criminal cases and *pro se* representation in civil cases remains utterly familiar. Despite almost a century of effort, more has remained the same than has changed.

Justice and the Poor was remarkably influential. Elihu Root wrote a glowing preface, and the ABA founded a Special Committee on Legal Aid. The ABA brought out the big guns for the project: Former Supreme

Court Justice and Governor of New York Charles Evans Hughes chaired it during the interim before he returned to the Court as Chief Justice in 1930. The Committee launched a nationwide effort to expand the number and reach of legal aid offices.

Right from the outset, there was tension over who should qualify for such services (Smith and others favored limiting them to the deserving/working poor), and whether to focus on law reform, individual representation, or both. Because bar associations were involved after 1921, legal aid lawyers tended to avoid controversial clients, causes, or aggressive tactics and favored individual cases.[8] Advocates disagreed about whether to provide legal aid through *pro bono* efforts of bar associations, private charitable societies, the government, or some combination thereof. They also differed about whether to focus on providing free lawyers or to include procedural reform as well. These tensions remain to this day.

By the middle of the twentieth century, virtually every city had a legal aid office, sometimes supported by the government. But even though legal aid offices had grown by 1951, population and needs had grown even faster. As a result, the poor's legal needs remained virtually unaddressed.[9]

The 1960s and 1970s:
The Boom Years for Lawyers (and Legal Aid)

The American legal profession grew dramatically between 1960 and 1980. The growth came after a trough, as the Depression was brutal for lawyers. From 1930 until the end of World War II, the absolute number of lawyers and their incomes shrunk.[10] Median lawyer income fell 8% between 1929 and 1933, and real earnings per lawyer were lower in 1940 than in 1929.[11]

From World War II until the 1980s, the legal profession grew exponentially. There were more total lawyers, more lawyers per capita, more law schools, more law students, and more law school faculty and staff. Even as the size of the profession *tripled*, lawyer income, from solo practitioners to corporate lawyers, rose steadily through the 1980s and frequently outpaced inflation. The absolute amount spent on legal services grew, and legal services grew as a percentage of GDP. This growth was multifaceted and much of it occurred in the corporate legal market, but the growth in the incomes of solo practitioners suggests that middle-class consumers were spending more on lawyers.

Part of the profession's growth came from government-supported lawyers, both legal aid and public defenders. The War on Poverty led the federal government to fund and formalize previously independent, charitable legal aid offices. In 1964, the Department of Health, Education, and Welfare hosted a conference on extending legal services to the poor. Attorney General Nicholas Katzenbach spoke, announcing a new federal interest in providing legal services to the poor and emphasizing the use of the law not just to represent individual clients but to change society.[12]

That same year, Congress passed the Economic Opportunity Act and founded the Office of Economic Opportunity ("OEO"). Two recent Yale Law graduates, Jean and Edgar Cahn, convinced Sargent Shriver to include legal services among the possible uses for OEO funds. Nevertheless, because the first wave of funding was controlled at the community level by community action agencies mostly comprising non-lawyers, little OEO funding went to legal aid.[13] Note the irony of the first wave of funding: When poor people chose how to spend federal largesse, lawyers were low on the list.

Later, the OEO just earmarked funds for legal aid societies regardless of community priorities. At first, the ABA and other bar associations resisted OEO funding on the grounds of lawyer independence. In order to gain bar association support, OEO funds went to several hundred existing legal aid societies, which remained under lawyer control. The budget grew steadily to $71.5 million a year in 1972. The program lived up to Katzenbach's vision, with funds supporting both individual representation and broader law-reform efforts through lobbying and lawsuits.

Note the back-and-forth in this battle. For the first sixty years of legal aid, individual representation was the primary focus. From the mid-1960s until the mid-1990s, the government allowed, and even briefly encouraged, law reform efforts through lobbying, constitutional cases, and lawsuits against government.

But legal aid soon grew controversial. For example, after a successful lawsuit challenging a $200 million cut in Medicaid in California,

Governor Ronald Reagan vetoed payment of the OEO grant to California Rural Legal Assistance.[14] A compromise was eventually reached, but legal aid had hardly heard the last of Reagan.

Because of this episode and others, supporters worried about political meddling and desired a more formal program. Thus, in 1974 Congress passed the Legal Services Corporation Act. The Act set up an independent Legal Services Corporation ("LSC"). It limited somewhat the types of legal services allowed (for example, it barred representation on non-therapeutic abortions and desegregation cases), but still allowed lobbying and broader law reform efforts.

The signature achievement of the next five years was a massive increase in funding.[15] LSC conducted a study of funding and service levels and found that over 40 percent of the nation's poor people lived in areas with no legal services program. LSC then developed a "minimum access" plan, with the goal of providing a level of funding to support two lawyers per 10,000 poor persons. The strategy proved extremely successful. In 1975, LSC took over a program with $71.5 million in annual funding. By 1981, funding had reached $321.3 million, an amount that met LSAC's "minimum access" level. LSC was providing funding to 325 separate grantees, covering every county in the United States, as well as Puerto Rico, the Virgin Islands, and Micronesia.

1980–Present:
Cuts, Limitations, and the Access-to-Justice Crisis

From the 1980s on, we have seen growing recognition of an access-to-justice problem that extends beyond just the poor. Civil case filings have risen precipitously since the 1960s, and reports of an increase in *pro se* litigation began bubbling up in the 1980s. Since then, we have seen the trend accelerate and transform from a problem for America's poor to a problem for America.

Across the same period of time, state and federal courts began to complain about the growth in *pro se* litigation. Some courts that regularly address cases involving the poor and middle class, like family, housing, and bankruptcy courts, became majority *pro se*—more than half of their caseload included cases where one or both of the litigants were unrepresented. The *pro se* phenomenon grew large enough that it was obviously not solely an issue for the poor. Middle-class Americans were likewise stuck pursuing justice on their own, often in hostile settings designed for lawyers.

The trend has been even clearer for the poor. The election of Ronald Reagan in 1980 and increased skepticism in Congress brought a swift end to LSC's two years of full funding. Reagan sought to eliminate the program altogether, but had to settle for a 25% cut in funding between 1981 and 1982. The cut closed almost 200 offices and caused LSC to reduce its staff and lawyers by a third. While there have been brief periods of respite since 1982, the overall trend has been sharply downward. LSC's budget was cut 14% to $348 million in 2012, continuing a long-term trend of shrinkage via one step forward, two steps back.[16] Adjusted for inflation, the 2012 amount was less than half of LSC's already reduced funding in 1982.

In 1996, Congress not only cut LSC's budget another 30%, but also changed its focus, banning large swaths of law reform and lobbying. From then on, federally funded LSC programs were limited to representing individual people in individual cases.

Despite the cuts and the limitations, LSC has done a lot with a little. Between unbundled legal assistance (such as just offering advice or answering questions), aggressive use of paralegals and staff, and representing the maximum number of people, LSC has reached as much of the need as possible under the circumstances.

Nevertheless, LSC has proven controversial and hard to maintain. Even at its absolute high point of funding and service, it claimed to offer only *two lawyers per 10,000* eligible persons. That funding level was doomed because of tight budgets, other priorities, and political opposition to LSC's mission. Legal aid is certainly part of the puzzle in addressing access to justice, but it has repeatedly fallen short of meeting the unmet need. There is neither the willpower nor the money to fund LSC vastly enough to reach the many legal needs of America's poor. And of course legal aid only reaches the very poor; by law, it cannot serve the needs of the middle class.

Counterintuitively, both the per capita and absolute number of lawyers grew continuously through this period. The competition on the low end of the market has been so fierce that real wages have shrunk by almost a third. At the same time, both the cost of going to law school and student loan debt exploded. This leaves small firm and solo practitioners between a rock and a hard place: Earning potential is lower and debt service is more expensive. And because lawyers are licensed by each individual state, and the process of joining another state's bar is expensive and often hard, lawyers cannot easily move to where the jobs are.

As the going has gotten rough, many have left the legal profession altogether. A comparison of the number of law school graduates with the number of working lawyers shows that almost a third of law school graduates since the 1980s are not working as lawyers. Some of these folks found better employment, but placement and survey data suggests that many of them were pushed out.

Why Are There So Few Low-Cost Alternatives?

If there is so much unmet demand, why has the market not provided a solution? The market for legal services is hardly a free market. Barriers to entry are steep and well enforced. Prohibitions on the unauthorized practice of law (UPL), or practicing law without a license, keep low-cost entrants out of the market. Every state in the Union prohibits UPL. The laws are purposefully vague about what exactly the "practice of law" consists of. At a minimum, every state prohibits representing another in court without a law license. States also prohibit giving "legal advice," but that is much more amorphous. Enforcement has waxed or waned with lawyer fortunes, with a particularly sharp uptick in the Depression. Historically, lawyers and courts have stated that they prosecute the unauthorized practice of law for consumer protection. Yet the vast majority of UPL complaints have come from injured lawyers, not injured clients, suggesting protectionism.[17]

Law schools account for some of the problem as well. Virtually every American lawyer was required to attend law school before practicing. Law schools generally teach law students only one way to handle a legal issue: individually and with a great deal of research and hedging. This means that lawyers are not trained in how to rationalize and routinize legal work. To the contrary, they are taught that good lawyering requires individual customization. The cost of law school also discourages discounting. Legal education is expensive in part because it requires three years of full-time, in-person classes, much of it in small to mid-size classes taught by tenured professors who are paid to do scholarly research as well. Debt loads are such that if prices fall too much, lawyers will pursue non-legal work.

Procedural and substantive complexity also plays a part. Lawyers are trained in complexity for a reason: American law is extraordinarily complex at all levels. Legal forms and in-court checklists will naturally fail to cover every applicable statute, case, or regulation, let alone the various procedures available. Consciously or unconsciously, American law and courts seem to have been designed to require an excellent lawyer to operate.

In a moment, we will discuss some of the various solutions to these problems for the poor: increased *pro bono*, law school clinics, or a constitutional right to civil lawyers for the poor. You may notice that there is not much discussion of solutions for the middle class. That is because, traditionally, reformers have not proposed solutions for that market. This book notes the new approaches that are promising—*pro se* court reform, technology, licensing non-lawyers to do legal work, etc.—but for years, the organized bar has vigorously enforced UPL and resisted many of these reforms. As constructed, the system is actually a wonderful advertisement for legal services. The harder it is to proceed *pro se*, the more likely anyone who can afford it will hire a lawyer.

In a famous episode of the TV show *The Simpsons*, overmatched beatnik parents bring a misbehaving child to a psychiatrist for help. Their plea to the psychiatrist? "We've tried nothing and we're all out of ideas." That quote encapsulates the legal profession's approach to middle-class legal needs.

Other Solutions: *Pro Bono*, Law School Clinics, and Court Appointments

In comparison, the bar has been concerned about the plight of the poor and there are some sources of free or subsidized legal help for the poor. There is, for instance, a longstanding tradition of representation *pro bono*. In 1836, the first written statement of an American lawyer's professional obligations provided: "I shall never close my ear or heart because my client's means are low. Those who have none, and who have just causes, are, of all others, the best entitled to sue, or be defended; and they shall receive a due portion of my services, cheerfully given."[18] University of Pennsylvania law professor George Sharswood's *Essay on Professional Ethics* likewise argued, "there are many cases in which it will be the lawyer's duty to work for nothing."[19] But this rhetoric was not matched by reality. It is unclear when or how often lawyers did *pro bono* work in the nineteenth and early twentieth centuries, and there is little evidence to suggest it has ever been particularly widespread.[20]

Since the 1960s, the ABA and other bar associations have encouraged *pro bono* work by adopting non-binding ethical rules and encouraging law firms and law schools. While *pro bono* work is increasing, it cannot begin to meet the legal needs of the poor.[21] There are not enough lawyers with the needed expertise, especially since many formal *pro bono* efforts focus on law firm lawyers or law students who likely have little expertise in the legal problems of the poor. Because *pro bono* is unpaid, it is often aimed at what most interests the individual lawyer, like non-profits or the arts, rather than the most desperate needs of the poor.

Another source of legal representation for the poor is law school clinics and externships. Law school clinics first appeared in the 1920s, became a part of regular law school curricula in the 1940s and, thanks to Ford Foundation grants, became widespread in the 1960s. Now, all American law schools have some type of experiential learning as an aspect of their curriculum, and many have quite extensive clinical programs. These clinics generally offer outstanding representation, but several bottlenecks confine them to representing a small number of clients. First, because faculty must closely supervise and teach the students, the student/faculty ratio is necessarily low, often as low as eight to one. This makes clinics very expensive to run in a time of tight law school budgets. Second, the clinics are often (and appropriately) run for the educational benefit of the students. This means they favor certain types of cases, like those that offer more opportunities for drafting or court appearances, or intellectual property disputes, rather than focusing on areas that help the most poor clients.

For more than five centuries, courts have also had the power to appoint attorneys in individual civil cases for poor litigants who are in particular need.[22] Many colonies and states continued this English tradition by statute.[23] In practice, however, American courts rarely, if ever, use this power.[24] In *Mallard v. United States*, the Supreme Court reviewed the historical record and concluded that civil appointments of counsel were infrequent, and courts had never sanctioned lawyers for declining such appointments.[25] The practice may have become more widespread recently, but there is no evidence that courts are willing to appoint lawyers in the huge numbers necessary to address the current need.

Other Solutions: Civil *Gideon*

Because of the relative failure of other solutions, advocates and bar associations have pinned their hopes on a civil *Gideon* right: a right to a free, appointed lawyer in some subset of particularly serious civil cases. Calls for a civil *Gideon* right followed quickly on *Gideon* itself. For example, in 1965, a poor Texas litigant argued that the Fourteenth Amendment required appointment of counsel in a property dispute, but the Texas appellate court rejected that claim.[26] Likewise, a 1967 *Yale Law Journal* Note argued for "The Indigent's Right to Counsel in Civil Cases."[27]

No court has adopted a broad civil *Gideon* right, but there were several hopeful signs from the Supreme Court. *In re Gault* extended *Gideon* to juvenile proceedings, even though juvenile proceedings were not strictly criminal in nature.[28] As noted in Chapter 4, in 1972, *Argersinger v. Hamlin* extended *Gideon* beyond felonies to any misdemeanor prosecution that resulted in jail time, regardless of how short that sentence might be.[29]

Taken together, *Argersinger* and *Gault* made civil *Gideon* look quite possible. *Gault* established that *Gideon* was a due process right that extended beyond criminal cases or Sixth Amendment protections. *Argersinger* set a low bar for the protected liberty interest. Civil cases dealing with termination of parental rights, deportation, or even housing and welfare seemed at least as important as a day or two in jail on a misdemeanor charge.

Nevertheless, like many other dreams of poverty lawyers, civil *Gideon*'s fate was essentially sealed when the (liberal) Warren Court drifted into the (more conservative) Burger and then Rehnquist Courts. Whatever law reform/constitutional projects remained uncompleted by the mid-1970s faced a substantially different legal landscape in the 1980s.

The Court finally turned to the possibility of civil *Gideon* in the 1982 case of *Lassiter v. Department of Social Services of Durham County*,[30] which dealt with Durham County, North Carolina's case terminating Abby Gail Lassiter's parental rights.[31] In many ways, *Lassiter* was an optimal civil *Gideon* case. After imprisonment, the right to parent one's children is perhaps the strongest constitutional liberty interest. *Lassiter* itself stressed that the parent's interest is "important," termination of her rights is "a unique kind of deprivation," and so the "parent's interest in the accuracy and injustice of the decision to terminate his or her parental status is, therefore, a commanding one."[32] If there were ever a civil case where the need for counsel seemed obvious, this was it.

But Lassiter herself was unsympathetic: a negligent mother who took no interest in her child and was convicted and imprisoned for first-degree murder. Nevertheless, to deny Ms. Lassiter's appeal, the Court still needed to place the case within its post-*Gideon* precedents. *Lassiter* drew a bright line at imprisonment: "The pre-eminent generalization that emerges from this Court's precedents on an indigent's right to appointed counsel is that such a right has been recognized to exist *only* where the litigant may lose his physical liberty if he loses the litigation."[33] With this generalization in mind, the Court created a "presumption that an indigent litigant has a right to appointed counsel *only* when, if he loses, he may be deprived of his physical liberty."[34]

Even though parents have a powerful interest in protecting their parental rights against termination, that interest does not require a lawyer in every case. Other procedural protections may suffice, such as written notice, a full hearing, and an appeal. The Court's description of the facts made it clear that a lawyer was not required in Ms. Lassiter's case and thus not in every termination of parental rights case. The case involved no particularly complicated law or facts. No experts testified. Ms. Lassiter had a chance to present her case and cross-examine witnesses. The Court left open the possibility that a lawyer might be needed in some termination-of-parental-rights cases, and some courts do so in some or all termination cases.

Despite defeat in *Lassiter*, civil *Gideon* remained a dream of poverty lawyers, bar associations, and judges. In the mid-1990s, federal district court Judge Robert Sweet and others relaunched interest in civil *Gideon*.[35] Over the next fifteen years, a flood of academics, the ABA, and state bar associations declared support for the concept. There have been a few close calls under state constitutional law[36] and a smattering of state legislative successes, but no state court has found any sort of broad civil *Gideon* right.[37]

The chances look even slimmer since *Turner v. Rogers* in 2011. If *Lassiter* did not permanently close the door on a broad civil *Gideon* right, then *Turner v. Rogers* did.[38] In *Turner*, a *pro se* mother sued a *pro se* father for not paying child support. The issue was whether the father had an automatic right to appointed counsel before he could be conditionally jailed for civil contempt.

Many activists hoped that the Court would overturn or narrow its earlier precedents and recognize a categorical right to counsel at least in civil cases that deprive someone of liberty. Instead, as discussed in Chapter 7, all nine Justices rejected the claimed right to counsel.

Turner foreclosed any federal civil *Gideon* right for the foreseeable future. While *Turner* split 5-4 on whether to require constitutional protections for *pro se* court procedures, it was 9-0 on the civil *Gideon* question. Thirty-six years ago, *Lassiter* rejected a civil *Gideon* right in a sharply divided 5-4 decision over a vociferous dissent.[39] In 2011, the civil *Gideon* argument could not garner a single vote.

This was true even though *Turner* dealt with actual imprisonment, and *Lassiter* had suggested that free lawyers might be needed when incarceration was possible.[40] The Court's unanimous decision against appointed counsel leaves little room for arguments that some other type of civil case (which would invariably involve a lesser liberty interest than a year in jail) might qualify.

The Upshot

After half a century of concerted effort to solve the access-to-justice problem, America has little to show for it. We have tried legal aid, we have expanded *pro bono* and law school clinics, and we have considered a concerted civil *Gideon* effort. Despite yeoman's efforts, all have failed,

We also have a large oversupply of American lawyers and American law school graduates, many of whom thought they were guaranteed a comfortable professional income, yet the market has failed to provide individual lawyers at an affordable rate for the middle class, let alone the poor. The answer should be obvious: Additional hourly work by individual lawyers cannot solve these problems.

Fortunately the answer is staring us in the face, and has begun to take hold. Court reform, legal simplification, and technology can make headway where free and low-cost lawyers have not, if only we properly refocus. Part II describes how we can.

CHAPTER 6

The Political Economy
of *Gideon* and Civil *Gideon*

Chapters 2 and 4 lay out how little access most Americans have to justice. Chapters 3 and 5 briefly trace how America reached this point. This chapter seeks to explain *why* these systems look the way they do. Our access-to-justice problems have persisted and accelerated for years. Why? None of the professionals, the ones who control the levers of power, feels the acute need to change.

Consider this common scenario. You are a single, divorced mother of two. Your ex-husband earns much more money than you do. Your divorce was ugly and your husband has never let go. Since the divorce, he has filed a claim for full custody of your kids every three years or so. Each time, he hires a lawyer and claims "changed circumstances," although to you the circumstances are very much the same. Your ex-husband is a vindictive man who is using his money to harass you in court.

The first time he filed one of these suits, you tried to handle it on your own. But the people in the clerk's office would not answer your questions. They do not see giving legal advice as part of their job and fear being blamed if they do so. The judge was impatient when you were confused about which witnesses or documents to bring or how to present them to the court. You went to the legal aid office, but you earned too much money to qualify for a free lawyer. You struggle to respond to a blizzard of letters and paperwork from your ex-husband's lawyer. After one particularly bad court experience, you decided you might actually lose your kids if you did not turn things around. You borrowed the money from your parents and hired a lawyer. You eventually kept custody and "won" the case. Now you simply accept that if you want to keep your children, you will find the money for a lawyer by hook or by crook.

In this example, the professionals all benefit, unconsciously, from the way the system works. The lawyers receive continuing sources of work. The judge does not have to deal with another *pro se* litigant, making processing the case much easier. And the clerk's office does not have to answer your confused questions. None of them suffers, so none feels pressure to change. Who suffers? You suffer. But you probably blame your ex-husband and his lawyer more than you blame the judiciary or the underlying procedures. The winners and losers in the story help explain why our broken system persists. The people who are in court every day are used to a system that funnels every litigant into hiring a lawyer. The rest of us do not have to face the problem because we appear in court pretty rarely.

Lawyers' Interests and Incentives

The answer to the "why" question differs somewhat for civil and criminal justice, but the fundamental answer is the same. Courts, court processes, and the regulation of the legal profession effectively benefit the repeat players: judges, clerks, prosecutors, public defenders, and lawyers. This effect appears at every level of the system, from micro decisions like requiring formal pleading and enforcing the rules of evidence in simple cases to macro decisions like requiring three years of law school.

Economists and political scientists often use what they call "public choice theory" to analyze the institutional incentives of government actors. Public choice theory, like classical economics, assumes that government actors are rational, self-interested, and maximize their own interests and happiness.

While the public choice assumptions about human behavior seem common-sensical, they actually represent a sea change in how we view the government. Early political scientists assumed that government actors sought primarily to serve the public good. Many lawyers and law professors assume that judges are motivated by a desire to do justice or at worst to pursue their own policy goals. Because judges cannot increase their salaries by working more, it was harder to see other incentives. Public choice assumes that other factors play substantial roles, like judges' incentives to make their jobs easier, win promotion to higher judgeships, and earn acceptance and admiration. The same is true for other repeat players in the justice system.

Legislators are easier to understand. They seek election or reelection, so they focus on garnering votes or campaign contributions. They will thus be especially solicitous of concentrated, well-organized, or moneyed interests, because those are the groups most likely to fund their own campaigns (or an opponent's).

Nevertheless, just as classical economists have had to accept evidence of human altruism and other economically irrational behaviors, public choice scholars have had to admit that government workers are often motivated by desires to serve the public, implement strong policy preferences, or simply do a good job. Though public choice cannot explain every governmental action, it is a simple, elegant, and powerful way to explain much behavior.[1] Note also that most of the incentives described below are unconscious. No one sat down and deliberately designed the flawed criminal or civil justice systems. No one wants to hurt *pro se* litigants or to tilt the playing field against them, and most would insist sincerely that they are serving (their conception of) justice. Nevertheless, the unconscious incentives that drive the system are probably more powerful and important than the conscious ones. Consciously, most of the players familiar with the current systems of criminal and civil justice are concerned and want to improve access to justice, including judges, defense lawyers, prosecutors, bar associations, and advocates for the poor.

These good motives make the ongoing deterioration of these two systems a puzzle. Why have they gotten worse rather than better, despite the sincere good efforts of well-meaning participants? Part of the answer is the insistence on a single, failed solution: more individual work by free lawyers, provided either by the government or *pro bono*. Part of the answer is that while the current system is unfair in many ways, it minimizes the pressures on the repeat players. Part of the answer is that access to justice presents a Gordian knot that no single player can fix without multiple other players' cooperation. These coordination challenges make it hard to organize realistic change and easy for any one player to blame the others.

Lawyer Regulation Is Run Almost Exclusively by Lawyers

American lawyers have a unique regulatory structure. Doctors, architects, engineers, teachers, and other professionals are all regulated in the first instance by state and federal legislatures. The legal profession, by contrast, is governed in all fifty states by state supreme courts. This means that state supreme courts have the final word on entry to the profession, discipline of the profession, and often on policing the profession's monopoly on legal work.[2]

What explains this unique setup? The obscure constitutional doctrine of "inherent authority." At the turn of the twentieth century, state supreme courts began to claim an inherent authority to govern the regulation of the legal profession. In most states, this authority was not explicitly granted by the state constitution. Instead, courts implied this inherent authority from the existence of a judicial branch and constitutional language barring one branch of the government (like the legislature) from exercising the powers of another branch of the government (like the judiciary).

The real question is whether regulating the legal profession is really an exclusive power of the judicial branch. Common-law courts come with some naturally implied powers, like the power to sanction litigants or lawyers. The new inherent-authority doctrine extended these powers to include control over the legal profession. Courts all over the country noted that lawyers are "officers of the court" and thus reasoned that courts, not legislatures, should govern their regulation, even though legislatures used to have or share this responsibility.[3]

State supreme courts have used this power in a number of ways, including controlling the admission and discipline of lawyers, requiring membership in the state bar as a condition of licensing, and defining, investigating, and punishing the unauthorized practice of law. State supreme courts have also overturned many legislative enactments that limit their regulation of the legal profession.[4]

The inherent-authority doctrine is a state constitutional doctrine. That means that it is not subject to legislative reversal or encroachment. Because these decisions are constitutional, citizens cannot do much to overturn them: They would have to amend the state constitution or lobby the state supreme court. Few citizens care enough to try to amend the constitution or to lobby state supreme court justices. This is especially so because few people know that state supreme courts govern the regulation of lawyers and state supreme courts are (for otherwise worthy institutional purposes) largely closed to citizen lobbying.

The inherent authority cases are rather thinly reasoned. There is intuitive appeal to the idea that the creation of a judicial branch naturally means the creation of common-law courts, complete with their common-law powers. Nevertheless, legislatures solely or jointly controlled lawyer admission throughout the 19th century, so it seems unlikely that regulation of the legal profession was one of the obviously included constitutional powers.[5] And state supreme courts have not limited their power to admission or discipline; on the contrary, they have stretched to the far reaches by punishing the unauthorized practice of law.

All state supreme court justices are former lawyers, so the American legal profession has a unique claim to self-regulation. Public choice theory suggests that self-regulation would prove quite protective of the profession's interests, and that has indeed been the case. This is partially because of empathy and sympathy. Justices will naturally see most regulatory issues from the point of view of the legal profession. It is partially because the public has limited access to the justices and the legal profession has extraordinary access. It is partially because justices have busy, full-time jobs they like (hearing and deciding cases), and regulating lawyers is tangential to their primary work. As a result, in many states, the justices have given as much of their regulatory authority as possible back to bar associations to handle.

Bar associations have taken the public interest into account, but when there is a conflict between the profession and the public, the profession has generally won. The regulation has proven helpful to the profession by any measure. It is beyond the scope of this book to detail the various examples of self-interest, but briefly consider how differently the organized bar treats admission (a topic of great importance to licensed lawyers) and discipline (a less beloved topic). The American legal profession is hard to get into, but much harder to get tossed out of. Bar admission is governed by a great number of quite stringent requirements. In almost every state, applicants must complete an undergraduate degree, three years of an ABA-accredited law school, and a lengthy character and fitness process, and pass the bar exam and the Model Professional Rules Exam.

By contrast, attorney discipline is and always has been weak. There are backlogs for investigations. In most states, the process is secret. As many as nine of ten complaints are summarily dismissed, especially if they concern "mere negligence," which is generally not covered by the disciplinary system.[6]

All of this means that some potential solutions for the access-to-justice crisis, like creating the lawyer equivalent of nurse practitioners or loosening the protections against the unauthorized practice of law, are unlikely to occur. State supreme courts are institutionally conservative and generally uninterested in taking steps that will harm the legal profession.

Legislators Lack Incentives to Change Courts Radically or Fund Free Lawyers

Aside from inherent authority, there are two other reasons for legislatures to tread lightly around courts and the legal profession. First, many legislators are themselves lawyers. The effect is not as great as with state supreme courts (where all the justices are lawyers), but it is still notable. Second, legislatures are appropriately leery of making wholesale changes to courts or court procedures without judicial and lawyer support. Judges are still quite popular in this country (usually much more popular than legislators), so legislators think twice before crossing them.

There are some areas that are largely within legislative control, such as funding. Despite lawyer lobbying, legislatures have resisted funding free or subsidized lawyers for the poor, especially during times of austerity. Poor people are less likely to vote or to contribute to political campaigns, making them a limited political force. Felony criminal defendants face a double handicap. Felons are unpopular with the general public and are also usually ineligible to vote.

Funding also suffers when pitted against other critical needs. Critics of the current system often describe the access-to-justice crisis in a vacuum, without weighing competing priorities. In recent years, state and federal legislatures have cut funds for medical care and insurance, food stamps, and direct cash assistance. Even though justice is important, it may pale in comparison to food, shelter, medicine, and education. Legislatures are naturally loath to fund court-ordered rights like *Gideon*, especially when they assist politically unpopular groups. If the governmental program at issue were popular, courts would not have to order it; legislatures would supply it naturally.

The sheer size of the problem and the suggested fix also makes triage the likeliest legislative result. The problems in civil and criminal court are serious enough that legislatures will never hire enough lawyers to solve them. In comparison, the *status quo* seems much more realistic. If the problem is insoluble, tinkering around the edges is not only appropriate, but the only available remedy.

Legislatures are also leery of funding for lawyers for the poor because victories for the poor may come at the expense of other, more powerful interest groups. This is obvious in criminal court: Crime victims, police officers, prosecutors, and prison guards are all more powerful lobbies than criminal defendants. Even in civil court, aggressive lawyers for the poor antagonize powerful interests such as landlords, government bureaucrats, and polluters. (Recall Chapter 5's account of Ronald Reagan's fights over the Legal Services Corporation's activities.) Thus, Congress has barred the LSC from lobbying, handling class actions, litigating prison conditions or desegregation, and representing most noncitizens apart from green-card holders. Consider also the periodic spats between state legislatures and aggressive clinical law programs over clinics' suing states or others for environmental or civil-rights violations.[7]

In short, legislatures stint on funding because money is scarce and other, more powerful interest groups do not favor it. The trajectory of LSC funding bears this analysis out. Except for a brief stretch in the 1960s and 1970s and a couple of years in the early 1990s, LSC has seen its funding and scope of practice continue to erode. Correlation does not equal causation, but note that the two eras of growth for LSC coincided with Hillary Rodham Clinton's chairing the Board of Directors (in the late 1970s) and being First Lady, so having powerful friends does help. LSC's survival itself is actually an impressive testament to the lobbying power of the ABA, advocates for the poor, and LSC itself.

Criminal defense has also suffered. Funding for public-defender offices and appointed counsel has been cut repeatedly over the years and lags well behind funding for prosecutors' offices, police departments, and jails. Spending more on criminal defense is a hard sell. Many Americans believe the criminal justice system is already too lenient on criminals and that spending more would free more of the guilty. (Recall from Chapter 3 the ambivalent, conflicting sales pitches that were needed to start public-defender offices in the first place a century ago.) This also explains why funding for the police or prosecutors is much more popular.

Why Don't Judges Order More Funding?

Judges have different incentives from those of legislatures. They sit in court every day and are often uncomfortable with the imbalances between the poor and everyone else. Why have the courts chosen not to order increased funding?

Part of the answer is that they cannot. Legislatures control funding, not courts. Except in the most exceptional circumstances, courts cannot order legislatures to make budgetary decisions. Courts hesitate even to order increases to their own budgets; they are much less likely to risk demanding a set level of funding for criminal defendants or *pro se* litigants. Some of this is appropriate institutional reluctance. Legislatures are in the best position to balance competing funding demands and, as long as criminal defense is funded at some sort of minimum level, courts are unwilling to order more.

Every time a court orders a legislature to fund something at a certain level, it plays a dangerous game of chicken. What if the legislature refuses? What if it makes offsetting cuts to the judicial budget? There is a reason that Alexander Hamilton, in *The Federalist Paper* No. 78, called the judiciary the "least dangerous" branch; courts must avoid overreaching in dealing with other branches, because, if other branches refuse to cooperate, they have few tools to enforce their orders. Judges regularly join bar associations to lobby for more funding for criminal defense or legal aid, but actually *ordering* a legislature to do so is much, much rarer.

Gideon + *Strickland* = A Workable Balance for Everyone but Criminal Defendants

Gideon and its progeny announce a powerful right to a free lawyer in ringing tones and much fanfare. And yet when it came time to put some teeth into the guarantee, either by requiring real lawyer competence or limiting individual lawyers' caseloads, courts have largely been silent. Why? Some of the answers are the institutional concerns listed above. But some of the reason is that the system works pretty well for everyone involved except for criminal defendants and, arguably, public defenders.

Judges, bar associations, and even prosecutors have been big fans of *Gideon*. Obviously, they appreciate that *Gideon* makes the entire process fairer, both in theory and in practice. *Gideon, Argersinger,* and their progeny also make everyone else's job easier. For judges, clerks, and prosecutors, handling cases is *much* harder when defendants lack lawyers. Non-lawyers are unfamiliar with laws and court processes. They also tend to be much more emotional about their cases. They interrupt. They ask weird questions. They ramble about legally irrelevant facts. This happens often even when they have defense lawyers. Without defense lawyers, the interruptions are constant.

Having a defense lawyer in every case that might result in jail time means that judges can count on a trained professional to expedite each case and handle the in-court part of proceedings, which the judge cares about the most. Judges are certainly upset when criminal defendants complain about defense lawyer indifference, but that hardly compares to judicial impatience if a lawyer repeatedly fails to appear in court or jams up the court's docket with sloppy lawyering.

Remember that judges are under tremendous pressure to clear their dockets. Since the 1970s, in both state and federal courts, the number of judges has risen much more slowly than the number of criminal cases. This has, predictably, resulted in a backlog of cases and powerful pressure to clear that backlog. Trials are long and usually follow various rounds of motions, hearings, discovery disputes, and the like, so trying to complete more trials or hear more motions is hardly an efficient way to clear the backlog. Instead, pleas came to replace criminal trials. Glenn Reynolds argues correctly that our system is now "basically a plea bargain system with actual trials of guilt or innocence a bit of showy froth floating on top."[8]

The plea-driven system serves both prosecutors' and judges' interests in doing their jobs. It makes their work easier, faster, and more under their control. It processes the maximum number of cases in the most efficient (read: quickest) manner. It avoids the unpredictability and expense of juries. Last, because it requires voluntary pleas, it seems at least superficially as fair and accurate as a system centered on trials.

That advantage for prosecutors and judges, however, is a disadvantage for defendants: The odds of avoiding conviction when pleading guilty are basically zero. The odds of avoiding conviction are thus always better at trial, even in an overwhelming case, because there are so many moving parts and juries are unpredictable. Defendants thus need some convincing to accept pleas over trials.

To sweeten plea deals, prosecutors offer plea discounts by dismissing or reducing the seriousness of some of the charges (which are called charge bargains), offering a suggested lower amount of punishment (sentence bargains), or both. The flip side of the plea discount is the trial penalty: Defendants who refuse to take plea deals face additional and more serious charges, and prosecutors push for more punishment if defendants are found guilty. Judges are key players in the system, because defendants and defense lawyers must believe that judges will impose lower penalties if defendants plead guilty but heavier punishments if they refuse to plead and are convicted at trial. Empirical evidence confirms that judges impose a trial penalty, which creates an increasingly wide spread between plea offers and threatened post-trial sentences.[9] All of this drives the system towards more and more plea bargains.

Overloading public defenders and underpaying appointed counsel also create pressure to plead. Defense lawyers for the indigent have so much work, or are paid such small, capped amounts, that they are forced to accede to plea bargains again and again. Trials require a long time to investigate, prepare, and conduct. If a well-meaning public defender decided to try even a quarter of her 100+ felony cases a year, there would not be enough business hours in the day to try the cases, let alone investigate and properly prepare them.

Likewise, because of low hourly rates and fee caps, appointed private lawyers often get paid the same whether they try a case or plead it out with minimal work, as Chapter 2 explained. This means that, when an appointed lawyer takes a case to trial, she is hemorrhaging money. Trial work for appointed lawyers is basically a costly pastime, because a quick disposition is always much more profitable.

There are also significant institutional incentives for defense lawyers not to rock the boat by filing too many motions or forcing too many trials. Judges and prosecutors are supposed to take each case on their own merits. But they are also only human, so if they decide a certain lawyer is pushing too hard or making their lives unnecessarily difficult, naturally they may retaliate. This is especially dangerous for appointed counsel who depend on judges for appointments. Consider game theory. When behavioral economists repeat the same game with the same players, cooperation between the players naturally rises. This is because, in a repeat-player game, defectors can be punished in the next game. When the economists run the game repeatedly with a mix of repeat players and new (non-repeat) players, the repeat players still drift towards cooperation, often to the detriment of the inexperienced players. In criminal court, the defendants are the obvious non-repeat players (along with the victims and witnesses). It is thus unsurprising to find the repeat players drifting into cooperation. Defense lawyers who refuse to play ball will stand out and may receive harsher treatment.

The result? Even the best-meaning criminal defense lawyers for the poor have become key players in the plea-bargaining assembly line. Some of these lawyers have been transformed from zealous advocates to cogs in the plea machine, explaining to their clients why they should take the plea offers they can get rather than risking trial. This account does not imply any individual malice or bad intent on anyone's part. To a certain extent, it may be vaguely analogous to an abuse victim's learned helplessness, fatalistically resigned to their role in a broken and overwhelmed system. All of the repeat players are victims of rising caseloads and limited time, money, and support. But whatever the actors' motivations are, the assembly line works. Cases disappear, and frequently disappear early enough to clear backlogs, before lawyers or judges must invest much time or effort.

This system also lets judges unconsciously ration precious trial time. Because the plea system punishes going to trial so heavily, the only defendants who will risk trial are those utterly convinced of their innocence (who can force trials by refusing all plea deals), those who can afford the very best defense lawyers and are willing to risk trial, and those convinced that the plea deal is very unfair. Prosecutors and defense lawyers alike agree that most criminal defendants are guilty of the crimes they are charged with, or something very close to those charges. The system wants to push them into pleas and extracts significant costs for demanding trials. That explains why only a few percent of all criminal defendants exercise their right to trial.

The current shabby funding of *Gideon* also mutes that case's obvious disadvantage: More lawyers with more time to work on each case would presumably mean more criminal defendants going free, including some guilty defendants. A fully funded *Gideon* would also likely result in more motions and especially more trials, meaning lots more work.

Perhaps more surprisingly, prosecutors prefer to face opposing counsel as well. We tend to think of prosecutors and defense lawyers as adversaries fighting in a zero-sum game, in which everything that hurts defendants must help prosecutors. But that is not so. When facing unrepresented defendants, prosecutors must endure their flailing around with the rules of procedure and evidence, and their overoptimistic expectations of being acquitted or receiving unrealistically low sentences.

By contrast, defense lawyers, like prosecutors, are detached professionals and repeat players. For the most part, they have seen plenty of convictions and sentences and lack their clients' overoptimism and self-serving perspectives, as well as their personal stakes in the outcomes. As repeat players, they also know the going rates for particular crimes and can develop bonds of trust with prosecutors, making it possible for them to strike deals. And, like prosecutors, they get little or no extra pay for investing more work. Both sides understandably prefer to minimize their workloads, clear their dockets, and avoid embarrassing losses and worst-case results at trial. Thus, the spread of lawyers on both sides, coupled with the increasing complexity that lawyers breed and thus the increasing benefits of avoiding long trials, gave rise to plea bargaining in the first place. Lawyers and judges are comfortable with this system, in part because they have grown used to it, in part because efficiency makes sense to them, and in part because it makes all the insiders better off.[10]

Most prosecutors are interested in maximizing their conviction rates as efficiently as possible. Plea bargains are the obvious way to do this. Prosecutors use the tools just described, plea discounts and trial penalties, to push for pleas. But they also have substantial and virtually unregulated authority to punish lawyers or defendants who step too far out of line. And the press of business forces most of their adversaries to be pliable.

One remarkable aspect of the current system is how heavily regulated every part of criminal justice is from arrest to trial to jail, *except* for plea bargaining. The Supreme Court has been largely silent on plea negotiations. There are lots of procedures that regulate the entry of a plea: For instance, judges must warn defendants of the various trial rights they are giving up and of any minimum and maximum sentences. And a few recent cases apply *Strickland* to defense lawyers' own performance, requiring them to provide minimally competent advice about the possibility of deportation and the advisability of a plea.[11] Otherwise, however, the substance of negotiations, and particularly the spread between the plea offer and the likely post-trial sentence, have been wholly unregulated thus far. This lack of regulation gives prosecutors tremendous discretion and all but bulletproofs guilty pleas from later challenge.

Gideon also works well for the legal profession writ large. The ABA and other bar associations have long supported free lawyers for criminal defendants, the more the better, with higher pay if possible. Consider Chief Justice Burger's concurrence in *Argersinger*. He quoted favorably and at length from the ABA's *Report on Standards Relating to Providing Defense Services*. The report argued that lawyers should be appointed "in all criminal proceedings for offenses punishable by loss of liberty, except those types of offenses for which such punishment is not likely to be imposed" because "[c]ounsel for the accused is an essential component of the administration of criminal justice. A court properly constituted to hear a criminal case must be viewed as a tripartite entity consisting of the judge (and jury, where appropriate), counsel for the prosecution, and counsel for the accused."[12]

Keep in mind that the ABA is, at bottom, an industry group that benefits if the government requires and pays for its members' services. Even if these jobs are not particularly well paid, they still employ more lawyers. There are multiple market reasons why the legal profession experienced a massive boom in numbers and pay between the 1960s and the 1980s, but the hiring sparked by *Gideon*, *Argersinger*, and legal aid were significant factors, generating a large new demand for lawyers.

The ABA and other bar associations are in the business of lobbying for full employment for lawyers, and government work for the poor has been a prime strategy. This is not to downplay the ABA's sincere and longstanding hard work on access to justice. Nevertheless, it is naive to assume only altruism on the part of an industry group. There were certainly self-interested reasons for supporting access to justice as well, as shown by the ABA's resistance to letting non-lawyers offer legal help to the poor.

Private criminal defense lawyers likewise benefit from the current state of affairs. Because of staffing loads, fee caps, and urban legend, criminal defendants fear that public defenders or appointed lawyers are not "real lawyers" and will do a bad job on their case. Even though many public defenders provide experienced, zealous assistance despite staggering caseloads, defendants have little way of knowing that. Thus, when asked whether he had a lawyer, one defendant unintentionally quipped, "No, I had a public defender."[13] Defendants are trained to know that if they value their freedom and can afford it, they should hire the best private lawyer they possibly can.

The treatment of the poor in an assembly-line justice system gives an edge to the sliver of defendants who can afford more justice. Wealthier defendants can pay lawyers and investigators to do all of the work the ordinary poor defendant does not receive. This alone is a massive advantage in a system based upon negotiated plea settlements: The wealthy are tougher foes who profit from having superior bargaining power.

A poorly funded *Gideon* unintentionally creates a two-tier justice system. There is the system available to those who can pay for a lawyer's time and energy, and the system for everyone else. The upper-tier system is full of opportunities to beat or (more often) reduce charges and sentences, but this requires significant amounts of time (read: money) for case investigation, expert analysis, and legal work on motions and at trial. Most well-off defendants still find plea discounts irresistible in the end, but these defendants can use their greater ammunition and greater readiness to go to trial to drive harder bargains. In the lower-tier system, the repeat players (judges, prosecutors, and defense lawyers) try to plead out the most cases in the least time. Overburdened, publicly funded defense lawyers are forced to be more pliable in bargaining, and prosecutors know it.

Law and economics scholar and federal judge Richard Posner sums up the strengths of the current system rather cynically:

> I can confirm from my own experience as a judge that indigent defendants are generally rather poorly represented. But if we are to be hardheaded we must recognize that this may not be entirely a bad thing. The lawyers who represent indigent criminal defendants seem to be good enough to reduce the probability of convicting an innocent person to a very low level. If they were much better, either many guilty people would be acquitted or society would have to devote much greater resources to the prosecution of criminal cases. A bare-bones system for the defense of indigent criminal defendants may be optimal.[14]

Posner's cynical economic calculation of the price of justice has proven predictably controversial. But whether or not you agree with his endorsement, he has correctly identified how the system works. Americans accept some level of wrongful conviction and poor lawyering because, system-wide, the plea-bargaining assembly line lumbers on at relatively low cost.

Some Solace for Criminal Defense Lawyers

Although this sounds like a tough deal for criminal defense lawyers, they are—like prosecutors and judges—largely shielded from external negative consequences, whether on appeal, by bar licensure agencies, or in legal malpractice.

Start with appellate review. *Strickland* guarantees that ineffective assistance of counsel will be handled with great deference to strategic decisions, making later reversals based upon poor lawyering vanishingly rare. Moreover, the strange logic of criminal appeals means that almost every appeal includes a claim of ineffective assistance of counsel, because most other alleged errors can also be dressed up as ineffectiveness. This has several benefits. Appellate courts are very much inured to these claims and assume that they are mostly strategic and specious. It also removes the sting for the criminal defense lawyer. Every lawyer loses sometimes, and when criminal defense lawyers lose, a challenge claiming ineffective assistance is inevitable and thus just a part of a day's work.

Strickland argues that courts must defer to criminal defense lawyers; if lawyers feared broad ineffectiveness claims, the Court reasoned, they would grow less willing to defend the poor. The *Strickland* Court should have known better. Virtually every criminal defense lawyer has faced a claim of ineffective assistance of counsel, so it is just par for the course. Being accused of ineffectiveness is largely meaningless, and courts ratify all but the most egregious examples as supposedly strategic decisions.

Nor is there much threat of legal malpractice liability. In most states, a former criminal defendant who sues for legal malpractice must prove not only that he would have won his criminal case, but also that he is actually innocent.[15] The actual-innocence requirement immunizes a great deal of criminal defense lawyering from scrutiny, such as failures to suppress illegally seized evidence or confessions made without *Miranda* warnings. It also means that many criminal defendants have no recourse if their lawyer misses obvious procedural or investigative irregularities in their cases, even if these oversights cost defendants their best hopes for acquittals or favorable pleas. Even innocent defendants find it extremely hard to prove their innocence after they have been convicted.

Furthermore, in most jurisdictions, plaintiffs cannot sue for legal malpractice until after they have been cleared of their previous charges on appeal. This requirement greatly delays malpractice claims.[16] And after a criminal court rejects a claim of ineffective assistance, in many jurisdictions the collateral estoppel doctrine bars a later malpractice action.[17] Thus, *Strickland* does double duty: It is both very deferential on appeal and also insulates many lawyers from later malpractice liability.

Nor will wronged criminal defendants have much luck with complaints to lawyer regulators. Attorney discipline is, and always has been, weak. Even with recent improvements, discipline is rare. In 2009, there was roughly one complaint filed for every ten American lawyers (125,596 complaints out of 1.2 million licensed lawyers).[18] The actual problem is probably greater, because filing a formal complaint is notoriously difficult. Moreover, these complaints are disproportionately filed against solo and small-firm practitioners, who are more likely to be criminal defense lawyers, as opposed to other types of lawyers such as in-house counsel, government, or big-firm lawyers.

Bar authorities dismiss many of these complaints out of hand. A majority of the 2009 complaints (66,160, or 53%) were dismissed without any investigation. After investigation, only one-twentieth of the complaints (6,900) resulted in formal charges. Only one out of every twenty-five complaints (5,009 lawyers) resulted in a public sanction, and only 0.6% (798 lawyers, representing 0.06% of all lawyers) were disbarred nationwide. Further, in most jurisdictions the only publicly available information is a public sanction, so as many as 120,000 of the 125,000 complaints remain hidden from public view.

The cases that actually end with a sanction tend to involve two types of lawyer misconduct that are easy to prove: (a) stealing from clients or (b) failing to do any work at all, often due to drug use or alcohol abuse. The number of lawyers who have been disciplined for run-of-the-mill poor performance is effectively zero. So bar authorities do far less to weed out incompetent lawyers than they do to keep non-lawyers from competing with them.

The Civil Side of the Ledger

As Part II notes, the *pro se* crisis in civil courts is a more hopeful and fluid situation, as courts slowly adjust to the reality that *pro se* litigants are a permanent and growing feature. Nevertheless, many courts remain uninterested in *pro se* reform, despite the many challenges unrepresented litigants face. Why?

The presence of lawyers greases the gears of the complex civil-justice system. Anyone who tries to proceed *pro se* is encouraged to get counsel. Clerks' offices refuse to offer legal advice; only lawyers can do so. Judges do not like to take the time to explain the rules of evidence or the order of the proof, or how to properly handle an opening or a closing statement; you need a lawyer to do that for you. Even something as simple as admitting a document into evidence will frequently be too complex for a typical *pro se* litigant. Throughout the process, the *pro se* litigant is told repeatedly to hire a lawyer. All a potential client has to do is sit in the gallery of a traditional American courtroom and watch five minutes of a confused and struggling *pro se* litigant before he will decide to spend the money to hire a lawyer.

Not only must a litigant hire a lawyer to navigate the complexity, but *it really matters whether the lawyer is good or bad*. And of course, quality alone is not enough without some measure of quantity. In short, the nature of U.S. courts encourages not just hiring a lawyer, but hiring the very best lawyer one can afford for enough time to tip the scales to victory.

Judges are also hesitant to change how courts operate. Virtually all American judges are former lawyers. They learned the "right" way to proceed in civil court as lawyers. They learned proper judicial behavior in cases where at least one party was represented.

It is also much easier logistically and emotionally for judges to proceed as detached, disinterested, neutral arbiters between two lawyered parties. The lawyers do the work and the judge shepherds the case along. Embracing the reality of *pro se* courts requires a whole different attitude and a much more involved judiciary. This requires more work and a fundamental shift in the judicial role that makes some judges uncomfortable.

As an example, consider how often judges come to legislatures asking for more funding for the poor in civil court. Frequently, these judges tell horror stories of having to sit on their hands on the bench as injustices are perpetrated against overmatched, unrepresented parties. Yet the State already pays someone with a law degree to sit in court and possibly address these issues: the judge himself. If a tenant is facing an eviction and the landlord has failed to provide the proper statutory notice but the unrepresented tenant does not know, the judge is not *required* to turn a blind eye. American judges have remarkable leeway in how they run their courts, so any judge could ask the landlord about notice in any case. The decision to favor neutrality over judicial involvement, and then to testify later to a legislature about the miscarriage of justice, shows how deeply entrenched the detached-arbiter paradigm is.

There are, of course, many advantages to the detached-arbiter approach. In the common-law system, there are significant dangers that judges may favor some litigants over others or become too involved in their cases. Nevertheless, the balance of the equities shifts significantly if one or both parties lack a lawyer. In those circumstances, judicial detachment is often less fair than judicial involvement.

Likewise, clerks' offices often are uninterested in wholesale change. Besides the judge, the other obvious source of assistance to *pro se* litigants is a court clerk. The clerks often know at least as much as the judges about the law and procedure of any particular court. Nevertheless, they rarely want to explain laws and procedures to unrepresented parties.

Clerks also have legitimate fears about offering legal advice. They hardly wish to be blamed if a litigant misunderstands their advice or loses. Questions from unrepresented parties often start off simple ("Where and when do I need to file these papers?") and quickly grow complex.

Nevertheless, the *pro se* crisis has grown so bad that many courts are pushing through reforms that make it easier to proceed without a lawyer, discomfiting judges and clerks alike. As Part II describes, some of the reforms are technology driven, some are attitudinal, and some seek to replace court time with mediation or other forms of dispute resolution.

The progress on these fronts, and the comparative stall in criminal courts, tells us much about the politics on the civil side. Judges do not like to deal with *pro se* cases, and they do not like to step outside of their comfort zone as neutral intermediaries between two represented parties. Nor do judges like to see injustice recur in front of them, as inevitably happens where one side is regularly represented and the other is not. Thus, courts have started to bend on their first preference and to accommodate reality. As a political matter, it has also undoubtedly helped that middle- and even upper-middle-class people now regularly find themselves in civil court without a lawyer. A majority of state trial judges face some kind of election, and many *pro se* litigants are now likely voters.

Lawyers have not been silent, however. For example, the Tennessee Supreme Court recently led a statewide effort to address a growing crisis for poor people seeking a divorce.[19] Many of the more aggressive reforms, notably form pleadings designed for more complicated *pro se* divorces, were non-starters. The divorce bar would doubtless block any changes that lessened the middle class's need to hire their services. Nevertheless, as Part II describes, the overall trend is positive, offering hope of a third way of addressing our access-to-justice problems.

Part II

=

How We Fix It

Lawyers, judges, journalists, politicians, and ordinary litigants who need legal help can all agree that, in some way, access to the justice system is broken. Equal justice under law means giving poor and middle-class people a fair hearing in court at an affordable price. Courtroom work is just part of the problem, however. Anyone who has children or owns a home should have a will. Anyone operating a small business should consider incorporation. Anyone in a dispute with an unreasonable neighbor or an employer could use legal advice.

For far too many, justice and law are out of reach. But it is far easier to diagnose a problem than to agree upon a solution. Lawyers instinctively respond that "there oughta be a law" (or at least a lawyer) and look to legislatures or courts to find a technical legal solution, coupled with a mandate for more lawyers as a new government entitlement. That response suits both lawyers' technical, intricate vision of justice and their self-interest in blocking competition.

But, as Part I demonstrates, that approach has failed. *Gideon* has made felony cases fairer, but the steady expansion of its scope has watered down its bite, spreading too few lawyers and resources too thin across too many cases. And civil *Gideon* efforts have neither gained traction nor proven their worth in practice.

The time is ripe for a new approach. We need to preserve *Gideon*'s core by not watering it down. Instead, America should concentrate its resources and efforts on the most serious cases instead of dispersing them. That means beefing up felony public defense while finding simpler, faster, cheaper ways to handle misdemeanor and civil cases. There also need to be less expensive ways to become a public defender or legal aid lawyer than a three-year, six-figure law degree. Paralegals, social workers, court clerks, and more active judges have bigger roles to play. Online mediation and self-help websites can also harvest some of the low-hanging fruit.

Modern technology, *pro se* assistance, plus more flexible professional roles can help to make justice in the twenty-first century simpler, cheaper, and fairer. Instead of propping up lawyers' monopoly and their expensive approach even to routine cases, we need a range of cheaper approaches. Just as urgent-care clinics, nurse practitioners, midwives, medical websites, and telemedicine are revolutionizing medical care and driving down costs, so too simpler procedures and more flexible legal assistance can help resolve civil and low-level criminal disputes with much less time and expense. Part II explores how America can and should do that.

CHAPTER 7

Against "More Lawyers, More Justice"

Those who cannot remember the past are condemned to repeat it.
George Santayana[1]

*Insanity is doing the same thing over and over again,
but expecting different results.*
Author unknown[2]

In July 1996, in rural Oconee County, South Carolina, 17-year-old Rebecca Rogers gave birth to a healthy baby girl. The father was her 19-year-old boyfriend, Michael Turner. Rogers struggled to support her daughter, and she eventually applied for state assistance. As part of that process, the South Carolina Department of Social Services helped Rogers prove that Turner was the father. In June 2003, Turner and Rogers agreed on a payment plan, and the Oconee County Family Court ordered Turner to pay $51.73 in child support per week. With this support in mind, Rogers told South Carolina she no longer needed state assistance for her daughter.[3]

Unfortunately, Turner followed the well-trodden path of the deadbeat dad. He made no payments in the summer of 2003 and, by September, he was $760 in arrears. From then on he moved from job to job at least eight times. Each time a court started garnishing his wages, Turner moved on. He continued to run up arrears. Apart from occasional withholding of wages, tax refunds, and government benefits, about the only time Turner paid down his debts was under threat of jail or when he was actually jailed.

Turner, and many other deadbeat dads, face jail under what is known as "civil contempt." Basically, civil contempt is supposed to stop someone from willfully disobeying a court order. In child support cases, it usually means that the father has refused to pay money that he has been ordered to pay and could pay. It is a powerful and effective tool for making deadbeat dads pay what they owe, especially when they work off the books or evade wage withholding. Turner was held in contempt four different times between 2003 and 2005. Each time, Turner (or someone paying on his behalf) coughed up the amount owed and Turner was released or avoided jail. The fifth and sixth times Turner was held in contempt he did not pay, so he served six months in jail in 2006 and twelve months in 2008.

Neither Turner nor Rogers had a lawyer at any of these hearings. The state of South Carolina did not voluntarily provide a lawyer, and no court had ordered them to do so. The issues in civil contempt are relatively straightforward. (1) Did you fail to pay? (2) If so, did you choose not to pay willfully—that is, could you have made payments? If the answer to both is yes, the court can find you in civil contempt.

For years, poverty lawyers have been hoping to expand the right to counsel, especially in civil proceedings. The so-called civil *Gideon* project was and is a cornerstone of the access-to-justice movement. Under that strategy, poverty lawyers hoped that courts would recognize a right to appointed counsel in more kinds of cases, and eventually we could eliminate the access-to-justice gap one mandatory free lawyer at a time.

Michael Turner's case looked promising for civil *Gideon*. The U.S. Supreme Court had previously refused to require a free lawyer for termination of parental rights, but had been much more generous when incarceration was at issue. Here, Turner had spent two different stretches of at least six months in jail without a lawyer to defend him. If he had been charged with a misdemeanor or criminal contempt instead of civil contempt, Supreme Court precedent would have required a lawyer (among many other constitutional protections).

So, there were reasons for optimism in *Turner v. Rogers*. Volunteer lawyers took Michael Turner's case on appeal in South Carolina and eventually on to the U.S. Supreme Court. They hoped the Court would see Michael Turner's liberty interest (his desire not to face jail time) as so important that it could not be restricted without a lawyer.

But the Supreme Court rejected that argument. While the Court acknowledged the father's strong interest in remaining free, three countervailing interests gave the Court pause. First, in routine cases, a father's inability to pay child support is straightforward, akin to the inability to pay a lawyer that criminal defendants must show on their own *before* receiving appointed defense counsel. Second, custodial mothers are often *un*represented and need money fast, and introducing lawyers "could make the proceedings *less* fair overall" by slowing them down and making them more complicated. More lawyers, the Court recognized, do not always breed more justice.

Third, a five-Justice majority found that alternative procedures would suffice in routine cases to help *pro se* litigants navigate the process by themselves. In child-support proceedings, courts may provide due process by (1) notifying defendants that ability to pay is a key issue; (2) asking defendants to fill out financial-disclosure forms; (3) questioning defendants about their finances and letting them respond; and (4) making express findings of their ability to pay.[4] For the first time, the Court acknowledged that *pro se*–friendly procedures were an alternative to providing free lawyers.

Many advocates for increased access to justice were aghast at *Turner* and pledged to continue to fight for civil *Gideon*. This is partly because the case essentially ends the civil *Gideon* movement (at least in federal courts) for the foreseeable future. It is also because these lawyers fervently believe that the best answer to the access-to-justice crisis is for courts to require the appointment of more lawyers. To lawyers and some judges, the obvious solution is to increase justice by increasing lawyers: more lawyers = more justice. In the progressive narrative of history, the march of progress leads from *Powell* to *Gideon* to misdemeanor lawyers and civil *Gideon* efforts such as *Turner*. The failures and impediments of the past should inspire us to redouble our efforts and try even harder.

But that response is misguided for three reasons. First, the history canvassed in Part I shows that this wishful thinking has consistently failed. And the political-economy reasons for that failure should give us pause. Beating our heads against the same brick wall for many more years is much less likely to break the wall down than to give us a chronic headache.

Second, the evidence that lawyers are necessary to justice in all cases is surprisingly weak. This is particularly true for simpler disputes with lower stakes. Even if lawyers are desirable, they are not essential across the board.

And third, even if America could afford to give them to everyone, lawyers might not be desirable. Adding lawyers imposes substantial costs—not just the money required to hire them, but also the complexity and delay that they introduce into proceedings. Felony criminal procedure and jury trials are already so complex that there is no going back: Lawyers are and will remain essential to protect defendants against professional prosecutors. But the lesson of history is that criminal lawyers brought not only fairness but also complexity and delay along with them, so much so that we feel the need to pressure most defendants into plea bargaining to circumvent the lengthy, elaborate procedures and rules of evidence that they developed. As the Supreme Court recognized in *Turner*, lawyers can make proceedings slower and less fair, when poor and middle-class litigants often need justice fast.

Rather than going down that road again, it is time to reverse course, to pursue simpler, swifter alternatives to lawyers. Advocating yet again for more lawyers will not result in more justice.

A Note of Realism: It's Just Not Happening

There is a classic Calvin and Hobbes cartoon in which Calvin's neighbor and erstwhile friend Susie Derkins is angry at Calvin for calling her names. She is so mad that she wishes for 100 friends to join her in taunting Calvin. After a pause, she rolls her eyes and says, "And as long as I'm dreaming, I'd like a pony. . . ." This is the exact circumstance in which the civil *Gideon* advocates find themselves. Twice, the Supreme Court has decisively rejected constitutional rights to appointed counsel across the board, most recently in *Turner*, just six years ago, by a 9-0 vote on the civil *Gideon* question. As with any other constitutional issue, it is foolish to say "never," but for now and the foreseeable future that dream is dead. This is partly because of the unanimous vote in *Turner*, but also because the liberty interest in *Turner* (a twelve-month jail sentence) is among the most serious of all possible interests, yet the Court still refused to require a lawyer.

Civil *Gideon* has not had much more luck in state courts. At one point, it looked like Maryland might be the first state to recognize a broad civil *Gideon* right under its own state's laws. In 2004 three of the seven justices on the Maryland Supreme Court wrote a concurring opinion in *Frase v. Barnhart* that called for a civil *Gideon* right based upon the Maryland Constitution's due-process and law-of-the-land clauses, and lengthy quotes from the Supreme Court dissents in *Lassiter*.

Nevertheless, two years later in *Touzeau v. Deffinbaugh*, those same three justices found themselves on the losing end of a 4-3 decision that closed the door on a civil *Gideon* right in Maryland. While there have been a smattering of limited state successes, no state court has found any sort of broad civil *Gideon* right. *Turner* does not dictate what state courts do with their own constitutions, but over the years most state courts have been heavily influenced by the U.S. Supreme Court's decisions, making a state civil *Gideon* right even less likely after *Turner*. Nor are legislative reforms picking up the slack. The Legal Services Corporation and similar legal aid budgets have been a tale of one step forward, two steps back. There have been some limited state-level successes, like California's recent civil *Gideon* pilot program, but these successes have been few and far between.

Even If It Happened, Why Would We Think It Would Work?

The more-lawyers-for-everyone solution is a dead end. Part I showed how far reality diverges from the hoped-for ideal and how little is moving in that direction. Eight decades after *Powell* and half a century after *Gideon*, the supposed march of progress is headed backwards fast. It would be one thing if civil *Gideon* was an expansion of a well-oiled machine into a new area; it is quite another to try to double down on a broken, overloaded system.

As Chapter 2 explained, in felony cases, there is little time or support for careful investigation, preparation, negotiation, and litigation. The standard of effectiveness requires only a warm body with a pulse, and the standard of prejudice makes it extremely hard to prove that an error would have changed the outcome. The lax standards of review are particularly problematic because most convictions result from plea bargains: Where there has been no trial, the record for review is thin, and in hindsight, after defendants admit their guilt, their convictions seem to have been inevitable.

In misdemeanor cases, "meet 'em and plead 'em" lawyers speed through three- and even four-figure caseloads, providing lawyering in name only. Many jurisdictions do not even provide lawyers in cases where they are supposed to, press defendants to waive their rights to lawyers, or make them languish in jail awaiting lawyers until they plead guilty in exchange for time served. Despite *Argersinger* and *Shelton*, evidently some jurisdictions routinely flout the law by failing to appoint lawyers for misdemeanor defendants. And, of course, *Gideon* and its progeny are limited to the poor. Middle-class defendants are out of luck, and on average, courts may deny requests for appointed counsel in perhaps 10% to 20% of cases.[5]

There are also particular reasons to be concerned in an area where judges require the appointment of lawyers. Are more lawyers or more due process really the answer to the problems of the poor and the middle class? Stated flatly, there are many reasons for advocates for the poor to worry when courts or bar associations announce that they intend to help the poor. The implementation of *Gideon* alone should offer a hint as to how these things work out in the long run.

As Part I demonstrated, *Gideon* is a hollow promise in death penalty and other serious felony cases, let alone misdemeanor cases. What are the odds that it would be enforced more stringently in landlord-tenant court? Even states that purport to guarantee free lawyers in some civil cases may in practice provide much less than meets the eye. Some states that have such rights on the books in child-support cases (such as Pennsylvania) routinely fail to provide lawyers in practice. Others (such as New Jersey) simply stop enforcing child-support orders because they have no budget for providing the needed lawyers. Still others (such as rural counties in North Carolina) offer lawyer-for-a-day programs that are the functional equivalent of "meet 'em and plead 'em" lawyers on the civil side, where lawyers meet their clients a few minutes before hearings and can do no investigation or research.

We cannot overcome the system's deafness by shouting more loudly. Advocates' wishful thinking cannot demolish the deep structural barriers to funding lawyers for all. As Chapter 6 explained, the political economy of *Gideon* should make us deeply pessimistic about redoubling our failed efforts. On the criminal side, criminal defense is deeply unpopular. Voters are loath to raise taxes, legislators are reluctant to seem to favor criminal defendants, and courts will neither reverse convictions tainted by mediocre lawyering nor order legislatures to increase funding. (That dynamic is particularly problematic in the many states where judges are elected.)

Under our separation of powers, there are good institutional reasons why courts leave budgeting and revenues to legislatures. So criminal-defense resources are spread far too thin across too many cases, providing breadth at the expense of depth. Prosecutors and judges have the comfort of dealing with repeat-player defenders on the other side; all the professionals' workloads and incentives incline them towards pleading out case after case quickly; and toothless review does not threaten to disturb their deals later on. This cookie-cutter justice efficiently disposes of the professionals' workloads, but it hardly probes the prosecution's proof of guilt.

On the civil side, the obstacles to funding more free lawyers are daunting as well. Cash-strapped legislatures are not about to create a massive new government entitlement for the poor, let alone lawyers for the poor. Poor and even middle-class citizens are a diffuse group, far less concentrated and politically organized than, say, landlords or employers on the other side of civil lawsuits. And lawyers who serve middle-class clients, such as domestic-relations or trust and estate lawyers, would mobilize to block any middle-class entitlement that could gut their core base of business. It is a testament to the ABA's lobbying strength that it has kept the Legal Services Corporation alive, albeit far from fully funded, but the ABA would never support expanding LSC's reach from the poor to the middle class if the expansion would undercut the market for its members' services.

Civil *Gideon* is a distraction. Time spent pursuing it through litigation or legislation is time not spent on better and more workable solutions. The tragedy is that its proponents mean well and share the same goals we do: a justice system that is fair, efficient, and worthy of our country's long dedication to the rule of law. Some civil *Gideon* proponents think that refusing to compromise is a sign of strength, not weakness. If the only route to a fair system is appointing a lawyer for every litigant, then nothing less will do, even if it means that the current system decays while we wait. But this myopia leads advocates for the poor to ignore, or worse denigrate, other solutions to the problem.

Lawyers Are Not Always Necessary

The second problem with the more-lawyers-for-everyone creed is that it assumes lawyers are indispensable to justice. There is good reason to think so in felony prosecutions, where motions, jury procedures, sidebar conferences, and rules of evidence and exclusion have intertwined to form a procedural maze. Moreover, the stakes are highest in felony cases: Defendants face not only years in prison, but felony criminal records, tremendous stigma, and collateral consequences such as deportation, loss of the right to vote, and loss of jobs or housing. *Gideon* was right to recognize that in felony cases, "lawyers in criminal courts are necessities, not luxuries." But the evidence for extending this conclusion to misdemeanors and civil cases is surprisingly thin.

To be clear, we are not claiming that lawyers make no difference. If we ourselves were prosecuted for misdemeanors, or faced eviction or firing, we would want to hire lawyers if we could. Our claim is only that fundamental fairness does not require providing free lawyers in all or most of these cases (particularly because there are cheaper, faster ways to promote justice). Not only are the stakes and stigma generally lower than for a felony conviction, but the facts and procedures are far simpler. In civil and minor misdemeanor cases (punishable by no more than six months in jail), there are usually no juries and thus no complicated rules of jury selection, jury instructions, and sidebar discussions with the judge. Nor are there likely to be motions to suppress. And in bench trials, judges need not enforce the rules of evidence as rigidly as if they were keeping inadmissible evidence from prejudicing jurors.

There is little evidence that lawyers make much of a difference in simple, nonjury cases. Lawyers, of course, assume that they do matter. (What professional thinks his own role is unimportant?) But the empirical evidence for this assumption is weak.

Criminal Cases: Felonies. In empirical research, the gold standard is a randomized, controlled trial, in which a random subset of cases receive an experimental treatment while the control group receives none or a placebo. We are aware of no randomized trials in which some criminal defendants were offered or given counsel while others were not. Indeed, there is little research at all on whether *pro se* criminal defendants fare better or worse than those with appointed counsel. But what little we know suggests that, in practice, *pro se* litigants fare about as well as those with appointed counsel. The only empirical study of felony defendants is a retrospective statistical analysis by Professor Erica Hashimoto of the University of Georgia. She found that the few *pro se* felony defendants in state court achieve results at least as good as (if not better than) their represented counterparts: They are more likely to be acquitted, have charges dropped, or be convicted of less serious charges. And the few *pro se* federal felony defendants achieve results that are not significantly worse: They are more likely to receive dismissals and at least as likely to be acquitted.[6]

Pro se felony defendants may be faring okay in part because the alternative, appointed counsel, is often not very good in practice given current resource constraints. More than half of the federal defendants studied were initially represented and then asked for new counsel before deciding to fire their lawyers and proceed *pro se*. That data point suggests that they were dissatisfied with their court-appointed lawyers' abilities, efforts, or resources. The samples are small and non-random (and so subject to selection bias), and many of the federal defendants in the sample had standby counsel available to help answer questions when called upon. But the data at least call into question the common assumption that anyone who represents himself has a fool for a client.

Criminal Cases: Misdemeanors. Likewise, there is little evidence that appointed defense lawyers make much of a difference in misdemeanor cases. In another statistical analysis, Professor Hashimoto found that appointed counsel for felony misdemeanor defendants "provide no significant advantage to their clients. Indeed, *pro se* misdemeanor defendants in federal court appear both to have lower conviction rates and to receive more favorable sentencing outcomes than represented misdemeanor defendants."[7] Unfortunately, we lack comparable data for the more numerous state-court cases, let alone randomized controlled trials. But given the simplicity of misdemeanor procedures and the staggering caseloads and funding limits on appointed counsel, it is hardly surprising that on average they cannot achieve much. Indeed, if a misdemeanor defendant is denied bail and must wait for a lawyer to be appointed, he will often be better off pleading guilty on his own in exchange for time served.

Civil Cases. While some studies have purported to find that lawyers make a difference in civil cases, most of the studies are tainted by selection bias. That is, judges sometimes appoint lawyers for the most meritorious cases, or legal-aid societies with limited manpower volunteer to take only the clients who deserve to win. Those clients are more likely to win because their cases were strong to begin with, regardless of whether their lawyers made a difference.

The half-dozen high-quality, randomized studies offer little evidence that justice requires free lawyers across the board, regardless of how complex the facts, laws, and procedures are. Studies of two juvenile courts found that providing a free, specially trained lawyer with an unusually light caseload improved outcomes in the jurisdiction that had relatively adversarial, formal proceedings, but that those effects disappeared in the jurisdiction with less adversarial, more informal proceedings.

A third study found that legal assistance made no significant difference in simple, nonjury unemployment benefits appeals. As discussed below, the only significant difference between the represented and unrepresented control groups was that the cases with lawyers tended to take longer. Two housing-court studies found that lawyers made a difference, while a third did not. That may be because the legal-services providers in the first two housing-court studies limited their help to cases that could benefit from representation, the facts required investigation, the governing laws were complex, the proceedings were aggressively adversarial with little judicial involvement, and the other side was almost always represented by counsel. In the third study, by contrast, the proceedings may have been more accessible to laymen, and actively involved judges and mediators helped to balance the scales.[8] In other words, half of the six studies found that lawyers made a difference, at least in a prescreened subset of cases, while half did not.

Political scientist Herbert Kritzer studied whether nonlawyer advocates could be as effective as lawyers in four administrative law settings: unemployment insurance appeals, tax appeals, disability appeals, and labor arbitration.[9] On the whole, nonlawyers did as well as lawyers, and better than lawyers who did not have experience in the particular tribunal. Kritzer's conclusion? "The presence or absence of legal training is less important than substantial experience with the setting."[10]

The lesson is that lawyers probably matter in some systems but not others. Some cases' factual, legal, and procedural complexities benefit from legal representation. But where the facts, laws, and procedures are simpler, more balanced, and more accessible to *pro se* litigants, there may not be much for lawyers to do. In other words, America may need to appoint lawyers in a subset of cases only if we choose to use a complex, adversarial system of laws and justice. The evidence is certainly too weak to justify a new, across-the-board entitlement program or constitutional mandate, regardless of the stakes or costs.

Adding Lawyers Imposes Substantial Costs

While the benefits of lawyering up are less than one might think, the costs are substantial. The most obvious cost, of course, is financial. At rates of $200, $100, or even $60 per hour, lawyers' bills add up fast. Representation in name only is not too expensive—think of lawyer-for-a-day programs, where the lawyer meets his client five minutes before a hearing, or unbundled services, where the lawyer may help with the initial filing but does no more—but that façade of help is hollow and unlikely to do much. Meaningful representation may require five, ten, twenty, or more hours per case, meeting with the client, interviewing witnesses, hiring investigators to dig up facts, writing motions and briefs, and preparing seriously for trial. Those costs quickly escalate into thousands of dollars or more per case; multiplied by thousands of cases, that works out to many millions of dollars per year. Consider the irony of the existing system in criminal courts: It is grossly under-funded and ineffective, yet still very expensive.

That money has to come from somewhere. So a right to a free lawyer may siphon money and support away from those who deserve it most, such as custodial moms seeking child support, to those who need and deserve it less, such as deadbeat dads and their lawyers. This has likely been the case in criminal court already, where guaranteeing an appointed lawyer in misdemeanor cases has probably leeched resources from felony cases and generally watered down expectations for the entire system. As the late, great Judge Henry Friendly put it, "At some point the benefit to individuals from an additional safeguard is substantially outweighed by the cost of providing such protection, and . . . the expense of protecting those likely to be found undeserving will probably come out of the pockets of the deserving." Though lawyers sometimes pretend otherwise, more law and more lawyers are not always worth it.[11]

Monetary costs are especially troubling when they deter otherwise worthwhile activities. In New Jersey, for instance, the state government had no budget for giving deadbeat dads free lawyers in child-support enforcement cases. So when the state supreme court held (before *Turner*) that defendants had a right to appointed counsel, New Jersey authorities had to start releasing indigent dads instead of using civil contempt to collect the child support they owed.[12] Giving this right to deadbeat dads came at the expense of needy moms and their children.

Lawyers also introduce many less obvious costs. For instance, lawyers naturally slow things down. Sometimes they have to do so to juggle all their cases; at other times, they use delay as a deliberate tactic. Judge Friendly put it well: "[w]ithin the limits of professional propriety, causing delay and sowing confusion not only are [the lawyer's] right but may be his duty." As one would expect, lawyers are much more likely to ask for more time (called "continuances"). The *only* statistically significant effect found by the study of unemployment appeals was that lawyers made cases take about 40% longer. In other words, adding lawyers had perverse effects—it did not increase clients' chance of success, but hurt clients by delaying their eventual recoveries. (Something similar happens when misdemeanor defendants cannot make bail and are jailed until lawyers can be appointed for them.) Likewise, in one of the housing-court studies, lawyers nearly doubled the length of proceedings, although delays in eviction cases sometimes offer the tenant the advantage of staying in the apartment.[13]

Delay is costly. As the old maxim has it, justice delayed is justice denied. The Supreme Court noted in *Turner* that delay can slow down payments to those who deserve it and need it fast. Custodial moms and their needy children must often wait years for the money they need to pay for food, rent, and medical care. But many deadbeat dads refuse to pay up until a court holds their feet to the fire. More rights for them equals more barriers to enforcement. Thus, deadbeat dads can use delay tactically, dragging out the day of reckoning.

This delay results in part from the complexity that lawyers breed. One way that lawyers delay proceedings is by filing more motions than *pro se* litigants. More generally, the history of criminal procedure over the last three centuries shows that lawyers have made the rules more technical and complex. The rules of evidence and procedure could not have developed until learned professionals came to dominate the system and use these levers of power. By the time the Court decided *Gideon*, technical rules of evidence, pleading, and procedure had grown too complex for laymen to grasp. Now, "lawyers in criminal courts are necessities, not luxuries," because only they have "skill in the science of law."[14] That complexity is now a fact of life for felony criminal cases, but that history should give us pause before requiring lawyers for civil cases as well.

In other words, introducing more lawyers has dynamic effects that reshape the entire system, making it slower, harder, and more complicated for unrepresented parties to seek justice or even understand the system. Complexity and opacity are real costs, and they are justified only when lawyers bring even greater benefits. Often, however, simpler, clearer, and faster are better. Lawyers, enamored of intricacy, forget that less is more.

Requiring a Lawyer Disadvantages the Poor and the Middle Class

Most American court procedures and American legal regimes are very complex. This is the heart of the "more lawyers" argument: The law and process is too much for lay people, so fairness requires access to lawyers. This apparent syllogism misses a critical point, however. Our current system privileges not just having a lawyer, but having a really good lawyer. Accepting a system that requires an outstanding lawyer to operate well puts the poor and the middle class at a significant disadvantage. Why? Simple economics. Some of the very best legal talent will take mission jobs serving the poor or the middle class for a while, but the wealthiest parties can afford to pay the best lawyers to do as much legal work as they need. Rather than ramping up the expensive arms race, we need to find ways to reduce the need for armament.

CHAPTER 8

Techno-Optimism
and Access to Justice

Colin Rule is an unlikely leader for a legal revolution. He is not a lawyer and does not have a J.D. He is not a computer whiz or a particularly adept coder. Earning money has never really been his first priority. He does not even like to argue. Nevertheless, if Colin Rule has his way, American dispute resolution will permanently change from a lawyer-driven, gladiatorial litigation system to one based upon mediated solutions. Rule is the most dangerous type of entrepreneur: the true believer. Mediation is his passion and he hopes to launch a worldwide revolution in dispute resolution. If he succeeds, ordinary people will have more access to inexpensive and fair dispute resolution than ever before.

Rule's first brush with mediation came at Haverford College, a small Quaker school outside Philadelphia. He majored in Peace Studies and managed the campus mediation program. After graduation, he worked at the National Institute of Dispute Resolution and got a master's degree in conflict resolution and technology from Harvard's Kennedy School. He also spent two years in the Peace Corps in Eritrea.

Rule has dedicated most of his life to the proposition that disputes do not have to devolve into full-blown wars. He believes that mediation offers the opportunity for disputants to hear and understand each other and then design their own best solution to the problem. When done properly, mediation does more than merely force a settlement to a dispute: It increases understanding and peace.

This is admittedly a somewhat naïve hope for the world, but Rule delivers it with a hopeful smile. He is deadly serious about the power of mediation to change lives and eventually the world. And with the advent of what he and others call "online dispute resolution" (ODR), he may well get the chance to prove it.

Rule wrote one of the first books about ODR way back in 2002,[1] and eventually landed a job at eBay and PayPal to help design and operate their ODR program. PayPal and eBay are natural sites for ODR. They have lots of low-dollar transactions that occur across state and even international lines, making litigation cost-prohibitive or impossible. Disputes are natural and somewhat predictable: For instance, Hummel figurines get chipped in transit, a small percentage of sellers or buyers are crooks, and Internet pictures can be misleading.

Settling these disputes satisfactorily is critical to the eBay and PayPal business model. PayPal and eBay benefit greatly from being the leaders in their field. But if consumers lose faith in the product, a competitor site is just a few clicks away. If that happens too often, the advantage of being the market leader can erode or disappear altogether. Consider the experience of Friendster, MySpace, and Facebook. A slow bleed of dissatisfied customers on the Internet can lead to hemorrhaging.

EBay understood this and wanted to build a simple, fast, and fair mediation system. But PayPal and eBay presented some unusual challenges. The system had to work for small- and large-dollar disputes and for a wide range of disputants, from one-time users to people who made their living buying and selling on the site. EBay disputes are also often about much more than money. Disputants tend to challenge each other's honesty and reputations as much as or more than their economic interests. As Rule dryly notes: "Dollar amount is usually not an accurate barometer of passion among eBay disputants." Nor do these disputants have much incentive to rebuild their relationship. Most disputes occur between buyers and sellers who have no previous relationship and will likely never interact again.

The system also needed to be able to handle a lot of disputes. Less than 1% of eBay's transactions result in a dispute, but that was still more than 40 million disputes a year when Rule designed the ODR program. Rule immediately realized he could not possibly hire humans to mediate all of these disputes. Even if he hired 1,000 human mediators, they would each need to settle 40,000 disputes a year.

Of course, Rule also had some special advantages. PayPal and eBay had reams of data about usage patterns and customer satisfaction. They also had the advantage of having a massive number of disputes and the power of interactive computing. They were able to find patterns and repeated issues, and how they were generally resolved. They were able to follow customer satisfaction with the process, even for small problems. This allowed for continuous tinkering and redesign, with immediate and measurable results.

The sheer volume of disputes also removed the incentive to try to simply reproduce human mediation online. For example, in mediation circles, it has long been an article of faith that mediation works best in person, in the same room, and in real time so the participants and the mediator can listen carefully to each other, begin to develop sympathy or empathy, and speak more cautiously and politely in person, and so that positions do not have time to harden during long, written back and forths.[2] When the eBay ODR system was created, videoconferencing was poor quality and very choppy, and of course many users did not have that technological capability. Rule knew he would have to create a different kind of mediation for online usage; it simply was not possible to re-create what had been done before. It was too expensive to hire a human mediator for each case, and it was not possible to have the parties videoconference in real time.

Rule decided to go with a "staircase" approach. The system begins by trying to get dissatisfied customers involved as soon as possible, so that simple problems like "late delivery" can be solved with no human interaction at all. This is a hidden advantage to ODR. Most mediations occur only after a full-blown dispute has been lodged in court or elsewhere. PayPal and eBay try to nip disputes in the bud before the parties have dug their heels in. Thus, Rule worked to find problems as soon as they occurred and to start the ODR process before the participants even knew they were headed for a dispute. This first step often does not even involve the other party. The ODR system simply tries to smooth the issue out on its own. For example, if an eBay client has ordered an item from the UK and is complaining about delivery time, the ODR system will remind them that international shipping by Royal Mail usually takes 7–10 days or longer.

If the complaint cannot be solved on this basis, the system engages the other party in a computer driven negotiation process. The users state what they think the dispute is. The ODR system locates areas of agreement and suggests possible solutions to the dispute. The disputants are also allowed to make offers to each other.

Only if these steps fail does eBay or PayPal step in to decide the dispute. All of the parties' interactions have been recorded and are used in this last step of the process, so parties have an incentive to be polite and forthcoming in the first levels of ODR.

The goal was to settle the maximum number of disputes as quickly as possible, with a minimum of human involvement or time. The eBay process proved exceptionally successful, eventually handling up to 60 million disputes a year and settling approximately 90% of them with no human input on the company side. PayPal and eBay's system worked better than what had gone before and saved tens of millions in customer service costs.

Customers expressed high rates of satisfaction with the process— even those who "lost." Rule found that parties who engaged in the process were more likely to return and purchase other items through eBay, a pretty remarkable result from settling a dispute. At first, this finding seems quite counterintuitive. Customers that were involved in a transaction that was problematic enough to result in ODR were not only satisfied with the process; they were actually *more likely* to return to eBay. Why? Rule speculates that a well-run ODR process increases users' trust in eBay. In this way, ODR is more than just an adjunct to eBay's core business model; it is a fundamental part of the company's appeal to its customers.

Colin Rule and others licensed the eBay software and launched Modria (which stands for "Modular Online Dispute Resolution Implementation Assistance"), an ODR system for hire. Modria sells a "Fairness Engine" that attempts substantive as well as financial settlement of disputes.

Like the eBay system, it starts with a "diagnosis module" that gathers and organizes the relevant information. Users can upload documents, videos, or pictures. This module finds areas of agreement, notes areas of disagreement, and suggests solutions.

If the diagnosis module fails to produce an agreement, the parties engage in a structured "negotiation module," where the parties negotiate directly and on the record. Modria uses an algorithm to further narrow down the areas of agreement and disagreement and pitch solutions.

If these do not result in settlement, a "mediation module" with a neutral third party begins. The final step is arbitration. Each step of the process works as a filter, separating the disputes that can be settled from those that are truly intractable. Modria claims that the vast majority of claims are settled in the first two steps without a human ever becoming involved. The system is extremely flexible and can be adjusted to local legal regimes or different cultural expectations. It can be set up to comply with the various international treaties governing binding arbitration, which means that the system's decisions would be binding on participants in almost every country in the world, or it can be set up as a non-binding process.

Both the diagnosis and negotiation modules are fully automated. Like other computer processes, Modria gathers a great deal of data from each use of the process and then tries to make sense of it through aggregation and experimentation. So at eBay, the system would gather information about every part of the dispute: How much was at stake? Were either the seller or the buyer eBay regulars, or were one or both novices? If there was partial agreement on what happened, did that make settlement more or less likely? When the system suggested a solution to the dispute, what proposals were most likely to result in settlements? Was it better to try to settle the dispute in one fell swoop with a dollar figure directly between the two parties? Was it better to go through several iterated steps? What sorts of information would move one party or the other off of their stated position? What role did seller or buyer reputation play in the negotiations?

These questions are just the tip of the iceberg. The eBay system allowed for a massive, fully voluntary, and unprecedented experiment in human dispute resolution. In this way, the sheer volume of disputes was not a bug, but a feature. PayPal and eBay handled over 60 million disputes in 2012, more than all the civil cases in state and federal courts combined. And unlike court dispositions, all of the results of these disputes were available for study and for fine-tuning the process. By using the data to track customer satisfaction and future behavior, Rule and his eBay team were able to tweak the system continuously to maximize settlements, minimize human involvement on the company side, *and* increase customer satisfaction and involvement.

Modria uses the bones of the eBay process, but is similarly flexible and interactive as it adapts its existing software to different countries and disputes ranging from property taxes to car accidents. In whatever setting, the system is set up to try to re-create the eBay and PayPal trifecta: more settlements, less human involvement, and greater overall customer satisfaction.

Modria was born in the crucible of eBay and PayPal: It was designed to deal with massive volumes of small claims disputes. Yet Modria is hardly modest in describing its potential applications. It is targeting a wide range of possible uses, including bigger-ticket disagreements or complicated issues like patent disputes.[3]

The American Arbitration Association recently chose Modria to design an ODR process for their New York no-fault auto insurance cases. Modria's system will handle more than 100,000 cases a year involving lawyers, insurance adjusters, and significant disputed amounts.[4] It will likewise prioritize settling cases without human intervention, leaving arbitration as the last option when it was once the main option.

Modria has also targeted online divorce mediation. Modria has created an online mediation program meant to change contested divorces into uncontested divorces—in other words, to change divorces from work for lawyers to work for online retailers. Wevorce is a similar site that uses an online "legal architect," rather than dueling lawyers, to design the parameters of a divorce settlement.[5] Both Australia and the Netherlands have experimented with ODR for divorces, and the early results in terms of settlements and satisfaction are quite promising.

Modria has also designed an ODR process for consumer complaints to British Columbia's consumer protection bureau.[6] Consumers with a complaint about a business are asked to try ODR. If they agree, Consumer Protection British Columbia contacts the business and invites them to participate.[7] From there, the Modria ODR platform does the rest and small claims court is saved a matter. Modria provides a similar process for property tax disputes in some large U.S. counties, including Davidson County, Tennessee (Nashville), Orleans Parish, Louisiana (New Orleans), and Durham County, North Carolina.

UNCITRAL, the U.N. working group on international law, has also sought to make this model the industry standard for cross-border e-commerce and business-to-business disputes.[8] The European Union is creating a single ODR site that will handle all disputes that arise from Internet commerce.[9] ODR is radically cheaper than using humans to resolve disputes, and theoretically it could replace lawyer-driven courts for dispute resolution when involving a lawyer is too expensive.

We begin with Modria because in our opinion it is emblematic of the most deeply disruptive of the many technological advances being made in the market for legal services. It does more than put legal documents or advice online. It is an attempt to wholly replace dispute resolution systems that require significant human time and energy and very costly lawyer fees. Lawyers and judges frequently forget that they are just *a* mode of dispute resolution, not *the* mode of dispute resolution.

British legal futurist Richard Susskind notes that there are two different uses of technology. In many cases, technology helps us by automating processes that once required significant human effort. For example, the printing press replaced handwritten manuscripts and the calculator replaced longhand calculations. Examples of this sort of legal automation abound, and some of them are discussed below. Sometimes technology does more than automate, however. Sometimes it *innovates*, which means it allows us "to perform tasks that previously were not possible (or even imaginable)."[10] Right now we are seeing a great automation of legal services, and that alone has revolutionized access to justice. The next step is even more exciting: legal technology innovation.

A Hundred Flowers Bloom

Modria is just one of many companies looking to change the way we deliver legal services in America. As late as 2011, Professor Gillian Hadfield was asking: "Where are the 'garage guys' in law?"[11] The last few years have answered this question quite emphatically. In 2012, legal tech startups took in an estimated $66 million in venture capital. In 2013, that amount was $458 million.[12] The startups run the gamut from well-known providers of legal documents like LegalZoom or Rocket

Lawyer to Judicata, a new legal research company that is aiming to "map the legal genome."

For years the legal profession has underserved the poor and the middle class, chasing after the more lucrative work of representing injured plaintiffs suing corporations or working for the corporations themselves. Many of these legal tech startups have taken the opposite approach. They are focused squarely on servicing the underserved part of the market, offering legal services as cheaply as possible to as many customers as possible.

Tech companies see the legal market as ripe for a revolution. For example, Forbes notes that Internet legal startups match the classic venture capital checklist: They offer a "disruptive model in a huge, decentralized business" and they often target "the high-volume, low-cost business of providing basic consumer and business documents."[13] The legal profession has woefully underserved this exact market.

For our purposes, it is worth dividing these innovations into three different categories, to match the three different kinds of legal work the poor and middle class typically need. We discuss them in order from the most promising to the least promising: access to the raw materials of law, access to legal documents and legal advice, and access to in-court assistance. Some of these problems are very close to being solved already and some will take more work, but progress is being made on every front.

There are two obvious caveats at the outset. Americans who are illiterate or lack access to a computer with Internet access will obviously not benefit much from the computerization of law. Access to the Internet is continuing to grow, however. Approximately 70% of Americans have a broadband connection at home, including more than half of households with incomes below $30,000. Almost all public libraries provide free access to the Internet and computers. New York and California offer a number of court-sanctioned online forms and provide free computer kiosks in clerk's offices or court law libraries for form creation and legal research. Many of these legal innovations are usable on a smartphone as well, and 68% of American adults own a smartphone.

Even fluency in English or literacy can be worked around. The most successful online document assembly programs aim their interactive legal forms at a middle school reading comprehension level. Likewise, the most successful programs are translatable into other languages like Spanish or Chinese.

But, even if it is true that technology can do little for the poorest of the poor, it can still help by harvesting the low-hanging fruit and allowing legal aid and *pro bono* to focus more narrowly on these neediest Americans. The problem is so significant now that advocates for the poor must reject a majority of requests for help and can offer only very superficial help to the clients they do reach. If computerized legal services could handle the simplest cases for the most able clients, it would be a massive benefit even to those who were unable to use them, because it could vastly expand the reach of our available resources.

Second, we are at the very outset of this revolution. So far, lawyer regulators have not tried to shut down computerized law via prosecution for the unauthorized practice of law. There is no guarantee this will remain true, however. State supreme courts, bar associations, and prosecutors are probably too late to reverse the progress and innovation that has occurred already, but that does not mean that they will not try.

Access to Legal Materials

We have grown so accustomed to the volume of information available online that we sometimes forget just how miraculous these times are. One hundred and fifty years ago, even lawyers and judges had a hard time gathering the applicable case law and statutes that could govern a case. The raw materials of American law were far flung and disorganized, and common-law courts were as likely to resort to Blackstone's 18th-century *Commentaries on the Laws of England*, common sense, or the Bible as they were to more formal sources of law.

The founding of West Publishing in 1872 was a quantum leap. For the first time statutes and cases were gathered in one place, with digests and a system for finding related materials. Still, unless an ordinary American had access to a large and well-stocked law library, she might still have no idea how to find relevant cases and statutes, and of course the books were written by and for lawyers, and were not easily navigated. Few individual lawyers could afford to have a comprehensive law library, which partially explains why corporate law firms tended to grow larger over this period. Law libraries were a fixed cost that could be defrayed across multiple lawyers, advantaging size.

Starting in the 1990s, electronic search engines like Westlaw and Lexis offered even better and cleaner access to these various materials. Because they were online, they also eliminated the need for a physical library for research. Nevertheless, these services were expensive and again designed for use by lawyers. The search terms and codes were clumsy and non-intuitive for ordinary people.

Over the last twenty years or so, free access to law on the Internet has become a reality. Federal, state, and local governments have made statutes, regulations, and published cases available for free online and nonprofits like the Legal Information Institute (LII) have gathered them in one place.

The LII was founded in 1992. Its mission is to provide free online access to law. The website is advanced enough now that it has statutes, court opinions, and regulations from the federal government and all fifty states. It also offers an online legal encyclopedia and other general legal help publications.[14] Wikipedia also includes a great number of sections devoted to legal cases and concepts.[15]

The availability of these materials is helpful, but the addition of advanced search engines like Google or Yahoo is the true value added. It allows easy access to particular cases, statutes, regulations, or rules if you have the citation or title (just Google any Federal Rule of Evidence, for example). More importantly, it also allows for relatively accurate natural language search. Google has gotten good enough at natural language legal search that Westlaw and Lexis are responding to the competition by improving their own natural language search engines.

None of these resources is perfect, and someone with a legal issue should certainly hesitate before relying on Wikipedia or a Google search if he has a serious legal need. And merely having the raw materials does not tell a layman how to use them; interpreting cases, statutes, and regulations and applying them to the facts can be tricky. Nevertheless, like Internet medical information, knowledge is power, and simply having access to the raw materials of American law is a massive leap forward. Americans now have more access than ever before to the raw materials of American law.

Legal Documents—Probono.net,
A2J, and State Supreme Courts

Access to the law itself is one thing; creating court filings and other legal documents is another. Between free documents provided by state supreme courts, probono.net, and low-cost document providers like LegalZoom and Rocket Lawyer, technology has radically changed the availability of legal documents.

The most obvious use of technology is to simply post forms and instructions on the Internet for download and use. In many cases, these forms are posted for free and are available to anyone with Internet access and a printer. Courts all over the country have started to offer free, online forms. California has long been a leader, and its "Online Self-Help Center" offers PDFs that can be filled in online and used for evictions, divorces, orders of protection, collection matters, small claims, and other issues.[16] In 2010 alone, over 4 million people visited the California self-help website.[17]

California is not unusual; the National Center for State Courts has a page with links to free, online court forms from 49 states and the federal government.[18] Much of the work on these forms has been done by state access-to-justice commissions. The ABA lists thirty-four different states with such commissions.[19]

How does it work? The Tennessee site for uncontested divorces is pretty typical.[20] It has five pages of instructions in English or Spanish. The very first set of instructions describes who may use the form: parties in uncontested divorces with no children or property. The instructions walk the applicant through the various forms, explain what to expect in court, and answer some common questions. The applicant then fills out the necessary forms, including the Request for Divorce, the Divorce Agreement, the various filing documents, and a draft Final Decree of Divorce.

These are the forms we use in the student-run University of Tennessee Homeless Legal Advocacy Project. While these forms are obviously not for every divorce, we have used them regularly since they came online a few years ago, and they have been a lifesaver. We would previously send the homeless to Legal Aid of East Tennessee, knowing that unless the divorce involved domestic abuse, the client was likely to wait for years or forever before gaining a divorce.

Forms are helpful, but much depends on the accompanying instructions and the clarity of the forms themselves. A recent Canadian study of *pro se* litigants found a high level of frustration with selecting which form to use and then reading and understanding the forms. A newer, more sophisticated solution is to make forms interactive. The Center for Computer-Assisted Legal Instruction and Chicago-Kent Law School jointly developed the A2J Author ("A2J"), a platform for creating interactive legal forms. Since 2009, A2J has been used to create over 145,000 different forms in 28 different states. The forms cover issues like child support and custody, domestic violence, debt collection, foreclosures, evictions, and divorce. The A2J Author is especially designed to deal with self-represented litigants who may be uncomfortable filling out a legal form or otherwise confused by legal processes.[21] It takes the user through a guided online "interview" that asks questions and elicits answers. Figure 8.1 shows a model first page.

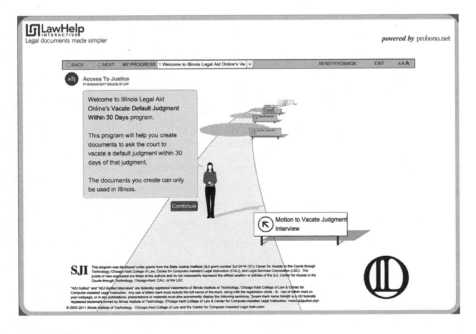

FIGURE 8.1

The program generally starts with a series of questions to make sure the user qualifies for the services and that the user is looking for the right form. It asks questions in simple language and records the answers. The questions become increasingly personalized, often using the user's first name and always proceeding towards the goal of producing a finished document. The programmer can add pop-up bubbles to answer frequently asked questions, define any confusing terms, or to embed audio or video to help explain forms or processes. The program can also be drafted in multiple languages. A2J allows hyperlinks to other websites, pointing users to helpful resources elsewhere on the web.

Users can save their progress and return later, and the forms are hosted on the web, so a user can start on one computer and finish on another. The program can also mandate answering some questions or confirming some answers already given, which limits human error in failing to fill out or misentering information. The program gathers all of the required answers and then selects and generates the necessary legal forms. In some cases this will mean creating multiple forms, like a divorce petition that includes proposed orders and an affidavit of service.

New York State has been a leader in utilizing the A2J software, and to great effect.[22] Like many other states, New York has faced a brutal budget crunch and its court system has felt the bite. Fiscal year 2011–2012 saw a $170 million funding cut in a budget of $2.7 billion. The cuts required layoffs, a hiring freeze, and a search for new solutions to an ongoing *pro se* crisis.

One answer was expanding New York's "DIY" forms program based upon the A2J platform. In 2012, New York offered 24 different programs across its 62 counties. There are free forms for unrepresented litigants available in every trial court, including New York State Supreme, County, Family, Surrogate's, District, City, Civil, New York City Housing, Town, and Village Courts. The areas available include housing, family law, small estates, name changes, guardianships, child support, custody, visitation, paternity, estates, consumer debt, guardianship, and name changes. In 2012 alone, more than 100,000 court documents were generated and filed using the program.

Early returns are very positive. User survey data (based upon over 65,000 user responses) shows a high level of satisfaction, and some of the individualized comments are positively giddy:

Excellent, I actually enjoyed this process, it allows us to become more involved and in control of the process. I love it.

This is an amazing service. Thank you for making a very complicated process (filing legal papers) such an enjoyable experience.

I found this program to be extremely helpful and saved me time from asking questions and trying to figure out what and how to file! Kudos!!

This program is great. New York cares about people who can't afford lawyers.

I don't know when I have ever used a government service that was so very helpful. This is GREAT!

This is the best thing I've experienced in this or any court.

Court personnel have likewise reacted well. Courts now have dedicated computer kiosks and a large number of interactive forms, so clerks have a place to send confused *pro se* litigants. The programs explain the forms and the questions, so the clerks answer fewer questions and avoid explaining forms line by line. The programs also make faulty or incomplete court filings much less likely. They also lessen litigant frustration and improve staff morale.

One of the big advantages to the New York program is that it has been largely court-driven. Court personnel take the lead in the drafting of the forms (in conjunction with judges, lawyers, and affected litigants) based upon what they see as the greatest *pro se* needs. Most importantly, the court system itself tries to ensure that the forms will work in every county in New York. The court system also leads training sessions for court personnel on how the program works. This means that clerks and judges are buying into the program, making it much more successful.

Legal aid societies are also turning to the Internet to try to help more potential clients. Most of the A2J programs around the country are hosted by legal aid societies. Lawhelp.org has an interactive map of the United States that sends the user to the relevant legal aid website in all 50 states.[23] Each of these sites contains a mix of forms, general information, and specific legal advice. For example, texaslawhelp.org offers advice and forms on a bevy of subjects, including divorce, domestic violence, bankruptcy, eviction, housing discrimination, estate planning, veterans' benefits, and many other topics.[24] Legal aid has long provided printed materials and forms to clients they cannot individually help. Just putting all of these publications and forms online is a tremendous leap forward.

For-Profit Online Legal Services— How May We Serve You?

The American restaurant business has seen a radical transformation over the last sixty years. In the 1950s, chain restaurants were largely unknown and there was little understanding of market categorization. Since then, the restaurant market has been micro-sliced into different categories and revolutionized by standardization, franchising, and national chains. Now, American consumers can choose a restaurant from a bevy of different market segments. If expense is the driving factor, fast food is the likely destination. If sheer volume is the key, buffet or family-style eating might be best. If a customer wants slightly improved food at a slightly higher price, but not wait service, "fast casual," like Chipotle, might be the choice. If wait service and alcohol are desired, but at a reasonable price, "casual dining," like Ruby Tuesday's, may be in order. For a special occasion, fine dining or a steakhouse, and so on. Over time, the borders between these categories have blurred, as entrepreneurs try to find the sweet spot to draw in customers and drive volume and profits.

By comparison, consumers in the market for legal services have been stuck with two different flavors of service for years: 1) pay a lawyer, often by the hour, a great deal of money to do the work, or else 2) try to do the work yourself. Intermediate options, like paying a paralegal or getting a non-lawyer friend to help, were largely banned by unauthorized practice of law statutes.

The last ten years have seen an abrupt end to this relative simplicity, and the market for legal services is now being micro-sliced into different levels of service and cost, just as the restaurant business once was. The most basic—the "fast food" of American law—is forms that users can buy and fill in themselves. Do-it-yourself law books of forms have existed for years, but are now more widely available and quite inexpensive on the Internet. For example, LegalZoom offers over 160 static documents "crafted by top attorneys" for download that the user can fill in herself.[25] The documents come with instructions and are listed from A to Z (or from "Academic Letter of Recommendation" to "Workplace Injury and Illness Report"). The individual forms are mostly priced under $20. LegalZoom also offers unlimited access to the forms for $7.99 a month. There are many competitors. Blumberg Legal Forms Online offers its forms at $9 each, although the price goes down if you buy in bulk.

This may seem very inexpensive, but it is actually quite expensive in comparison to free, and many of the forms that LegalZoom and others sell are already available free or basically free on the Internet. Rocket Lawyer has noted this, and offers its customers the first legal document "free." LegalZoom was not amused and has sued Rocket Lawyer, claiming false advertising,[26] which is surely a sign of the effectiveness of Rocket Lawyer's approach.

LegalZoom also offers interactive forms. These forms take users through a series of questions, and then LegalZoom uses the answers to generate a legal document. For many documents, LegalZoom offers final review of the document by a non-lawyer scrivener or a lawyer for an additional fee, sometimes for as little as $39 depending on the document.[27] Interactive forms sites are like "fast casual" restaurants: slightly more service at a slightly increased price.

Take, for example, drafting a living will. LegalZoom's basic living will is $39. The site offers a helpful page that differentiates between a Last Will, a Living Trust, and a Living Will, explaining what each is for. When you select "Living Will," you begin to answer a series of relevant questions: name, address, county of residence, etc. Then the site asks a series of questions about life support. Would you want it if you are unconscious and have a terminal condition with no hope of recovery? What care would you like if life support is withdrawn? Do you have any additional comments or instructions? Next, you decide whether to appoint a health-care agent and what powers you wish to grant the agent. It closes by asking for your burial wishes. After spending $39, LegalZoom creates a document from your answers and then prints it out and mails it to you. The process is simple, inexpensive, and quick.

Not every interactive document is as inexpensive. The basic last will and testament is $69 and the basic living trust is $249. More contested matters are costlier or unavailable. For example, LegalZoom offers documents and support only for uncontested divorces, starting at $299. Bankruptcy by LegalZoom actually requires a lawyer and a higher fee ($1,599 in Tennessee, for example). Rocket Lawyer likewise steers users toward hiring a lawyer for bankruptcy.

The list of LegalZoom interactive documents covers almost every type of non-court document you can imagine, including entity formation, trademark searches, contracts, leases, patents, and promissory notes, just to name a few. All told, LegalZoom's "products available" page lists more than seventy interactive documents.

The next level of service is forms plus legal advice. LegalZoom charges a fee to have a lawyer review its interactive forms. It has also started a legal advice program. Users can purchase unlimited "attorney support" from the "Legal Advantage Plus Attorney Plan" for as low as $9.99 a month (if you purchase 12 months).[28] The plan offers lawyer document review and brief legal consultations with a licensed lawyer in your state. If more work is needed, especially in court litigation, the user will have to contract separately with the lawyer.

Rocket Lawyer offers "free" forms to try to hook users on a similar model. The first week of membership is free and then there is a monthly charge of $39.95. Rocket Lawyer's membership includes unlimited access to their interactive forms. Like LegalZoom, work beyond legal advice or reviewing forms requires an extra payment, although Rocket Lawyer offers pre-negotiated flat fees for different types of legal work.

Jacoby & Meyers, the law firm that pioneered mass-marketed legal services, has adopted a similar approach, purchasing USLegal Forms, Inc. and the domain name legalforms.com in 2012. That site now offers do-it-yourself forms for purchase, as well as assistance from a lawyer in creating the documents, on a sliding scale. If more work is needed, the users are forwarded to a Jacoby & Meyers lawyer for assistance.

Rocket Lawyer and LegalZoom are trying to make a subscription model for legal advice work, but other websites are offering free advice. Avvo is a website that serves as an attorney evaluation service and offers free legal advice. Users post questions anonymously and attorneys answer them publicly. Avvo encourages lawyer interaction by providing a "contributor level" for each lawyer. The level goes up as lawyers answer questions. Avvo works like "Ask.com" or other crowdsourcing Q&A sites: The answers are stored, browsable, and searchable.

Avvo also has listings of lawyers, with a controversial (at least among lower-ranked lawyers), multi-factor rating system, like a TripAdvisor ranking for lawyers. Several lawyers have sued Avvo over low rankings, thus far with poor results.[29] Avvo makes money through advertising on the site and selling "Avvo Pro," a subscription service for lawyers to track their Avvo profiles. Avvo thus leverages its ratings and traffic to draw lawyers into giving free advice with the hope of gaining paid work. Avvo draws traffic/potential clients to the site with free advice and lawyer ratings.

Avvo provides a service that lawyer regulators have long declined to offer: a public forum for ranking lawyer effectiveness. In addition to user rankings of lawyers, Avvo searches for any public disciplinary actions, so potential clients can find that information in a single location. (Martindale Hubbell also offers lawyer rankings, though its model depends on lawyers seeking to be reviewed and then using positive reviews in their own marketing.) For years, defenders of our unwieldy system of lawyer regulation have claimed that law is what economists call a "credence good," meaning that customers cannot tell a good lawyer from a shyster, so regulation is necessary. If it ever was true that the public lacked information about American lawyers, it is certainly false now. Even information that many regulators have tried to bury—public discipline of lawyers—is now available with an Avvo search.

There are other sources for free legal advice. There is the truly free provision of advice on sites like Wikihow. A Google search for "How do I write a will on my own?" leads to ads from LegalZoom and Rocket Lawyer, but one of the first results is from Wikihow.com and is entitled "How to Write Your Own Last Will and Testament." There are also online communities like Reddit or other chatboards. The acronyms "IANAL" ("I am not a lawyer") and "IAALBNYL" ("I am a lawyer, but not your lawyer") are common intros to question and answer sessions on legal matters in these forums. The advice is general and informal, but is permanent and available to the public. Freeadvice.com also offers community chatboards and "ask a lawyer" areas, with the answers saved for future use or search.

The next layer up is the virtual law firm, the "casual dining" of law. Richard Granat was a pioneer in the field with his fixed-fee divorces in Maryland at mdfamilylawyer.com.[30] A simple divorce for a couple with children can be handled by a lawyer for as little as $229, or without children for $199.[31] Granat has expanded the idea with Directlaw.com, which sells an online platform to lawyers so they can likewise set up virtual law offices. Virtual law firms can save lawyers time and money in a number of ways, from automating functions formerly handled by secretaries or accountants, to allowing lawyers to time-shift client communication and offering easy access to reusable legal templates.

Some solo practitioners are now essentially fronts for online forms providers. The National Law Foundation offers "fully editable forms" to lawyers for "as low as $19," covering virtually every type of legal drafting.[32] Similarly, state bar associations are creating online databases of interactive forms for use by their members, with an explicit eye towards "competition from web-based companies like LegalZoom and Rocket Lawyer."[33]

Other portals combine ratings and reputations with posted menus of services and prices, like fast-food restaurants. JustiServ first asks users multiple-choice questions to figure out what subject area and kind of services they need, and then displays lists of lawyers who handle those kinds of cases. Like Amazon.com, JustiServ displays ratings, reputations, and posted prices for various kinds of services, allowing consumers to shop intelligently for the right combination of credentials, experience, customer satisfaction, and price. Needless to say, posted price competition promises to hold down costs and limit sticker shock later on. And attorneys who need more work can advertise and adjust their prices to competitive market levels, benefitting unemployed law school graduates as well as clients.

The top level is individual lawyers working by the hour on individual matters, the "fine dining" of law. As with fine dining, it runs from the bistro level (a solo practitioner charging $100 an hour) to the five-star treatment at a white-shoe corporate law firm (could run upwards of $850 an hour). This portion of the market is now for the knottiest problems or bet the company/bet the family type cases where money is not an object. The good news for consumers is that they were once forced to eat fine dining for even basic meals like simple wills or incorporating a business (or go hungry). Now they can choose a level of service that best suits their needs.

There are a couple of other takeaways from this brief overview. First, there has been an explosion of new providers of inexpensive and free legal advice and forms. Second, these providers run the gamut in terms of formality and expense.

Third, it is amazing just how much legal information is now available online, for free. Americans with Internet access can find statutes, regulations, and even relevant case law online. They can ask for legal advice for free and can probably find some version of the forms they need for free as well. LegalZoom and Rocket Lawyer are already very inexpensive, but they may actually be overpriced. LegalZoom filed for a possible IPO in 2011, but withdrew later that year due to market conditions (it has since sold out to European private equity firm Permira, putting an IPO on hold for the foreseeable future). One of the concerns was that LegalZoom faces stiff competition from free forms. This is, of course, exceptional news for access to justice: One of the investor worries about LegalZoom is that it is *too expensive*.

Lastly, note that this first level of digitization is very basic. The provision of the raw materials of law is simply placing searchable documents online. The same is true for the provision of legal forms. Even interactive legal forms are a very basic use of technology: Most of these programs just populate a form with the answers to simple questions, which computers have been able to do since the 1980s. Online legal advice is similarly just a variant of the same question and answer format that chatboards have used for years.

But the technology does not need to be so basic. In particular, as these sites mature and gain more experience, there is the chance that LegalZoom and its competitors will be cheaper *and* better than flesh and blood lawyers. LegalZoom is already operating on a scale that no law firm can match, serving millions of customers. LegalZoom may eventually do a volume of business that will allow it to surpass the quality of any individualized work. As LegalZoom puts it: "The high volume of transactions we handle and feedback we receive from customers and government agencies give us a scale advantage that deepens our knowledge and enables us to further develop additional services to address our customers' needs and refine our business processes."[34]

LegalZoom may be able to use its volume business to rapidly adopt new elements in its forms that have been approved by the courts or have proven especially effective. If LegalZoom is able to focus on what works best nationwide, it could stay ahead of the curve in a way that an individual lawyer probably could not, and could even affect the course of the law by bringing certain types of will codicils or LLC provisions to the fore.

In Court

LegalZoom, Lawhelp, and other online providers of legal services generally do not offer in-court legal services. Online court forms are meant to be used *pro se*, or the users must hire a lawyer to represent them. In-court litigation looks likely to stay a lawyers-only activity for the foreseeable future. In-court representation of clients is the easiest type of unauthorized practice of law for judges to police, and it is the area least likely to be attacked by political opponents or lawyer competitors. Since the turn of the twentieth century, American judges have insisted that only lawyers may represent clients in their courts, and that will not change anytime soon. As Chapter 9 argues, *pro se* courts have become friendlier to self-represented litigants. There are some limited cracks in the lawyers-only façade in housing and other specialized courts, and those trends will continue. Nevertheless, in-court legal work is and will remain a bottleneck to the technology-driven access-to-justice revolution.

That said, technology is also helping here. First, it is making it easier for lawyers to streamline their work. Overhead is less expensive. Mobile technologies and laptops make it possible to work anywhere, anytime, including while waiting in court for another matter to be called. A solo practitioner can run a decent office with a cellphone, a laptop, and a regular table at Starbucks. Legal research, drafting, and client management are also becoming more efficient. From corporate law on down, American lawyers are spending less time on relatively mundane tasks, freeing them to focus on work that *must* be done by a lawyer.

Middle-class consumers will also benefit from a trickle-down of innovation from corporate law firms. Right now, corporate law firms are going through wrenching changes of their own. These large firms had an amazingly profitable run from the 1960s through 2008, relentlessly growing in size, revenue, and profits. The cost of these services grew to the point where clients started looking for ways to save money, eventually turning to outsourcing and computerization. Right now, these methods are replacing only high-end corporate work, but as the technology and methods become more settled, they are likely to become cheaper and to drift down the ladder to save money for even middle-class clients.

One of the prime drivers of the expense of litigation is what lawyers call discovery. This is the process where opposing litigants share relevant information and documents with each other in advance of trial. Discovery is helpful because it eliminates trial by ambush and it encourages settlement, as both parties learn more about their opponents' strategies and evidence. Nevertheless, it spawns side disputes and can be extremely costly and time consuming, especially in a digital age when thousands or even millions of documents or emails might be relevant. The biggest expense in modern litigation is not time spent in court; it is time spent on discovery.

Corporations have found two ways to slash the cost of discovery and other types of relatively straightforward drafting or document review. The first way is outsourcing. Corporations hire lawyers (or literate nonlawyers) in foreign countries (usually India) to handle issues like document review or drafting discovery pleadings. Pangea3 is a fast-growing "legal process outsourcing" firm that employs English-speaking, common-law-trained lawyers in India to handle document review or due diligence that used to be done in the U.S. by lawyers. Pangea3 claims to have grown 40%-60% a year since its founding in 2004, and currently employs 850 lawyers. Pangea3 was successful enough to be purchased by the legal information giant Thomson Reuters in 2010. As of yet, outsourcing legal work has passed muster under state prohibitions on the unauthorized practice of law because the outsourcing companies work under a licensed lawyer, who is ultimately responsible for the work. Outsourcers do have to supervise and audit work to ensure quality control. But with those caveats, outsourcing is a promising way to bring down costs.[35]

The second way is using computers and predictive coding. Basically, a computer does the work of culling relevant documents for litigation.

Typically a human lawyer looks over a small number of documents and tells the program the key terms to look for and which documents are useful or not, and which may be privileged from discovery. Then the computers use that information to run through the rest of the documents. Rather than pay a human by the hour to go through boxes (and sometimes warehouses) full of documents, the computer does the work. Both *The Atlantic* and *The Wall Street Journal* have highlighted the advantages in accuracy and cost of using computers to do large-scale discovery work.[36] The computer programmers claim that these programs are cheaper *and* more accurate than humans.[37]

Outsourcing and computerization presume that legal work can be broken into constituent parts, and that not everything needs to be done by a highly paid human in the United States or by a human at all. Corporate legal work has been opened up into a production chain. Over time, these technologies will become more accepted and cheap enough for small firms and solo practitioners to use. All of these changes will make it much less expensive for lawyers to service more clients more efficiently.

That is fortunate for lawyers, because the cost of hiring a lawyer will continue to fall. The Internet makes it easier to shop for the best deal on a car or a pair of pants. It does the same for lawyers. Before the Internet, it was very difficult to get comparative information on either lawyer price or quality; that has all changed. Avvo and other sites offer a great deal of consumer-driven information about both quality and expense. The Rocket Lawyer and LegalZoom subscription models ask lawyers to provide advice to customers at very low prices. Even if that advice turns into a more extensive representation, the lawyers are required to offer discounts and to clearly state their fees ahead of time.

Internet sites like LegalMatch seek to connect clients and lawyers for the lowest price. One of us (Barton) briefly signed up for LegalMatch just to see how it worked and received a number of potential client matters to review and bid on. If I were an underemployed solo practitioner, I certainly would have been sorely tempted to pitch some of these potential matters. But LegalMatch provides customer reviews and my proposed fees to each potential client, so I would face significant pressure on both price and customer satisfaction. Lawyers desperate for work and clients looking for the best deal naturally drive down costs.

Between online sites packaging the work of actual lawyers and selling it for peanuts, and regular lawyers feeling the pressure and adopting their own forms-based practices, the price of a real lawyer is falling significantly. As Chapter 10 demonstrates, law schools have also been pumping out an oversupply of lawyers for years, increasing competition. The price of a lawyer will never fall far enough to make it cheap for a middle-class consumer to have a contested divorce or a will contest, but it is making relatively simple matters more affordable.

Modria and other sites are also attempting to make an end run around the legal profession and the courts altogether. The vast majority of civil and criminal cases never see trial, so what is it exactly that only a lawyer can do? If the issue is negotiating out a final resolution to a dispute, mediation, direct negotiation, or arbitration become more attractive and are also much cheaper.

But Consumer Safety?

What about consumer safety? Bar associations agree that there is an access-to-justice problem, but argue that the only safe response is more licensed lawyers. A 2011 letter to the *New York Times* by ABA President William Robinson is emblematic:

> The American Bar Association strongly agrees that our nation must expand access to justice for low-income Americans. However, a rush to open the practice of law to unschooled, unregulated non-lawyers is not the solution. This would cause grave harm to clients. Even matters that appear simple, such as uncontested divorces, involve myriad legal rights and responsibilities. If the case is not handled by a professional with appropriate legal training, a person can suffer serious long-term consequences affecting loved ones or financial security. It also could lead to a violation of the law. . . . We must expand legal services for those in need, provided by first-rate trained lawyers.[38]

For years, the objections to unbundled legal services or other self-help aids has been that the poor deserve the same quality of legal work that the wealthy receive, and that LegalZoom and other online aids are clearly deficient. It is true that these first-generation online services may not be as good as a live lawyer, although anyone reading this likely knows a lawyer whose work is worse than what LegalZoom provides. Over time, these programs will continue to adjust and improve. Regardless, LegalZoom, Rocket Lawyer, and LawHelp Interactive are already clearly superior to nothing, which is what most poor and middle-income Americans can afford.

There are other reasons for skepticism. First, the ABA is a trade group, and it is not particularly surprising that it sees cheaper competition as too dangerous.

Second, consider the speculative nature of the claimed harm. Historically, lawyers and courts have stated that they prosecute the unauthorized practice of law for consumer protection. Yet the vast majority of UPL complaints have come from injured lawyers, not injured clients, suggesting protectionism rather than any threat to consumers.[39] For example, LegalZoom has faced complaints of UPL in several states over the years. These suits appear to arise out of bar association and lawyer concerns, not consumer complaints. The discovery in these suits is not publicly available but the complaints are, and thus far those complaints do not allege any specific harms to any customers, just that LegalZoom is involved in UPL.

Given LegalZoom's high profile and the threat it presents to existing lawyers, if its legal work had caused a flood of serious injuries, one would expect lawsuits or significant publicity by bar associations or both. The absence of this publicity or lawsuits is telling. For what it is worth, LegalZoom claims customer satisfaction rates in the 90% range and an A+ rating with the Better Business Bureau. The relative dearth of reported harm from LegalZoom, which has existed since 2001, speaks volumes. If we are going to ban or curtail vastly less expensive online legal services for consumer protection, we need actual evidence of harm. As of yet, there is none.

Third, the sheer scale of these companies offers some protection. Disruptive technology companies must expand their reach beyond early adopters and on to more mainstream customers. LegalZoom and Rocket Lawyer have spent millions advertising and building a national brand identity so that consumers will see them as safe, national, well-capitalized alternatives to hiring a lawyer or going it alone. Especially in the early days of this industry, customer satisfaction and public perception are critical to future success. Compare the reputational pressure on these large national companies with any individual lawyer or small firm and it is obvious that the market itself will help to hold LegalZoom and Rocket Lawyer accountable.

Fourth, the danger of harm on the Internet is, ironically, greatly reduced by the availability of the Internet. The Internet is the single greatest engine of consumer information ever created, and online merchants and sites are now assiduous about maintaining a good reputation. For a hotel, one online story of bed bugs can be devastating. For a restaurant, an online picture of mouse droppings can close the doors. Lawyers are finding this out as they confront online ratings at Avvo and other sites. If there are very harmful legal forms or legal advice on the Internet, soon customers will be warning others about it, blunting the potential for harm. Comparelegalforms.com is a review site for various online forms providers. The site compares various providers on cost, accuracy, and customer satisfaction.

Last, lawyers made the same quality-control arguments when title insurance companies largely replaced lawyers on residential real estate closings. Real estate law was too complicated, and the danger to the clients too great, to allow non-lawyer involvement.[40] These concerns have proven to be largely unfounded. By 1986, even the ABA gave up the ghost, admitting, "It can no longer be claimed that lawyers have the exclusive possession of the esoteric knowledge required and are therefore the only ones able to advise clients about real estate closings."[41]

There is also a great irony in lawyers and bar associations complaining about the danger online providers pose to potential clients: The lawyer disciplinary system itself does not offer much protection. Given the relative indolence of lawyer regulators and the fact that many solo practitioners do not have malpractice insurance, a potential client might have better luck suing LegalZoom or Rocket Lawyer for faulty legal work than a licensed lawyer.

Will the Empire Strike Back?

As of yet, attorney regulators have been relatively quiet about the online provision of legal services. As the oldest and most notorious, LegalZoom has faced the greatest UPL scrutiny. Every state in the

Union bans the unauthorized practice of law. The exact parameters of the ban, however, are notoriously mushy because most states do not define "the practice of law." At a minimum, no non-lawyer is allowed to file papers or appear as a representative for another in court. That is the easy part. The ban stretches to "legal advice," however, which covers a much broader swath of activity and gets into existential discussions of what exactly constitutes "the practice of law."

The Washington State Attorney General investigated LegalZoom for UPL in 2010. LegalZoom settled by paying $20,000 in costs and agreeing not to violate Washington law, while continuing to operate in the state with no changes in their business practices.[42] In 2011, a private lawyer in Missouri filed a class-action UPL suit against LegalZoom.[43] The case was settled before trial when LegalZoom agreed to a small payment and unspecified changes in its business practices. The CEO of LegalZoom stated that the settlement involved "little change in [the] business" and that the main result was an agreement "to pay lawyers' fees."[44]

The Supreme Court of South Carolina recently found that Legal-Zoom's interactive forms did not violate UPL because they matched many free forms available through the State Supreme Court's own website.[45] LegalZoom also brought suit against the state bar in North Carolina, seeking a declaratory judgment that it was not engaging in UPL.[46] At first, the bar resisted mightily and the case looked like it was headed for trial. But in 2015, the U.S. Supreme Court decided an antitrust case called *North Carolina Dental Board v. FTC*, which cast doubt on the viability of state licensing boards dominated by the regulated profession. A settlement on the UPL case came soon afterwards.

Thus, the results have been largely positive for LegalZoom. As a matter of *realpolitik,* this makes sense. LegalZoom and other online providers are now well known and established; an effort to shut them down would come with significant political costs. Any effort to put it out of business in any particular state would bring considerable negative attention to that state's lawyer regulators. For example, the Texas Bar Association successfully prosecuted an offline program called "Quicken Family Lawyer" for UPL in the late 1990s, only to be briskly overruled by the Texas legislature.[47]

There is also a broader enforcement problem: Even if UPL could destroy LegalZoom, what about the websites that promise that a lawyer "reviews" the documentation? Thus far, Rocket Lawyer has avoided UPL enforcement by tying a local lawyer to its sale of forms. Rocket Lawyer and similar sites are priced competitively with LegalZoom and are much cheaper than a traditional lawyer, so inexpensive online forms will persist even with aggressive UPL enforcement.

A full-scale attempt to bring computerization to heel via UPL or other aggressive regulation would require a great deal of political will and capital from state supreme courts and other lawyer regulators. Truly aggressive moves would be likely to draw federal antitrust and congressional attention. This sort of brinksmanship would hardly be worth it, however, because UPL would be unlikely to bar the hybrid forms providers where lawyers are nominally involved in reviewing the documents.

But the various lawsuits against LegalZoom warn against underestimating the power of bar associations and state supreme courts. Vigilance is necessary.

CHAPTER 9

Court Reform

Fern Fisher grew up on Long Island with a single, working mom. She graduated summa cum laude from Howard University in 1975 and headed off to Harvard Law School, at a time when not many women or African-Americans went to law school. She pretty quickly decided to dedicate her life to public service and promoting access to justice. Since then, she has spent the bulk of her career working in and around the trial courts in New York City.

She cut her teeth as a Harlem Legal Aid lawyer in the infamous Manhattan Housing Court, ground zero for the access-to-justice crisis. It is a classic example of what we call a *"pro se* court," a court where the majority of cases feature one or more unrepresented litigants. But Housing Court is a particularly pernicious example because the vast majority of cases feature a lawyer on *one* side of the case—the landlord's lawyer.

When Fisher arrived in the late 1970s, the scene was chaotic. There were packed courtrooms, with litigants spilling out into the halls and waiting areas. The bailiff would call the cases in the courtroom and another clerk would call the names in the hall. The daily docket of cases regularly ran into the hundreds, and some tenants did not speak English or understand what was going on. These tenants faced a cadre of lawyers that specialized in processing evictions.

Unsurprisingly, this system worked out quite well for the landlords. New York City has some of the most tenant-friendly law in the United States, from rent control to exacting requirements before eviction. Nevertheless, law is helpful only if one knows how to use it, and Fisher saw tenants repeatedly waive their rights, misunderstand the questions, or simply fail to appear. All too often, this happened in cases that a lawyer could have won or that judges should have known were deficient.

In Housing Court in the 1970s and the 1980s, many of the judges ran things as if everyone had a lawyer. The judges expected the litigants to argue the law, correctly examine their witnesses, and proceed *pro se* as if a lawyer were handling the case. To Fisher, this was more than a little unfair. Even as a Harvard Law graduate, she found Housing Court law and procedure byzantine and challenging. How was an unrepresented tenant supposed to navigate the system? She promised herself that when she had a chance to make the system fairer, she would.

And she has fulfilled that promise in spades. She was appointed a judge in Housing Court in 1989 and pledged that all litigants would get a fair shake. She explained the process to unrepresented litigants and made sure that landlords had followed the proper eviction procedures.

She was fair and hard working and moved her way up the ladder all the way to her current position as the judge in charge of New York State's Access to Justice Program. As a housing court judge, Judge Fisher could affect the litigants before her. In her new role, she is changing courts all over the state. Fisher runs one of the most aggressive and innovative state access-to-justice programs in the country. She encouraged New York State to become one of the first jurisdictions to adopt the A2J online document production platform discussed in Chapter 8. She started in 2005 by working with Columbia Law School's Lawyering in the Digital Age clinic to create an in-court kiosk for tenants to create fileable answers to eviction actions. The interactive program from the kiosk was based upon the A2J platform and eventually migrated online and then throughout the state. Fisher wanted to be even-handed, and next helped create a program to help property owners of single- or double-unit rentals file eviction papers, a growing area of *pro se* litigation. The housing experience was then duplicated in other areas of need and spread throughout the state.

To make sure these reforms succeeded, she has led training programs for judges and court personnel all over the state on how to use the kiosks and online forms and how to help *pro se* litigants. She has formed task forces covering all of the areas where *pro se* litigation is common, from housing to divorce to child support, and pushed to simplify and regularize forms and procedures. She has also tried to boost the number of free lawyers, lobbying for increased legal aid funds and creating *pro bono* and volunteer programs to bring volunteers to problematic courts. She has done all of this on a shoestring budget and often through the sheer force of her personality.

Has it been easy? No. Organizing judges is like herding cats. Convincing court clerks to change their default setting from "filing papers drafted by lawyers" to "helping guide confused *pro se* litigants through the process" is not easy. Entrenched interests like landlords' attorneys and collection lawyers are opposed to most changes that benefit *pro se* litigants. Nevertheless, it is the work that Judge Fisher was born to do. Progress is slow, but palpable, and changes have only just begun.

All over the country, there are people like Judge Fisher fighting to change the nature of *pro se* courts. The work has been slow and hard, but the advancement is unmistakable. This chapter discusses the most promising strategies, ranging from the easiest to implement to the most radical, and argues that this is where America should be spending its precious funds.

In most courts in America, judges, clerks, lawyers, and litigants are partying like it is 1899, running paper-heavy court dockets by hand through individual human activities. Our current approach is at odds with the changing realities of American law and willfully blind to technological advances. Of course that is also good news: There is much, much low-hanging fruit here.

Information, Simplification, and Standardization

The most basic form of *pro se* assistance is also probably the furthest along: providing information to litigants. Legal aid and clerk's offices have long provided this information, but placing it all on the Internet, along with usable, fillable forms, makes a massive difference. For example, the Indiana Supreme Court has its own YouTube channel containing more than 129 videos, most less than ten minutes long, which explain various court processes to *pro se* litigants.[1] As of July 2014, these videos had been viewed over 360,000 times. The New York Access to Justice Commission has a Twitter account that shares information about its services. California has also been a leader. Its State Supreme Court self-help website has over 900 pages of forms, instructions, and legal overviews, and is visited by over 100,000 people a month.[2]

Information can bring us only so far, though, especially given the very substantial differences in court forms and procedures across jurisdictions. It seems crazy to non-lawyers that different counties in the same state would handle basic activities like divorces or evictions differently, but that is in fact the rule, not the exception. So online self-help often has to do more than provide statewide forms; it has to provide forms by the county. It is also hard to provide generalized advice about what *pro se* litigants can expect in court when the procedures themselves differ from county to county and even courtroom to courtroom. With more than 3,000 counties in the United States, the extent of variation is staggering.

State supreme courts and access-to-justice commissions are taking a leading role in this battle. For example, in New York State, Judge Fisher and others are working on uniform procedures and paperwork for areas dominated by *pro se* litigants, including divorce, landlord-tenant, foreclosure, and consumer debt.

The process is challenging. Different constituencies disagree about what to include in any uniform legal pleading. For example, in some housing courts, a landlord barely needs to explain the basis for the eviction, and if the tenant does not ask, the landlord does not need to present any evidence of compliance with the eviction procedures. This is pretty helpful for landlords and speeds along many eviction proceedings. Tenants' rights advocates thus prefer a uniform eviction pleading that requires the landlord to attach evidence of breach (such as a list of the back rent owed or a picture of the damage to the apartment) plus a copy of a proper eviction notice (which often requires 30 days' notice). Landlords would prefer uniform pleadings that require much less. The bottom line is that uniform pleadings can actually have a powerful substantive effect on every case in the state, which makes them politically charged.

They also may impinge upon lawyers used to monopolizing an area of law. When the Texas Access to Justice Commission tried to move forward with uniform forms for uncontested divorces, it encountered significant opposition from the Family Law Section of the Texas Bar.

Naturally, the section did not come out and say that its members worried about losing business. Rather, it argued that the forms were misleading and dangerous. They went so far as to question whether there was an actual need for the forms. The battle got picked up in the national news by *The Wall Street Journal*[3] and *Bloomberg News,*[4] and eventually the Texas Supreme Court put its foot down and promulgated the forms over the bar's objections.

Attempting to manage courtroom procedures is also politically fraught. American judges have a long history of firm control over their own courtrooms, including the power to call their docket in the manner they prefer, to decide whether or not to ask questions of litigants, and to decide how they will (or will not) explain the business of the court to the assembled litigants. This means that, in some courtrooms, a judge will take the bench and give a short speech aimed at the *pro se* litigants explaining what issues are on the docket, the order in which they will be called, and what will happen when their case is called. Other judges will arrive and start calling cases with no explanation. Even something as straightforward as the order of calling the cases can be radically different. Some judges will take the cases with lawyers first. Others will take the cases from oldest to newest or alphabetically by case name. Others will take cases that seem simple before cases projected to be more complicated, and so on.

Nevertheless, the benefits of standardization are well worth the struggle. In a system where everyone arrives with a lawyer, it is possible (although not preferable) to accommodate different forms and procedures from court to court. Trial lawyers are accustomed to figuring out those sorts of variations. In courts where the majority of litigants are *pro se* individuals, it is palpably unfair.

State supreme courts and their access-to-justice commissions have taken the lead on this front by generating form documents for all sorts of cases that lower courts in the state are *required* to accept. This means that a litigant in any county in the state can download a form for name changes or an uncontested divorce, and then file and prosecute it. Many of these websites also include advice about what to expect in court—exactly the kind of advice that non-lawyers would be hesitant to offer lest they run afoul of the prohibition against the unauthorized practice of law.

Changing the Clerk's Office

Right now, somewhere in America, a court clerk is refusing to answer a question and is telling a *pro se* litigant that the clerks are not allowed to answer legal questions. In most clerks' offices in America, a sign announces that "Court Clerks Cannot Give Legal Advice." Canon 1.7 of the ethics code for court clerks (ironically entitled "Assisting Litigants") states that clerks "shall not give legal advice unless it is required as part of one's official duties."[5] On one level, this prohibition makes sense: Court clerks have not typically gone to law school and should not be offering advice beyond their expertise. And, as court administrators will happily point out, they are barred from the unauthorized practice of law, and giving "legal advice" is the practice of law.

Nevertheless, this ban does more to make the clerks' jobs easier than it does to protect the public. It is not exactly clear what "legal advice" consists of, which means that clerks can interpret the prohibition broadly or narrowly. Because a broad reading avoids a great deal of work, some clerks refuse to answer almost any question about court processes or underlying law. Other clerks will answer certain questions depending on whether the questioner is polite or rude, and in some offices different clerks in the same office handle the prohibition differently.

By any definition of "legal advice," most clerks know a lot about their courts, including what documents to file and when, how court appearances are handled, and even what legal avenues are most likely to succeed in any particular kind of case. In fact, court clerks often know more about their court and the underlying law than many local lawyers, let alone *pro se* litigants.

California has been at the forefront of changing the nature of court services. It has an extensive self-help website and has at least one self-help center in every county in the state. Some of these locations are more comprehensive than others, but at a minimum each of these centers has a real live human who is dedicated to helping *pro se* litigants through the process. Many of these centers feature a "Family Law Facilitator," a court employee who specializes in helping *pro se* litigants navigate divorce and child custody matters. Others feature a Small Claims Advisor who helps with collections matters. These services are free and not limited to poor people.

143

San Diego and Sacramento have pilot "one-day divorce" programs.[6] If the spouses can agree on the division of property, spousal support, and a parenting plan for children, they can come in, meet with a court clerk who reviews the paperwork to make sure it is all in order, and then appear before a judge the same day to finalize the divorce.

Self-help centers have been launched in places as diverse as Missoula, Montana and Pinellas County, Florida. Nacogdoches County, Texas has a self-help computer kiosk that is staffed by a legal aid attorney. Federal bankruptcy and district courts have followed suit in Illinois, Arizona, and elsewhere. In Hawaii, the Ho'okele Court Navigation Project supports a "court concierge" desk located at the entrances of their main court buildings.

Paying for staff or kiosks in self-help centers can be expensive, but as the National Conference of State Courts has noted, "usability is free."[7] Some courts have designated one or more court managers as a *"pro se* clerk." Over 25% of federal district courts have a dedicated *pro se* clerk.[8] Others have retrained all of their staff, focusing on the areas most likely to involve *pro se* litigants.

Some clerks' offices have also taken a much more muscular role in managing *pro se* cases: checking them at the outset to see that the paperwork is correct, pointing out potential areas of concern, and then shepherding the case and the litigants through the process. Traditionally, court clerks have simply filed court papers and then relied upon the lawyers to take the necessary steps from there. *Pro se* cases require more oversight and guidance. This necessitates more work from the clerks, but saves a great deal of time on the back end: *Pro se* litigants are better prepared for court and less likely to fall afoul of procedural traps.

There are myriad training programs and approaches, but the bottom line is that court clerks need to change their default setting from "I do not answer those sorts of questions" to "What can I do to help you and how can I best explain the necessary steps?" This is a bigger deal than it sounds like, because it requires the firm support of the local judges and in some cases elected heads of the county clerk's office.

It also significantly expands the duties of a clerk's office. It is hard work to answer questions calmly and provide guidance about such a complicated and often irrational system. These efforts work hand in hand with standardized forms, because clerks have a much easier time answering questions when they can provide a specific form that will work or a helpful website.

Most court managers are justice professionals who care quite a bit about their courts, judges, and dockets and do not want to stand by as *pro se* litigants flounder. If one adds up divorce, child custody, foreclosure, eviction, and debtor/creditor cases, there are a lot of *pro se* litigants these days, and these litigants are often facing very serious outcomes, including losing their housing, cars, or even their children. Court clerks are wary of getting too involved, but by and large they are professionals who care about the administration of justice, so training them to provide more information and assistance can be a win-win. This is especially so when part of the solution is standardized, online forms and advice, because the most basic questions can be handled by a courthouse kiosk or online, lessening the workload on clerks and providing better information to litigants.

Changing Courts—Low-Hanging Fruit

America's common-law courts have a long and proud tradition of judicial independence. This independence includes the general power to run one's court as one pleases, within the bounds of the rules of procedure and due process of law.

American judges are also inherently conservative in the non-political sense, which is only natural in a system built on adherence to precedent. Most American judges are not specially trained for their jobs; they simply start working as judges after careers as practicing lawyers. When you combine these factors, it is not surprising at all that American courts have proven resistant to change, especially when it comes to operating as if every litigant has a lawyer.

Remember that every judge in America (excluding the occasional justice of the peace and traffic court judge) is a former lawyer. Everything he learned about court processes pre-appointment came as a lawyer. Thus, by definition, the bulk of any new judge's courtroom experience involved cases where at least one of the parties was represented and often where both sides were represented. Most judges are more senior than most lawyers (because they must first have a law career before becoming a judge), and many judges stay on the bench for years. This means that much of the American judiciary cut its teeth before the *pro se* crisis grew to its current levels. As a result, the model case in every lawyer's (and thus every judge's) mind includes lawyers ferrying the case through the various complicated legal and procedural steps.

If a judge did have any prior experiences with *pro se* litigants, it is likely to have been unpleasant. *Pro se* litigants often file papers late, feature topics outside of the litigation, mangle legal arguments, and the like. Ask any trial lawyer how she feels about dealing with *pro se* litigants and you will hear a litany of complaints (and sometimes chuckling over how easy it was to defeat them). This attitude of disdain and irritation is a natural carryover to becoming a judge.

Even with all of this, the *pro se* crisis means that judges, especially the great majority of American judges who worry about fairness, must change their procedures. And they are starting to do so. There are two seminal documents that describe the state of the judicial revolution in *pro se* matters. The first is the American Judicature Society's *Reaching Out or Overreaching: Judicial Ethics and Self-Represented Litigants.*[9] The second is Richard Zorza's 2002 book, *The Self-Help Friendly Court: Designed from the Ground Up to Work for People Without Lawyers.*[10] Both books argue that court clerks and judges are not ethically barred from offering extra assistance to *pro se* litigants and offer sensible, if pretty basic, solutions about how to do so.

Consider Zorza's book. Zorza has been working in technology, self-help, and access to justice since the 1970s. "Self-help-friendly courts" are the passion of his life. The book is remarkable in two ways.

On the one hand, it is notable and visionary because it does not ask how current court processes can be amended or appended to suit the occasional *pro se* litigant. It starts from the opposite end. In many American courts, *pro* se litigation is the norm, not an exception. If we redesigned those courts from scratch to serve these litigants, what would they look like? It is not enough simply to supply *pro se* litigants with more information on how to operate the existing system: We must rebuild them from the ground up.

On the other hand, even with this brave and salutary approach to the topic, Zorza's actual suggestions are very modest. Part of that is its timing. In 2002, the technology had not advanced to the point where it was realistic to automate much of what courts do. Part of it is the audience and the publisher. Zorza wrote the book to win over open-minded judges, and the National Center for State Courts (the primary national organization for state court judges) published it. Thus, he naturally downplayed more radical solutions.

So what are the suggestions? The most basic is to adjust the attitudes of everyone in the justice system towards successful, fair, and transparent dispute resolution for *pro se* litigants. This means that judges and court administrators must reevaluate and redesign every step of the process with laymen in mind. Courthouses must include clear signage and lists of what cases are being heard in which courts. Clerks must simplify and standardize forms. They must post the forms in courthouse kiosks and online, along with clear instructions for filling them out and filing them, and then following up in court. Court clerks' offices need to be ready and willing to answer questions, provide guidance, and actively advise litigants through the process.

And most importantly, judges must change how they run their courtrooms. These suggestions are particularly basic. Judges should explain the law and process to the *pro se* litigants politely and simply. Judges should reserve time to answer questions patiently. They should not be afraid to ask pertinent questions of any witness or litigant or to summarize the proof as things proceed so that everyone is clear on what has and has not been established. Judges should be flexible with the rules of procedure and evidence, especially in non-jury cases. When the case is completed, the judge should rule on the case, explaining her reasoning orally and then following up with a written order on the case.

Readers who have not spent much time in an American court are probably a little surprised by this list of common-sense suggestions. Don't most courts explain the relevant law and procedures at the outset of a hearing? And don't most judges announce clear decisions and rulings at the end of a case and follow it up with a written judgment and order? Actually, no. Take issuing orders after a trial or hearing. In many cases, a trial judge will ask the winner's lawyer to "draft an order" that summarizes the holding, provide the order to the opposing lawyer for approval, and then give it to the judge for signing. This is a relatively mundane task for an experienced trial lawyer, although most lawyers will still remember the panic that set in the first time a judge asked her to "write up an order for my signature." Consider how challenging and strange it would seem to a *pro se* litigant. Even the formatting of the document would be hard, let alone properly stating what has been ordered, and then getting a hostile opposing lawyer to agree on the wording.

One of the biggest challenges in addressing the *pro se* crisis is just how much American courts count on lawyers to handle every step of the litigation process. The lawyers draft the court documents, often including documents the judge signs. The lawyers explain the law and process to their clients. The lawyers gather the relevant documents and witnesses and shape the testimony to match the relevant law. The lawyers even handle much of the legal research and argumentation for the judges. In *pro se* cases, all of these assumptions are turned on their heads: Judges and clerks must carry the freight for the litigants if there is to be any semblance of fairness.

Part of the objection to these changes from judges and clerks is that they require much more work and patience and time. Another challenge is that they require a fundamental shift in the judicial role, from reactive or even passive to active. American judges seek, above all, to appear neutral. Judges fear that if they try to help *pro se* litigants along with asking pertinent questions or explaining how to admit a document into evidence, they will seem to favor one side over another.

This is especially so when one side has a lawyer and the other does not. Take this very common example. A *pro se* litigant seeks to admit a bank record in his divorce case. The lawyer on the other side objects: "Hearsay, authentication, and foundation, Your Honor." Everyone in the courtroom believes that the record is not a forgery. Everyone agrees that the record is relevant to the issues in the trial. Yet the objection puts the judge in an awkward position. If she explains to the litigant the steps to lay a foundation for a hearsay exception and authentication, the opposing lawyer may cry foul. Judges rarely help lawyers when these sorts of problems arise, so why should they help *pro se* litigants? On the other hand, if the judge simply sustains the objections with no explanation, the *pro se* litigant may be barred from presenting a key part of his case. The choice in this case seems relatively easy to a non-lawyer. The document is not a forgery and the information is necessary for the case, so how is it biased to just let it in?

This sort of dilemma recurs in every *pro se* case. This example should clarify that much of the most important work in *pro se* court reform has been changing judicial hearts and minds—convincing them that their ethical duties do not bar asking questions or giving frank advice to a confused *pro se* litigant. To the contrary, their ethical and moral duty to provide justice demands that they do so.

Zorza tells a great story of a *pro se* training he ran for a group of judges. When they got to the point of the training where Zorza suggests asking pointed questions from the bench to clarify a *pro se* litigant's case, a judge exclaimed: "We can't ask those sorts of questions. That would be unconstitutional!" Zorza held back from pressing the judge on exactly what part of the Constitution would bar balanced judicial behavior, but this judge's reaction actually speaks volumes about the deep-seated nature of judicial resistance.

Nevertheless, courts are making progress. The National Center for State Courts and state supreme court justices all around the country have been advocating for what they call "engaged neutrality," which includes almost all of the suggestions above. They have backed this concept with research papers, national resolutions, training sessions, and a slow, but steady, trickle down into the courts that actually matter.[11]

The Federal Courts in the Eastern District of New York (which covers Brooklyn, Queens, and the rest of Long Island) have created a special magistrate's court that is exclusively set up for *pro se* matters, and other city and state courts have followed suit.[12] State supreme courts have established access-to-justice commissions in almost two thirds of American states, and each of these commissions is trying to create usable, standardized forms and encourage adoption of reforms to courts and clerks' offices.

The Self-Represented Litigation Network and the National Conference of State Courts have launched a very promising "Triage Protocols" project.[13] The project suggests a strategy for remaking *pro se* courts. Each project starts by collecting data on *pro se* cases and ranking priorities based upon the greatest need. This is an obvious thing to do, but it is impossible to analyze data that has not been gathered, and historically *pro se* litigation was discussed anecdotally rather than numerically.

Once the needs are ranked, all of the stakeholders (judges, clerks, legal aid lawyers, other lawyers and litigants who handle these cases regularly, and groups representing the litigants themselves) assemble in an effort to streamline and regularize the process. The goal is to produce standardized forms and procedures, so that each player in the system can have a set "protocol," similar to the checklists that have become popular in medicine.

The process results in a set protocol for each player. And any *pro se* litigant in one of those cases can work from her own "triage protocol," a list of documents that are necessary, dates and places for filing, and next steps once the case gets to court. When she interacts with any other player in the system, that person can likewise refer to the protocol and send her on to the proper forms and instructions.

The Legal Services Corporation (the central hub for legal aid offices) has bought into this vision and has hosted several technology summits. It has taken the protocol effort seriously and is trying to organize a legal "portal" in each state, where *pro se* litigants can find information, download documents, and eventually process their cases. All of this is backed by data gathering and continuous updating of processes and forms based on litigant and court experiences.[14] The ABA has climbed on board with "Hackcess to Justice, an Access to Justice Hackathon." At this point there are no shortage of good ideas; the need is for implementation and leadership.

The successful efforts just described have been necessitated by the sheer volume of *pro se* litigation and have been assisted by the popularity of streamlining court processes. Funding for legal aid or public defenders is always a challenge. Funding for *pro se* court reform, however, has proven much more popular, especially when framed as a middle-class access-to-justice issue. Consider two recent "state of the judiciary" speeches by the top justices in New York and California, two of America's most populous states.[15] Both speeches heavily feature the progress made on access to justice through computerization and self-help tools and evince a willingness to push through any bar association or judicial reticence in a way that would have been unthinkable even 10 years ago.

Changing Courts More Radically

One can think of possible judicial behavior along a spectrum. At one pole, there are courts that are lawyer-centric and staffed by passive, neutral judges. This has been the traditional common-law and American model. The lawyers do the work and the judges sit back and decide the issues raised by the lawyers. Few American courts follow this model all the time, but passive neutrality is our baseline.

At the other pole, the judges are fully involved and in control of every element of their cases. Judges take the lead on gathering the facts, calling the witnesses, asking the questions, and finding and applying the law. Most courts around the world outside of the Anglo-American tradition are closer to this model of full judicial control. In technical parlance we call that system "inquisitorial," because the judges inquire—they ask the questions.

Most of the *pro se* court changes have barely nudged judges away from disinterested neutrality. A more radical redesign would ask judges and court clerks to take a much more inquisitorial role in their cases. This would be an ever larger and more controversial change in judicial behavior, but would greatly balance the scales for *pro se* litigants. Rather than trying to come into court and imitate lawyers' behavior, *pro se* litigants could come to court comfortable that the judge would run the show, greatly blunting any advantage held by a represented or more knowledgeable *pro se* opponent.

While this suggestion seems radical, this exact system is in use both in America and throughout the world. "Inquisitorial" sounds rather ominous and Monty Python-esque, but it is actually quite familiar. One obvious model is small-claims court, where judges assume that the litigants will be unrepresented and proceed accordingly, asking the necessary questions, guiding the witnesses in telling their stories, and deciding the case without hearing any legal arguments from the parties.

In fact, many Americans are likely to be *more* familiar with the inquisitorial model than the traditional model because of the popularity of television shows like *Judge Judy*, *Judge Joe Brown*, and *The People's Court*—all settings where the judges take much more aggressive roles in managing cases. When one describes the inquisitorial system to lawyers or even laypeople, there is often some bewilderment about the change in the judge's role. But when you add that judges ask questions and define issues "like Judge Judy does," the proposal is clearer and less threatening.

Small claims court is not the only inquisitorial system in America. Most administrative proceedings, from disability appeals to unemployment hearings, run on the same model. Lawyers are allowed but not expected. Often, non-lawyer advocates are also allowed. The procedure is simplified and clearly explained at each step of the process. The rules of evidence are relaxed or ignored. Court clerks proactively subpoena standard forms of evidence, such as doctors' records in disability cases. The parties bring the witnesses and documents they want the administrative law judge (ALJ) to consider, but the ALJ takes the lead on questioning and accepting and considering the documents.

If you are wondering whether the proposed changes would actually make a difference, remember Chapter 7's discussion of the substantial and growing body of first-class empirical research demonstrating that having a lawyer in these settings has no effect or even a negative effect. Harvard Law Professor James Greiner led a blind, randomized study of outcomes in unemployment appeals before an ALJ and reached the conclusion that lawyers made no detectable difference in outcomes, other than delaying the results for about two weeks.[16] Herbert Kritzer led a similar study in Wisconsin that compared the results of administrative cases handled by lawyers and by non-lawyers. The study concluded that non-lawyers were at least as successful (and sometimes more successful) as lawyers in these administrative settings.[17] The determining factors were experience in the setting and some familiarity with the underlying law, *not* a law degree.

And of course the American inquisitorial systems are only the tip of the iceberg. Most courts in the world, including virtually all of the courts in continental Europe and most of the courts in Asia, South America, and Africa, run on an inquisitorial system.[18] Litigants are allowed to bring lawyers, but not required to. The lawyer is allowed to press a litigant's case, but in an inquisitorial system the judge is always in firm control of the proceedings. Lawyers are deemphasized; judges do most of the work.

There are obvious disadvantages to this approach. Judges can abuse their case-management powers to affect case outcomes, and zealous judges certainly can tip the scales of justice. It also likely requires a different sort of appointment and training for judges. In many American states, judges are elected, sometimes in partisan elections with little regard for qualifications and expertise. In the inquisitorial jurisdictions, judges are trained on a different track and spend their whole careers working as civil servants/judges, rising based on aptitude and seniority. It is harder work for the judges. It also offers an uncomfortable amount of control to judges that many Americans already feel are too powerful.

Nevertheless, there are reasons to favor a more inquisitorial system regardless of these objections. First, we are not suggesting a wholesale substitution of the French system for the American one. The focus of this book is on the courts that ordinary Americans are stuck navigating without a lawyer, what we call *pro se* courts. The courts where lawyers staff most cases can remain unchanged, including more serious criminal courts (as opposed to those handling traffic tickets and misdemeanors). There are reasons to favor simplification of law and process in those courts, but their problems are distinct from those of *pro se* courts.

Second, even neutral American judges already have plenty of power to affect case outcomes. Every trial lawyer can tell a story of a judge who had it out for him, or his client, or both. There are innumerable ways for these biases to carry weight behind a veneer of neutrality. Though inquisitorial judges may be biased too, their biases may be more obvious, making some judges more hesitant. At a minimum, some types of bias should be more detectable and possibly easier to correct on appeal, or at the ballot box in states with elected judges.

Third, studied judicial passivity is quite distinct from judicial neutrality. A passive judicial posture actually confers a massive and hugely unfair advantage on parties with access to lawyers and especially on parties with access to the very best lawyers. The inquisitorial system could actually begin to balance the scales of American justice between the haves and the have-nots.

Fourth, as judges become more involved, procedural simplicity and streamlining is much more possible. Involved judges can guide *pro se* litigants through evidentiary or procedural issues and pare down the issues to what really matters: applying the substantive law to the important facts to reach a just result.

Fifth, while it is true that an inquisitorial approach may take more time and effort, the gain in fairness is worth it. Currently judges may in fact speed cases along to clear their overburdened dockets, but that is precisely when inserting a speed bump could create more caution and care. And finally, a more inquisitorial approach would require some additional training. Currently, most federal ALJs start off with a month and a half of orientation and training. More initial training plus continuing legal education each year could supplement this foundation, cultivating the requisite expertise.

Bypassing Humans Altogether—ODR

Recall our discussion of Colin Rule, Modria, and online dispute resolution (ODR) from Chapter 8. Technology makes it possible to solve disputes, even complicated or very entrenched disputes, with little or no human involvement. This is especially so in common types of cases where certain issues and types of settlements recur. As disputes get more unusual or unique, computers struggle with what statisticians call "out of sample" problems, situations where there is limited data for the machines or humans to work from.

Fortunately, the types of disputes handled by *pro se* courts generally fall within pretty well-defined boundaries. Each divorce carries its own sad story of discord (Tolstoy warned us that every unhappy family is unhappy in its own way), but the legal issues—how to divide property, how to split parenting duties—are pretty repetitive and settlements and court decisions fall into patterns. This is even more so with child support, evictions, and consumer-debt cases. And if a substantial number of these disputes could be handled through ODR, the data on which cases settle and how would become richer, and the ODR programs would get even better. Computers make it possible to collect and use the data in a positive feedback loop, ever improving the process.

As such, the cases that are clogging our *pro se* courts are particularly well suited to online dispute resolution. Maybe the market could solve this problem as individuals simply choose ODR rather than traditional court? There is some proof of this happening. Wevorce and other online divorce mediation sites are examples.

Nevertheless, even after ODR, Wevorce and other sites ask the participants to file papers with the local family law court. Why? Because our government courts are the *only* location where a state-granted marriage license can be dissolved.

This explains why ODR has limited appeal for eviction, child support, or consumer-debt cases. In America and all over the world, government court systems hold the monopoly in exercising the unique powers of the state. If you want an enforceable judgment that allows you to garnish wages or seize property, you must head to court. If you want an eviction proceeding that ends with the sheriff coming to the apartment and forcibly removing the tenant from your property, housing court is your sole venue. In fact, self-help evictions or seizures of property are explicitly barred by law, so courts are truly the only show in town.

So, in cases where settlement can be reached and the opponents can trust each other to follow through on the agreement, ODR is an easy fit. But, in the great mass of disputes where a court may be necessary to enforce any settlement, one way or another a court proceeding is necessary.

That does not mean that the *process* of gaining or enforcing a final judgment has to remain the same. Many courts have already instituted voluntary or even mandatory mediation programs before trial and often before any significant court proceedings begin. Congress passed the Alternative Dispute Resolution Act of 1998 (28 U.S.C. § 651), which encourages and supports federal ADR programs. Many states have followed suit and mandatory mediation is relatively common in civil matters, including matters dominated by *pro se* litigants. For example, more than two thirds of the states have some form of mandatory mediation for divorce or child custody.[19]

Almost all of these mediation programs are staffed by human mediators and require quite a lot of human time and effort. Litigants with settlement authority must set aside a period of time to all meet together with a mediator and their lawyers (if they have lawyers). Other, more formal types of ADR like arbitration or summary trials are even more labor-intensive.

The foundation for an ODR revolution is already in place, however, since courts are already accustomed to sending a case out for mediation first. Given how much cheaper and more efficient ODR is, a court system could replace human mediation altogether or simply add ODR as a required first step to be followed by human mediation as eBay does, culling out the easiest cases to settle. And as these ODR programs improve, they could eliminate an increasing number of cases.

There are, naturally, objections to court-ordered mediation and those objections would also apply to ODR. Critics have long objected to mediation in settings where one litigant is much more knowledgeable or powerful than the other. The classic example is divorce mediation in cases of abuse,[20] but many eviction or consumer-debt cases will likewise feature represented and knowledgeable plaintiffs who are repeat players facing off against unrepresented and less knowledgeable defendants.

In both ODR and in-person mediation, it is axiomatic that the parties are to make their own agreement, without reference to statutory rights or the basis of the suit. Parties are encouraged to speak broadly about terms and conditions of settlement. They are discouraged from focusing on "positions," especially legal positions, since this tends to deter settlement. If the parties are happy with their settlement and the settlement is otherwise legal, it is not the mediator's job to tell one side or the other that they might have gotten a better deal or have underestimated the strength of their case.

This may explain mandatory mediation's mixed results post-settlement. Proponents have long claimed that mediation results in better solutions because the parties themselves create them, and that satisfaction with the process and compliance with the agreements will thus be higher than with traditional adjudication. The empirical studies are more of a mixed bag, however, with some studies showing mediation working better than traditional court and others showing little improvement.[21] If it is not true that mediation is better, critics ask, why bother?

These are objections to all mediation programs, not just ODR, and mandatory mediation looks like a permanent and growing feature of American courts whether it heads online or not. Further, ODR offers the opportunity to at least partially address systematic imbalances. It does not occur in person or in a set and pressurized period of time, so arguably personal power imbalances are lessened. Part of the ODR process could include educating each party about his legal rights and remedies, which could lessen information imbalances. And just as divorces that feature charges of abuse are often excused from mandatory in-person mediation, a class of similar cases could be exempted from ODR.

ODR also naturally blunts the effect of having one represented party. Typically, unless they are barred from doing so, lawyers come to in-person mediation and offer their advice and thoughts to their client throughout. Further, even though experienced mediators try to bar discussion of the law, lawyers in mediation often launch into an explanation of the legal rights and remedies, frequently slanted towards their positions. In a situation where one side is unrepresented, the lawyer often gets to frame the issues and influence the settlement terms.

ODR, by contrast, is done anonymously and at a time lag, offering each litigant the chance to research his case along the way as they move towards settlement. If one side has a lawyer and makes claims about how the law or process will work along with his settlement terms, an unrepresented party has time to research the question or to decide that she really needs a lawyer regardless of the cost. These options are much harder to exercise during in-person mediation.

A Vision for the Future

The current progress and the current batch of solutions are very heartening for anyone concerned about access to justice in America. In a short period of time, we have seen pretty substantial changes to the nature of American dispute resolution. The amazing thing about where we find ourselves, however, is how very rudimentary our initial efforts have been. We are barely using technology right now. Interactive forms and explanatory online instructions are extraordinarily helpful for litigants who used to have to pay a lawyer by the hour. But the technologies that underlie that usage have been available for at least twenty years. Imagine what these resources will look like as they take advantage of data collection and personalization.

The technology is already available to offer a much better experience. That potential is stifled by unauthorized-practice-of-law rules, adherence to tradition, and the failure to combine human expertise, data collection, and computing power. If America could combine those changes with the increased use of technology and triage protocols in *pro se* courts, we would create something truly exceptional: a simple, transparent court system aimed at assisting litigants politely and efficiently. Today's *pro se* courts are far from those ideals.

Imagine a world where there are special courts set up for the poor and middle class that operate so well that they are the envy of the wealthy who are still using a lawyer-driven model that persists from seventeenth-century England. This hypothetical is not only possible: If access-to-justice advocates can convince legislatures and courts that this approach would alleviate the *pro se* crisis, make better use of precious judicial resources, save money, and (as a bonus) produce better, fairer outcomes, it may be probable.

CHAPTER 10

Cheaper Lawyers and Paraprofessionals

On July 20, 2004, Ernest Chavis visited his neighbor, ninety-one-year-old Annie Belle Weiss.[1] Chavis was an insurance agent by trade and had known Weiss personally and professionally for years. Weiss's daughter, Sara Crossman, had died that May, and Weiss was trying to settle her revised estate plans. During their chat, Weiss expressed to Chavis that she wanted to write a new will, and wanted help from "somebody objective." As a later lawsuit proves, there was some jockeying among Weiss's heirs, and she wanted to make sure her wishes were carried out. She asked Chavis if he might be willing to help her make a will. Chavis agreed, and Weiss told Chavis how she wanted her property divided. She also wanted to sell some property and asked Chavis to help with that as well. She left nothing to Chavis in the will and paid him nothing.

Chavis took the information with him and, using Quicken Family Lawyer, he drafted a simple will. According to Chavis, the program took him through a series of simple questions and answers that he filled in with Weiss's information. He also drafted a power of attorney so he could help sell Weiss's property. By July 31, Weiss was in the hospital. Chavis brought the will and power of attorney documents to the hospital, and Weiss signed them both. Chavis then proceeded to sell Weiss's property, again for no payment. Weiss died on September 27, 2004. Under the will, Chavis served as the personal representative to the estate (basically the executor).

In the "no good deed goes unpunished" category, a dispute broke

159

out among Weiss's relatives, and Weiss's grand-nieces (who each received 10% of the estate under the new will) sued the will's primary beneficiary—Weiss's nephew by marriage Michael Lehman, who received 60% of the estate. The thrust of the lawsuit was that Michael Lehman had exercised "undue influence" over Weiss. But in a will contest, plaintiffs will frequently pull out all the stops to invalidate a will, so the disgruntled heirs argued that the new will was void because Chavis had engaged in unauthorized practice of law. This accusation was no joke: In South Carolina and many other states, the unauthorized practice of law is a felony, with a maximum sentence of 5 years in prison and a $5,000 fine.

The unauthorized practice of law portion of the case eventually made it to the South Carolina Supreme Court. South Carolina, like most states, differentiates between being a "mere scrivener" and practicing law. If you only write down what another tells you on a legal form, that is not the practice of law. If you offer "advice, consultation, explanation, or recommendations," however, you are illegally practicing law. The South Carolina Supreme Court determined that Chavis did illegally practice law when he helped his elderly neighbor with her will and her power of attorney. The fact that he did it for free was no defense. According to the Court, that made Chavis *even more dangerous*:

> Indeed, the public may well be in greater need of protection from the unauthorized practice of law where it seems to be done without charge than where a charge is openly made for the services. In the former situation, the public, through natural cupidity, are the more readily attracted to something which appears to be a "give-away" project or a chance to obtain "something for nothing."

The Court made two rulings. First, it punished Chavis by disallowing the statutory fee he would have earned for administering the estate, the only payment Chavis was to receive for his trouble. Second, the Court issued an injunction barring Chavis from illegally practicing law again, which Chavis did not object to, since he had no plans to ever do anything of this nature again. Last, the Court refused to remove Chavis as the personal representative of the estate or to declare the will void.

Consider the strangeness of these rulings. On the one hand, the will was valid and Chavis was to stay on as the executor. This suggests that the will and the power of attorney were not harmful in operation. But, because Chavis did more than type in Ms. Weiss's information (although the Court is quite unclear about what he specifically did wrong), he violated the law and forfeited a fee he earned under another statute.

This case tells you much about UPL: It shows how broad the protection is. Chavis never claimed he was a lawyer. Chavis did not solicit business as a lawyer. Weiss knew that Chavis was not a lawyer; she had done insurance business with him in the past and they were neighbors and friends.

This case shows how mushy and standardless UPL is. The Court states the relevant standard (mere scrivener vs. scrivener plus legal advice), but never states exactly what it is that Chavis did wrong. Chavis did not appear in court and did not draft a complicated legal document from scratch. If anyone seems to have committed unauthorized practice, it is Quicken, not Chavis. Why does the Court stick it to Chavis and not Quicken? Because courts have unsurprisingly had an easier time punishing unauthorized legal practice by individuals than by big companies like Quicken or LegalZoom, which have the money and political clout to fight the charges. For example, in Texas, the Unauthorized Practice of Law Committee of the Texas State Bar convinced a federal court that Quicken Family Lawyer software was engaged in the unauthorized practice of law. The court reasoned that such planning and consideration of alternatives requires legal judgment, and laymen might be misled into trusting the software's accuracy and legal judgment. After the decision, an intense lobbying battle broke out, and the Texas state legislature amended its law to allow such self-help software.[2]

The Chavis case also shows that UPL is often disconnected from consumer protection. Who exactly was harmed in this story? Chavis charged nothing for writing the will or handling the power of attorney. The Court rejected the argument that the will or the power of attorney were faulty solely because Chavis was not a lawyer. Who then was harmed? The lawyer whom Weiss failed to hire to redraft her will was harmed.

UPL is one half of the protection of the American lawyer's "monopoly" over legal practice: It keeps outsiders from encroaching upon lawyers' turf. UPL explains why American title companies, notaries public, and paralegals offer very limited services. UPL also explains why, until

15 years ago, Americans had two choices for handling a legal issue: hire an expensive lawyer by the hour or do it themselves with no outside help. Any outside helpers, even friendly neighbors working for free, face the threat of UPL prosecution.

The second half of lawyers' monopoly is law school, the bar exam, and the various barriers to entry into the profession. It is harder and more expensive to become a lawyer in America than in most other countries. The requirements include years of expensive schooling, multiple required standardized tests, and a lengthy character and fitness process.

Bar associations and judges claim that these two limits on the practice of law are for consumer protection. There is some truth to that claim. Surely if Chavis had wandered into his neighbor's home and claimed to be a lawyer for the purposes of stealing her inheritance, prosecution for UPL (and criminal fraud) would be appropriate. Likewise, consumers should have some idea what a licensed professional knows how to do and educational requirements could serve that informational purpose. Nevertheless, the current levels of protection go well beyond what is needed to keep consumers safe. Some have examined the system and found a protectionist cartel: Bar associations and courts are protecting their own turf against lower-cost competition that might serve people who would not and could not otherwise hire an expensive lawyer.[3]

As we explain in this chapter, the status quo is hardly inevitable. Law training used to be much cheaper and faster, and non-lawyers were able to do much more. The same is still true in many other countries. America should go back to the future, both by lowering the cost of legal education and by letting paraprofessionals help with routine legal matters. The high-cost lawyer should be one of a range of options instead of the only game in town. The alternative is that many poor and middle-class people simply go without legal help, lumping it instead of choosing among cheaper, simpler alternatives to a lawyer.

Legal Training in America: A Brief History

Only in the last century did America make a long, expensive sequence of postgraduate education and training a prerequisite for anyone to offer any legal assistance. Well into the nineteenth century, most lawyers became lawyers by "reading law"—that is, learning as an apprentice to an existing lawyer. Indeed, some, like Abraham Lincoln, read law on their own, studying classic legal books without apprenticing to anyone else.[4]

As the size of the legal profession tripled between 1860 and 1900, apprenticeships could not expand enough to keep pace. Two types of law schools emerged to meet the demand: elite academic schools within universities, in the mold of the Harvard Law School, and cheaper, proprietary law schools—what we might call trade schools. Trade-school teachers were not professors but largely part-time adjuncts, judges, or practicing lawyers, and their institutions often operated as night schools. Students did not have to show any particular education to be admitted, and they tended to be immigrants, Jews, and the working class.

Elite law schools and bar associations railed against these newcomers as diploma mills, in part out of snobbery, nativism, and anti-Semitism. Raw protectionism also played a role, as the elite bar tried to protect itself against a flood of new competition. For example, from the ABA's inception in 1878, the group argued against both apprenticeship and proprietary law schools and in favor of the Harvard model. The ABA also helped to launch the American Association of Law Schools, the elite law school industry group, in 1900.

Though at first the ABA had limited success in strangling the proprietary schools, it eventually succeeded. During the Great Depression, demand for legal work collapsed and bar associations and state supreme courts sprung into action. State supreme courts claimed an inherent authority over lawyer regulation and rapidly raised barriers to entry. State supreme courts also stepped up the prosecution of the unauthorized practice of law.

By the end of World War II, the fight was over and the Harvard model had won. The ABA began to accredit law schools and require various elite model features, such as a full-time faculty that produces legal scholarship and a permanent law library. Eventually, graduation from an ABA-accredited law school became the dominant mode of entry to the profession. To become a lawyer in most states, students first needed a college education, followed by three years of full-time study at an ABA-accredited school (as opposed to an apprenticeship or unaccredited school), and passing a tough written bar exam. Between 1930 and

1950, 70 law schools folded; 69 of them were unaccredited. Proprietary schools either added the features required for ABA accreditation or went out of business. Outside of California, which allows graduates of unaccredited law schools to sit for a more challenging version of the bar exam, very few remained.

State supreme courts and bar associations claimed these changes were a triumph of consumer protection, but they hardly discussed the associated costs.

Our Unsustainable Model: Cadillac or Nothing

In Milton Friedman's iconic book *Capitalism and Freedom*, he tells a great story about lawyer over-regulation. An economist is speaking to a group of lawyers, arguing against the current, high barriers to entry: "Would it not, he said, be absurd if the automobile industry were to argue that no one should drive a low quality car and therefore that no automobile manufacturer should be permitted to produce a car that did not come up to the Cadillac standard?" The lawyers turned the argument on its head, asserting, "Of course, the country cannot afford anything but Cadillac lawyers!"[5]

Our current regulations and licensing requirements hold legal education to the gold standard, with a price to match. Other countries, such as England, France, and Germany, allow students to study law in college. But here, students must first earn a bachelor's degree in another subject from a college or university, which usually takes four years and costs tens if not hundreds of thousands of dollars.

Thereafter, aspiring lawyers must ordinarily study full-time for three more years to earn a Juris Doctor (J.D.) degree. A few grueling programs compress three years of classes into two, but still charge three years' tuition. And there are still some night law school programs, which require as many credits and take even longer. But for the most part, a law degree costs three full years of a student's life and can often run as much as $200,000 in tuition and living expenses. And that is not even counting what economists call "opportunity costs": the earnings that people would otherwise have made if they had not had to spend all three years in school. Law schools have made a bad situation worse by increasing their tuition far more than inflation. Between 1985 and 2012, tuition at private law schools increased by 440%, nearly four times as fast as inflation. The growth was a whopping 1,005% for in-state tuition at public law schools.

Law school is so expensive in part because of the ABA accreditation requirements and in part because of the race to look better in *U.S. News'* annual law school rankings. Tenured or tenure-track faculty, not practicing judges or lawyers, are supposed to do most of the teaching. But they are allowed to teach four or at most five regular courses *per year*. (At some colleges, by contrast, lecturers teach four undergraduate courses per semester.) Teaching loads are low in order to subsidize professors' academic research, though many professors publish little. Student-faculty ratios are capped, and distance learning is restricted. Law schools have to maintain large libraries at great expense.

But the accreditation requirements have hardly changed since the 1980s, and certainly have not changed enough to explain the run-up in tuition. Law school is expensive because almost everyone who wants to become a lawyer must attend one. Easier access to student loans and an unrealistic view of job and earnings prospects drove students into law school, heedless of cost. Some argue this is just the market at work and that law students should have learned the Latin phrase *caveat emptor* before they attended law school. This is not exactly a free market, however. Law schools are required to meet the ABA requirements, and law students are required to attend before joining the profession.

Worse yet, legal education is hardly tailored to what students will need once they enter the profession. Most classes are abstract lectures across a wide range of legal fields, many far afield from a lawyer's ultimate specialty. This array of classes teaches breadth and can cultivate critical thinking and analytical reasoning, but at the same time can sacrifice depth. There is too little focused legal work of the sort that real lawyers do, such as negotiating and drafting contracts, and not much hands-on learning.

Moreover, three years is too long. Many students and observers agree that the third year is largely repetitive.[6] As the law school adage goes: "The first year, they scare you to death. The second year, they work you to death. The third year, they bore you to death." Some students do manage to specialize in technical areas that require advanced coursework and skills training, such as tax law or corporate deals. Others take clinics or externships that resemble apprenticeships and help them to transition into practice. So it makes sense to offer a third year as an option. But for most, especially those on a tight budget, the last year or year and a half are wasted.

Ironically, even after three years of general law, students still do not know the nitty-gritty rules. They must still spend another two months and thousands of dollars for a bar-prep class to study for their state's bar exam. The bar exam remains a barrier even after students take and pass it. Because each state licenses lawyers on its own and only a minority use the same exam, a lawyer who moves to a different state sometimes has to take another bar exam tailored to the wrinkles of that state's laws—which helps to keep out competition.

There is a terrible irony about these entry requirements: They are not even particularly effective as consumer protection. An American law student can graduate from most law schools without ever having tried a case, written a contract, or even spoken to a client. Aside from an ability to read appellate cases and to memorize and then apply legal rules on the bar exam, American law graduates have no other guaranteed skills. This makes the consumer protection extremely limited: A newly minted lawyer can hang out a shingle and start taking cases with virtually no experience in handling the work and consumers would be none the wiser.

The situation only deteriorates over time, because lawyer discipline is so soft. If consumer protection were truly the concern, one might expect to see more lawyers disbarred or suspended for poor performance. The profession is extremely difficult to join but, once lawyers are in, they tend to stay in, barring truly gross misconduct like stealing from a client.

Students jump through all of these hoops in the hopes of landing a six-figure job at the end. Top law firms in the biggest cities tempt new associates with starting salaries of up to $180,000. But only a small fraction of students grab that golden ring. Many more work as solo practitioners or at small firms for perhaps $46,000 per year or less, and huge numbers graduate without jobs or land jobs that do not require a law degree. Marc Gans estimates that between 1985 and 2011, roughly one in three law school graduates could not find work as a lawyer, and that there are as many as 600,000 J.D. holders who are not working as a lawyer.[7] Some of these are businessmen or financiers by choice, but many are not. Recent graduates have done even worse, with legal employment numbers as low as 50%. Yet they are saddled with decades of loan repayments, which graduates will struggle to make unless they earn substantial salaries.

The situation is puzzling: There is a glut of newly minted lawyers who want to be associates at large firms. But, at the same time, there is a dearth of affordable divorce, housing, and criminal defense lawyers. That may well be because law schools teach their students the high-cost, high-overhead, individually tailored model of client services which we previously discussed in Chapter 6. After one factors in the costs of rent, secretaries, paralegals, and careful personalization of services, lawyers have to charge more per hour than most middle-class people can afford.

True, there are programs that help law school graduates with their student loan debts. A handful of super-elite law schools subsidize loan repayments for graduates who enter low-paying public-service jobs. Also, the federal government's current income-based repayment program caps payments and forgives outstanding loan balances for those who remain in specified government or public-service jobs for ten consecutive years, or after twenty-five years for those outside of public service.

These programs, however, at most soften the edges of the problem. First of all, they are primarily targeted toward traditional public service, which itself is far too underfunded to hire the current flood of law school graduates and can also accommodate only a fraction of the clients who need help. Second, their income thresholds are too low to tempt people to go to law school in order to serve underserved communities. Third, though some Democrats proposed to expand loan-repayment programs, given fiscal austerity and discretionary-spending caps, they are far more likely to be cut.

Fourth, they pose a serious risk of becoming the next mortgage bubble and financial crisis. Creating a new entitlement encourages excessive, risky borrowing and will likely lead to far more loan defaults and forgiveness than optimistic initial cost estimates suggest. The hard truth about student loan programs is that they actually do more to help university bottom lines than student well-being. One reason why law school tuition has risen so rapidly is the availability of almost unlimited federal loans and the hope of future loan repayment assistance.

Finally, and most fundamentally, student-loan programs tinker at the margins, rather than solving the deeper structural problem. They double down on a high-cost model, allowing law schools to continue to raise tuitions in the hopes that Uncle Sam will foot the bill. The root problem here is that students are spending too long in law school and racking up too much debt with too little reward to pay it off. Loan-forgiveness programs cloak this problem, with an eventual hidden transfer of wealth from taxpayers, instead of solving it. It is far less clear that any benefits will trickle down to poor and middle-class people in the form of more affordable legal services. Far more likely, law schools will soak up much of the gains, just as the rest of higher education has consistently grown much more expensive in tandem with increased financial aid.

There is a lively debate among scholars about whether, from the perspective of applicants, law school is worth the cost. Brian Tamanaha and others argue that it is not; Michael Simkovic, Frank McIntyre, and others offer evidence that it is, for the large majority of graduates. But that debate is largely beside the point from the perspective of access to justice. Whichever side is right, no one disputes that loan payments, overhead costs, and other financial realities drive lawyers toward more lucrative, higher-end practice and away from bare-bones legal services for the poor and middle class.

The signs of the times suggest that multiple crises are brewing in legal education. Disgruntled students at lower-ranked law schools have been filing false-advertising lawsuits, claiming that their alma maters inflated or distorted the likelihood of finding a good job after graduation. Applications to law school are down and many law schools are shrinking, buying out faculty through early retirement or even laying them off. Many student borrowers are in default, and surprising numbers are delinquent from the very beginning. And we may see a credit bubble resulting in massive loan forgiveness, borne by taxpayers.

The word *crisis* comes from the Greek word for decision or turning point, as in the course of a disease. Legal education and training are now in crisis, in both the original and current senses of that word. Over-medication has not worked, so it is time to try a different approach.

Rather than doubling down on the high-cost, gold-plated elite model, it is time to go back to the older varieties of legal training and licensure; to let a hundred flowers bloom.

Cheaper Ways to Become a Lawyer

We do not purport to know the single best and cheapest way to train and license lawyers. It is likely that there is no single way. We can state confidently that possibly well-meaning but protectionist regulations are stifling competition and inflating the cost of legal services beyond what much of the market can bear. The elite model ought to remain one path for those students who want it, and for those clients who can afford those graduates. But the choice for many people with legal problems is cheaper help or nothing; inflated costs should not force them to go without. Bar authorities should not be so paternalistic and restrictive. We should let potential clients choose among a broad menu of types of help at a range of price points. Cheaper help should take two forms: cheaper ways to become a lawyer and cheaper alternatives to lawyers.

First, states should loosen their accreditation and credentialing requirements to open up cheaper ways to qualify as a lawyer. There is no shortage of ideas as to how to accomplish this. One obvious possibility is to eliminate the law school requirement altogether, while making the bar examination harder and more comprehensive. Ironically, if the bar exam was expanded to include testing of certain core legal skills (drafting a contract or a civil complaint, some type of live advocacy, drafting a will, etc.), future lawyers would have *more* guaranteed skills for consumers, not less, and at a greatly reduced cost.

Another obvious route is to keep everything the same and make law school shorter. Legal scholars as diverse as Richard Posner, Deborah Rhode, and Brian Tamanaha (not to mention former President Obama) all agree that the basic law degree, a Juris Doctor (J.D.), should be readily available through two-year programs, requiring only two years' worth of credits for two years' tuition. The third year could be an optional part of a J.D., or it could be part of a combined program for earning a business degree (M.B.A.) or an advanced law degree, such as a Master of Laws (LL.M.), in a technical specialty such as taxation or intellectual property.

169

These rules should be especially flexible in allowing students to specialize in underserved areas such as poverty law, family law, or indigent criminal defense. Why should specialists have to pay to train as generalists? Donald Dripps has proposed letting law schools offer a year-and-a-half degree in Public Defense Law, in which students would take most of the traditional first-year curriculum except for civil procedure, as well as ethics, evidence, and two semesters of criminal procedure. Graduates of these programs could take the bar exam but would be limited to specialized criminal practice for at least a decade. The tuition, time, and opportunity cost of the degree would be cut in half. Public defender offices could hire more new defenders for roughly the salaries of teachers and social workers, meaning more defense lawyers at less expense and with much less debt.[8]

Law school should be not only shorter, but also cheaper. The accreditation standards should be stripped down to the point where the proprietary schools of yesteryear could reopen. Night schools or part-time programs staffed by adjunct lawyers and judges are very inexpensive to operate, and there is limited evidence that they are worse than many accredited law schools. And, of course, "worse" is not the relevant standard—dangerous to consumers is. Shorter B.A./J.D. programs could also help. More importantly, we need to bring down the cost per credit hour. The ABA and AALS are acting as a giant cartel, restricting the supply of lawyers and thus driving up the price. They are effectively protecting their turf by restricting market competition, much as taxicab drivers use regulatory barriers to keep Uber, Lyft, and similar smartphone taxi and ride-sharing services out of the market.

The market should be able to experiment with different, cheaper ways to deliver a legal education. In an era of Internet legal research, a library with a certain number of bound volumes is no longer essential to learning. Faculty tenure has at best a marginal relationship to the classroom educational experience; while faculty scholarship can sometimes improve teaching, plenty of judges and practicing lawyers make great teachers too. Student/faculty ratios have surprisingly little impact on educational outcomes. And limits on distance learning are at odds with the experience of bar-review classes which help thousands of students to pass the bar exam, often via videotaped or online lectures supplemented with educational software.

Relaxing the rules would also let law schools experiment with massively open online courses (MOOCs), teaching thousands of students at once. The early evidence from these programs is mixed, and it may be that MOOCs should be combined with some supervision, evaluation, small discussion groups, or even apprenticeship. But even if MOOCs do not supplant traditional classroom instruction, they can certainly supplement it. And they can also spur promising educational reforms. The Khan Academy, an online nonprofit, has recorded and posted thousands of lectures and problems, allowing teachers to "flip the classroom" by assigning lectures as homework and letting students work on problems in class. William Mitchell College of Law has received a waiver from the ABA for what they call a "hybrid" program: half online education and half in person. The details are still being ironed out, and tuition will be the same as the in-person program, but the change is at least a promising sign of flexibility on the ABA's part. Celebration will be more appropriate when such programs are rolled out at a lower cost, however.

We can even revive the apprenticeship route to legal practice. Paralegals could gradually take on more responsibilities over the space of years, while reading key legal books supplemented perhaps by online coursework at night. And even those who pursue J.D. degrees could incorporate apprenticeship-like aspects, doing supervised *pro bono* work or taking externships for credit as part of their degrees. This could provide much of the practical experience of clinical programs at substantially lower cost and tuition.

Critics will naturally oppose reform, dismissing shorter, cheaper paths as producing a two-tier profession of second-class citizens. But this critique harkens back to the elite school versus trade school debate of a century ago, and may conceal some of the same snobbery and class bias. It denies applicants the freedom to choose whatever course they have the time and money for, deterring would-be lawyers who balk at taking out six-figure student loans.

Most basically, critics confuse the interests of lawyers and law schools with the interests of clients and of society. Poor and middle-class clients need cheaper options. Right now, many have nothing. Instead of being told to buy a new Cadillac or walk, they should be free to buy a bicycle, scooter, motorbike, or used Chevy. It may not be perfect, but it will probably get the job done and is far better than having to limp on foot or remain trapped in one's legal problem. Consumers should be free to choose, not stifled by paternalistic regulation and excessive cost.

If you doubt that protectionism is driving barriers to entry, consider the other half of bar regulation: discipline for misbehaving or incompetent lawyers. If bar regulators were truly passionate about protecting consumers, you would expect to see bar discipline and legal malpractice given equal billing to entry regulation. Of course, the opposite is true. It is too hard to get into the profession and it is far too hard to get thrown out. Legal malpractice suits are difficult to win, and bar authorities are notoriously unwilling to disbar incompetent lawyers unless they pilfer client funds. In most states, lawyers are not even required to carry malpractice insurance to practice law, so it is hard to say with a straight face that protectionist regulations are really protecting clients, not lawyers.

The better way to protect clients is to offer information that helps them to weigh a lawyer's cost against his quality. Ratings websites such as Avvo.com already rank lawyers and offer consumer reviews. Broader-based websites such as Angie's List could easily do so as well, particularly if bar authorities made client complaints public and required lawyers to solicit feedback by email after each case. Bar regulators have hardly been interested in providing consumers with information. The lawyer discipline system in most states is run completely out of the view of the public. Consumers learn of only the tiny portion of complaints that result in public discipline like suspensions or disbarment. The vast majority of consumer complaints are kept confidential.

The high cost of legal education is a big part of the problem, and freeing the market to lower costs is an important solution. The other half of the solution would likewise free the market, by letting social workers, paralegals, and other paraprofessionals offer legal help. We turn to that idea next.

Cheaper Substitutes for Lawyers

UPL is prohibited in all fifty states. The definition of the "practice of law" and the levels of enforcement differ from state to state, but at a minimum, non-lawyers are barred from appearing in court for another and from offering "legal advice." Though these rules are supposed to protect consumers, they also inflate the price and depress the competition that might provide legal services cost-effectively. These rules keep graduates of apprenticeships and non-ABA-accredited schools out of the market and restrict lawyers' ability to move and compete across state lines. And they restrict or forbid non-lawyers' ability to provide legal services, such as tax advice by accountants.

America is an outlier. Many other countries let paralegals, social workers, and notaries handle routine legal transactions, both in and especially out of court. As Gillian Hadfield has shown, people in other countries hire lawyers at rates comparable to Americans. But many more foreigners overall have some kind of representation, because foreigners can turn to cheaper options in situations where Americans must either proceed *pro se* or lump it without legal help.

Things are much better in England, for example. The United Kingdom's UPL rules do not restrict who can give legal advice. Thus, both volunteer and proprietary centers dispense legal advice to those who need it. When Hadfield compared the two legal systems, she found that Americans were half as likely as the British to receive legal advice when confronted with a legal issue. Likewise, Americans were much more likely to simply live with their legal problems than the British. Dutch, Slovakian, and Japanese respondents were also more likely to receive third-party assistance from non-lawyers and less likely to lump it than Americans.[9]

This problem has not gone unnoticed. Washington and a few other states are experimenting with what they call "limited-license legal technicians" (LLLTs). These LLLTs will be required to complete a prescribed course of study, pass an examination, take continuing education classes, and (unlike lawyers in Washington State) carry malpractice insurance. The first wave in Washington State will have to specialize in domestic relations work and will not be allowed to appear in court. They will be allowed to offer advice and draft documents.

There are two different ways of reading this development. On the one hand, it is somewhat ominous that the Washington version was created by the state Supreme Court, but will be governed by the Washington State Bar Association (WSBA), exactly the professional group that LLLTs might compete with. The WSBA has not been shy about its double role in regulating the LLLTs: "WSBA's role is to maintain the high standards set for the *legal profession* while serving as the regulators of this new rule. The goal is to ensure quality implementation aimed at *supporting WSBA members* and upholding protection of the public." (Emphasis added.)[10] In fact, the LLLT program may well be a stalking horse for increasing prosecution of UPL by paralegals or others.

A less cynical view is that Washington State is finally considering loosening UPL and allowing lower-cost alternatives to flourish. If the program becomes a success, it could easily be broadened. Why not allow these technicians to appear in court, at least for specialized subsets of smaller cases? New York State has started a pilot project allowing non-lawyer advocates to appear in case areas of great need, like housing court. Each of these reforms makes the next step easier.

There is, of course, an easier route than creating a new level of licensure: simply define UPL more narrowly and concretely. The obvious dividing line would be defining the practice of law as filing papers or appearing in court. Legal advice and drafting would be open to lawyers and non-lawyers alike, subject to normal tort liability for harmful advice or documents. This would allow consumers to collect damages if they were harmed, but would also allow them many more options.

Another possibility would be to limit UPL prosecution to situations where the consumer was harmed or defrauded during the transaction. The most irrational part of the current UPL regime is that a truly victimless "crime," like Ernest Chavis helping out his neighbor Annie Belle Weiss, can be punished at all.

How Paraprofessionals Are Improving Medical Care

If anything is even more important than good legal help, it is good medical care. The harms that might occur in the typical case of medical malpractice are usually much worse than the typical case of legal malpractice. The worst-case scenario in medicine is death or significant pain and suffering. The typical legal malpractice case is about money. Obviously, criminal malpractice can result in loss of liberty or even one's life, but ironically that type of legal malpractice is the very hardest to prove.

Because we value our health above all, many people's instinctive reaction is that they would never want anyone other than a licensed doctor, ideally a fancy specialist, to treat their medical conditions. Yet classic fee-for-service medicine has grown not only ruinously expensive, but also slow and bureaucratic. The American Medical Association, like the ABA, has tried to keep barriers to entry high both to ensure quality care and to protect doctors' livelihoods. Nevertheless, medical care continues to grow more flexible, as paraprofessionals play increasingly important roles in delivering quality care.

Foremost among these are nurse practitioners. Registered nurses must earn a bachelor's degree, but nurse practitioners typically practice for a few years as registered nurses before going on to specialized training as part of a master's or doctoral degree, including clinical training and certification. Nurse practitioners typically specialize in an area such as family practice, pediatrics, women's health, gerontology, neonatal care, or mental health/psychiatric care, and may sub-specialize within one of these areas. They may practice under the supervision of a doctor or, in some places, independently. Particularly because there is a shortage of primary-care doctors, nurse practitioners have stepped in to fill a void. They may do much of what doctors have traditionally done: order and interpret tests, prescribe certain medications, diagnose and treat both acute and chronic conditions, and educate patients.

Likewise, physician assistants work together with doctors to deliver care. They must earn a master's degree but need not complete a residency, and may examine and diagnose patients, order and interpret diagnostic tests, prescribe medications, and refer patients to specialists. Like nurse practitioners, physician assistants can thus not only treat patients but also triage cases, screening those that present typical symptoms and require only routine care from the fraction that require advanced medical knowledge and training.

Then there are midwives, who specialize not only in delivering babies, but in prenatal, postpartum, and well-woman care. Some midwives receive formal education, certification, and licensure, while others learn through apprenticeship. Today, midwives deliver about 1 out of every 13 babies in the United States—sometimes at home, but often in a hospital or birthing center. They cost much less than obstetricians, but many women who could afford obstetricians choose midwives instead because they prefer the care. Evidence suggests that in many respects midwives deliver superior care: When they deliver babies, there are significantly fewer complications, babies are more likely to remain with their mothers for their entire hospital stay, and mothers are more satisfied with their care. And obstetricians' financial incentives may lead to excessive caesarean sections to suit their schedules, while midwifery patients are much less likely to have elective c-sections.[11]

Paraprofessionals are making possible new, cheaper, faster venues such as urgent-care centers and minute clinics. Urgent-care centers are walk-in clinics that treat injuries and illnesses not serious enough to require an emergency room's facilities and staff, including sprains, broken bones, sore throats, influenza, bronchitis, moderate cuts, and minor burns. They also offer immunizations and physicals. They may have diagnostic tools such as x-ray machines on hand and can suture wounds and (in many states) dispense medications. While a majority have a doctor on hand at all times, they also use nurses, physician assistants, and medical assistants to deliver care. They typically open before and close after traditional office hours and are open seven days a week. They cost less than emergency rooms and keep patients waiting for minutes, not hours at a time.

Much of the same is true of retail clinics, such as CVS' Minute Clinic or Walgreens' Healthcare Clinic. These clinics, typically inside retail pharmacies, are staffed by nurse practitioners or physician assistants. They not only treat moderate injuries and illnesses (including chronic conditions such as asthma, diabetes, and high cholesterol) but also provide preventative care. They cost up to 80% less than emergency room care and 30%–40% less than primary care physicians, yet appear to deliver comparable care.[12] They are also markedly more convenient, with posted prices, longer hours, weekend appointments, walk-in service, and online scheduling and waiting times. Clear guidelines delimit what care they can provide, and they refer to doctors or emergency rooms cases that are beyond their expertise.

Paraprofessionals can also assist by using information technology to provide advice and answer questions. There are, for example, nurse hotlines that can question patients about common symptoms and provide guidance on when a condition is serious enough to require going to the emergency room. Nurse-staffed websites and chat rooms can do much of the same. Smartphone apps such as iTriage enable patients to compare their symptoms to those of common maladies, helping them to figure out when to seek further treatment. And telemedicine creates video and audio links between doctors in central hospitals and nurses examining patients in faraway small towns. The nurses can take vital signs, question patients, and examine bodies and symptoms, allowing doctors to diagnose and treat many more patients without travel.

No one expects doctors, whether family practitioners or specialists, to go away. But it is silly to demand that every patient see either a medical doctor or else no one at all—given that Hobson's choice, far too many went without. The expense, time, and inconvenience of scheduled doctor's visits meant that people often did without preventative and minor care, or waited until they got sick enough for the emergency room. Making care much cheaper and more convenient, by loosening licensure and allowing paraprofessionals to do much more, lets people get health care that is cheaper, faster, *and* better. And paraprofessionals can serve as front-line responders, helping to do triage according to checklists and diagnostic criteria. If an adult flu sufferer has had a 102° fever for three days, it is time to refer him to a doctor; if a baby remains in the breech position at 38 weeks, the midwife can refer the mother to an obstetrician.

The analogies to legal practice should be obvious. Some medical or legal conditions are severe enough that a specialist doctor or high-priced lawyer is called for, and some patients are wealthy enough to hire one even when doing so is optional. But for less serious cases and less-wealthy clients, a range of treatment options can improve coverage, convenience, and cost. The key is not to denigrate paraprofessionals or less-expensive lawyers as second-class citizens, but to welcome their constructive role. The alternative is not the unattainable ideal of fancy doctors or lawyers for everyone, but rather giving most people little or no care at all.

Legal Offices Pushing the Envelope

A handful of innovative, well-regarded public defenders have broken outside the box of traditional, reactive, lawyer-only services. One example, Neighborhood Defender Services of Harlem, represents its clients with teams of criminal and civil lawyers, social workers, investigators, paralegals, law students, and social-work students. It proactively tries to address clients' underlying problems, such as drug or alcohol addiction, medical care, and housing. That can also include trying to resolve cases before they get to court by negotiating settlements and restitution. Nationally renowned for the quality of its services, Neighborhood Defender Services leverages its attorneys by using private investigators, social workers, and other nonlawyers to interview witnesses and do much of the legwork and counseling that would otherwise be done by lawyers.

Like Neighborhood Defender Services, the Bronx Defenders uses teams of lawyers and social workers to address clients' needs for drug treatment, housing, education, and employment in order to break the cycles of addiction and recidivism. Bronx Defenders, like Neighborhood Defender Services, strives to listen to clients and their families and treat them with dignity. The involvement of social workers and interns allows the lawyers to leverage their legal time, allowing nonlawyers to do much of the interviewing, hand-holding, and mentoring needed to resolve disputes, address underlying pathologies, and get clients back on their feet. This holistic, problem-solving approach yields dividends: When counselors have gotten a client to make restitution and enter drug treatment or housing, or get a job or education, they can credibly ask judges for lower sentences because their clients pose less of a danger.[13]

The moral of the story is that nonlawyers can play greater roles in triaging, interviewing, and delivering legal services, and their involvement need not mean watered-down, mediocre help. Some of the best public-defender offices in the country trust trained, specialized paraprofessionals to deliver top-notch care, freeing up lawyers to handle more cases. By breaking out of the high-cost, individualized box, these offices point the way forward to flexible, innovative, specialized service delivery. Lawyers matter greatly for a certain fraction of cases. But lawyers' protectionist desire to guard their own turf must not keep out cheaper paraprofessionals for the many cases that cry out for cheaper, faster alternatives. Even where lawyers are needed for some stages, they can unbundle their services, leaving it to lower-cost nonlawyers or even *pro se* litigants to handle many other parts of the case at lower cost.

Winston Churchill supposedly quipped that we should never let a good crisis go to waste. Between the roil in the market for legal services, the access-to-justice problems, the growth in *pro se* litigation, and the drop in law school attendance, we have a large-scale crisis occurring all around us. In response, lawyer regulators may be tempted to batten down the hatches by redoubling efforts to battle UPL and sticking with their outmoded and very expensive licensing system. Our best hope is that innovation and common sense triumph over attempts to shove an ever-escaping genie back into the bottle. Our current crisis can mark the beginning of a market for legal services that is more diverse, cheaper, more efficient, and much, much more accessible to the middle class and the poor.

CHAPTER 11

Criminal Case Triage

The University of Pennsylvania Law School, where one of us (Bibas) teaches, is blessed with one of the largest law libraries in America and a world-class staff of researchers. We asked the librarians a pretty simple question: Find us examples of criminal courts that are using technology to innovate and streamline criminal proceedings, making them cheaper and more accessible. Despite repeated requests, we could not find a single example. Sure, there are some courts (though not enough) that are using technology to provide judges and probation officers with more accurate information more quickly, or to track defendants' histories and case outcomes or train lawyers and court personnel. But in Chapter 8's terminology, these are modest automations, not innovations. Unlike eBay, Modria, or even small-claims courts or administrative tribunals, these criminal-court experiments do not disrupt the lawyer-driven, adversarial model of resolving disputes one case at a time by bringing all the parties, lawyers, and judge together, almost always in the same physical location. It is possible that there are innovators who are hiding very well; more likely, this void illuminates the power of inertia. Technology has revolutionized the private sector and opened up new ways of resolving disputes that were unimaginable half a century ago. But courts are technological backwaters and have neither the incentives nor the expertise to try out new ways of resolving criminal cases. Even if they did, the Supreme Court's constitutional dictates would limit courts' freedom to experiment with different ways of providing justice. The contrast between civil innovation and criminal stagnation is one of the biggest downsides of *Gideon*'s approach.

The American Bill of Rights is an unusual document in many ways. When it was written, it included the most comprehensive list of rights for criminal defendants ever assembled. Colonial Americans, like modern Americans, were not particularly enamored of criminals. If you doubt this statement, browse a list of the severe criminal punishments of the time. Nevertheless, the Framers of the Bill of Rights were very concerned about government overreaching. The Bill of Rights starts from the premise that every criminal defendant is also a citizen facing off against a very powerful government, and thus deserves substantial protections.

The United States was founded as an idealistic project of a government of limited powers, hemmed in by rights guaranteed to every citizen. Every citizen, from the poorest to the richest, should get a fair shake when facing off against the State in a criminal court. Equal justice under law is promised to all; not just the wealthy, not just the powerful, and not just the innocent.

Gideon v. Wainwright is a powerful restatement of that ideal. But to suggest any solution that trims back the guaranteed right to a lawyer has been seen as a heretical rejection of the fundamental right to equal justice under law. The ideal of *Gideon* has blinded us to the reality of today's criminal courts. Equal justice under law is almost as distant today as it was in the 1960s, and there is almost no chance of infusing enough money to fix the broken system.

We suggest a more realistic strategy of triage and a grand bargain that would make *Gideon* narrower but deeper, concentrating funding at its core. Felonies, particularly the most serious ones with plausible claims of innocence, would get more time, money, and attention. In return, misdemeanors that carry no serious collateral consequences would be handled without lawyers on either side. Misdemeanor courts would greatly simplify their procedures and evidentiary rules; assist *pro se* litigants; let paraprofessionals help; and even use e-adjudication to streamline dispute resolution. Specialized non-lawyers, or occasionally appointed lawyers, would help youths, mentally retarded, mentally ill, and non-English-speaking defendants. Done right, these reforms could reduce pretrial detention and delay and promote alternatives to prison. They could also give prosecutors incentives to push for felonies and substantial jail time only in the fraction of cases that truly require them.

People instinctively dislike triage, especially when it comes to critically important items like medical care or justice. Nevertheless, we live in a world of finite resources, so some level of triage is not only likely, but inevitable. The question is whether we want to handle triage rationally and openly, or to back into a system that spreads out resources without any plan or purpose. Our current system of indigent defense exemplifies such a thoughtless division of resources. We have a system that claims to treat every case the same and to eschew triage, but actually underdelivers to everyone in the system.

Principles for Triage

Triage requires principles for rationing services. During battle or natural disasters, medics must identify and treat the gravely wounded before attending to patients with modest injuries. In doing so, medics must weigh both the severity of the patient's injuries and the likelihood of improving the patient's health. And they must make these judgments quickly and imperfectly, based on rules of thumb, past experience, and preliminary observations of the patient's wounds and vital signs.

Similar principles should operate in criminal defense. To some extent, criminal practitioners do some trading off already. For instance, they rarely ask for expert-witness funding in less serious cases, in part because courts are stingy about authorizing it. But most of this triage is covert, inconsistent, and incomplete. Criminal defense lawyers for the indigent often have very high caseloads. As such, they are forced to pick and choose which cases to focus on. Many defense lawyers will choose among their cases rationally, by prioritizing defendants they think are likelier to be innocent or focusing especially on cases that might change the law and affect a whole class of defendants. Others may work more on the squeaky-wheel cases, or just choose based on the luck of the draw. And some lawyers may make the economically rational decision to do as little work as possible on all of their cases.

More candid triage could eliminate some of the vagaries of the current system by explicitly separating those cases that need the most attention from those that do not. It would also allow for cheaper substitutes in many cases, rather than the façade of defense lawyers across the board.

The *seriousness* of the crime charged is the simplest and most obvious dividing line. Felony convictions, which typically carry prison terms of a year or more, are by definition serious. Lengthy terms of imprisonment are devastating for defendants and their families. Inmates lose not only years of freedom, but usually their jobs and their houses or apartments. Prison breaks up or strains family ties, particularly when inmates are shipped off to far-off state or federal prisons rather than the county jail.

Felony convictions also carry grave stigma. Being branded a felon is shameful, and it may make the convict unemployable not only because of social stigma, but also from laws specifying collateral consequences of convictions. Many states' laws bar felons from working at dozens of jobs: not only as doctors, lawyers, and cops but as plumbers, beauticians, and undertakers as well. Felons may also lose student financial aid, not to mention the rights to vote, hold public office, serve on a jury, or carry a gun. And noncitizens who are convicted of felonies can generally be deported, even if they are green-card holders who have lived here for decades.

Misdemeanors are as a rule less serious than felonies. Though states' definitions vary a bit, generally a felony is punishable by more than a year in the state prison. A misdemeanor, by contrast, is punishable by a year or less in the county jail.

Nevertheless, some misdemeanors are serious because they carry collateral consequences comparable to those of felonies. For instance, even misdemeanor sex crimes may require convicts to register as sex offenders and to live far away from any schools, day care centers, parks, churches, and the like. (Because cities and suburbs are full of schools and churches, in practice residency restrictions force some misdemeanants to move out of their homes and neighborhoods.) And even misdemeanor drug convictions may make noncitizens deportable. So not only felonies but also misdemeanors carrying these weighty collateral consequences need to be treated as serious cases.

Therefore, we propose preserving the right to appointed counsel in all cases that are felonies, misdemeanors punishable by six months' imprisonment or more, or misdemeanors carrying major collateral consequences. The nice thing about this dividing line is that it clearly separates two different types of cases up front, with little room for misunderstanding or discretion. An entire category of cases would be removed from the highly complex system we have now and pushed into simpler courts designed to be operated *pro se*.

This dividing line roughly sorts between complex and simple cases. Complexity, it turns out, goes hand in hand with a case's seriousness. As a rule, a defendant has no right to a jury trial unless he is charged with a felony or a misdemeanor punishable by more than six months' imprisonment. So six months of imprisonment is the line for whether the Constitution requires a jury trial.

Jury trials bring with them myriad procedural complexities such as jury selection, jury instructions, sidebar conferences, and strict enforcement of evidentiary rules such as hearsay. Lawyers and judges developed these complicated rules of evidence and procedure, and unsurprisingly, a lawyer is often necessary to understand them. Many of these rules are aimed at shielding juries from prejudicial information or guiding them in their decision-making. If we select petty offenses, we have a natural group of cases to simplify: those cases where we do not have to worry about shepherding or protecting a jury. Without a jury, we should be able to strip away much of what makes the system impossible to operate without lawyers.

Of course, a jury trial is an imperfect proxy for a case's complexity: Some felonies are cut and dried, while some misdemeanors involve tricky mental states, defenses, or constitutional challenges. And even most felony cases result in plea bargains rather than jury trials (though the trial rights can prove relevant as plea-bargaining chips). But in processing large volumes of cases, the legal system must rely on proxies and checklists just as emergency rooms and battlefield medics do. As discussed below, these rules of thumb for automatic appointment of counsel could be supplemented with discretion to appoint counsel in other exceptional cases. And volunteer lawyers could also bring occasional test cases challenging unconstitutional patterns or practices and the like.

Another possible criterion for appointing defense lawyers is *inno-*

cence. The worst thing our criminal justice system can do is to convict an innocent man, and we should focus our efforts on preventing these injustices. But it is hard to define ahead of time a category of innocent defendants. Police and prosecutors do not charge defendants who are obviously innocent; they have better things to do with their time than to pursue losing cases. And courts, knowing little about the evidence up front, can hardly discern innocence at the time of arraignment. Innocence does not amount to a judicially manageable rule for appointing counsel in the first place.

Innocence can, however, guide defense lawyers, courts, and legislatures in allocating extra resources among cases that already qualify for appointed counsel. In recent years, DNA testing has exonerated many hundreds of defendants, in the process exposing recurring sources of error: Eyewitnesses are often mistaken, particularly when identifying suspects of different races or when tainted by suggestive lineup procedures. Jailhouse snitches and informants frequently concoct incriminating stories in the hopes of monetary rewards or leniency in their own criminal cases. There has been a spate of recent cellphone tower cases where police and prosecutors have misused cellphone data to "prove" a defendant's location at the scene of the crime. Forensic testing is sometimes misunderstood, tainted, or even occasionally fabricated. And suggestive interrogation techniques induce even innocent defendants to confess falsely, particularly if they are young, mentally retarded, or mentally ill.

These recurring sources of error should guide discretionary funding decisions: Public defenders can steer more of their limited funds towards these cases. Courts can be more generous in funding expert witnesses in such cases. And legislatures, prodded by innocence commissions, can earmark extra funds for investigating the factors that contribute to wrongful convictions, which is more politically appealing than funding indigent defense generally.

A last relevant criterion is whether the defendant *cannot speak for himself.* Youths are, as a rule, less able to explain their plight in court. The same is true of mentally retarded and mentally ill defendants. Non-English speakers cannot make their cases alone. While these kinds of defendants need some help, they may not need a lawyer (depending on the complexity and seriousness of their cases) as much as they need a guardian, social worker, or translator. The legal system needs to assist these defendants, but as we discuss below there are often other ways to do so.

Our bottom line, then, is that *Gideon*'s original scope was about right. Felony defendants need the guiding hand of counsel at every step to navigate complex criminal procedures and to check long sentences, stigma, and collateral consequences. The most serious misdemeanors, punishable by more than six months in jail, belong in the same basket, as do those that trigger deportation, loss of a job, residency restrictions, or sex-offender registration. Conversely, misdemeanors should not qualify if they carry only short jail sentences, suspended sentences, or fines.

Our proposal would slash the number of criminal cases that require lawyers across the board. There are just over a million felony convictions per year, but nearly ten times as many misdemeanors. Criminal justice resembles a pyramid, and serious misdemeanors appear to be dwarfed by those below the six-month threshold (though good misdemeanor statistics are hard to come by). In those states that have struggled to provide lawyers for misdemeanors, this six-month line would bow to reality. And states that have been appointing counsel for many misdemeanants would gain the freedom to concentrate their limited funds on cases that need them most.

Making the Cut: Beefing Up Felony Defense

Serious cases—those that would still require appointed counsel across the board—need many more resources. The savings from restricting *Gideon*'s breadth must go part of the way towards increasing its depth. Our adversarial criminal justice system depends on a zealous defense lawyer with the strength, time, and money to probe the other side's case and build his own. To be effective, defense lawyers need more support.

First and foremost, they need manageable caseloads. A lawyer cannot represent his client vigorously and well without getting to know him, getting or figuring out the other side's likely evidence, and collecting his own. That requires caseloads in the dozens, not hundreds, at a time. Lower caseloads remove the pressure to meet 'em and plead 'em, allowing professionals to gauge each case instead of presuming guilt. They also give lawyers time to elicit their clients' stories and build their trust. Some defendants will admit guilt immediately and want to plead right away, but defense lawyers should not have to pressure them from the moment they first meet.

Second, defense lawyers need salaries commensurate with those of prosecutors. Leveling the playing field promotes fairness. And comparable salaries and caseloads help public defender offices to recruit and retain talented, experienced defense lawyers. We should favor public defender offices and move away from relying on low-bid, flat-fee contract attorneys. Courts can help to ensure that defense lawyers' salaries, caseloads, and other resources are pegged to those of prosecutors. This gives defendants no unfair advantage, but simply treats them equally.

Third, defense lawyers need funding for paraprofessional support. Paralegals help with everything from client interviews to research to filing. Private investigators do much of the legwork, locating and interviewing witnesses, verifying alibis, and pursuing alternative suspects. Forensic, medical, and psychiatric experts probe weaknesses in the state's case and can prevent wrongful convictions. All of these kinds of support mirror those already enjoyed by prosecutors, who can call on police, coroners, ballistics experts, and their own paralegals for the same support. Guaranteeing the same resources to defense counsel simply levels the playing field.

Fourth, defense lawyers need time. It takes time to understand the defendant's story and the witnesses or other evidence that could corroborate it or challenge the prosecution's version. That means time to locate and interview witnesses, pursue discovery from the prosecution, negotiate plea bargains, file motions, and prepare for trial. Defense lawyers who are overburdened and underpaid can hardly dig up evidence and challenge the prosecution's version of events, so they have little negotiating leverage.

More vigorous defense lawyering can make a big difference at various stages. In discovery, defense lawyers can negotiate with prosecutors to turn over more information and can counteract prosecutors' tunnel vision and jumping to conclusions. At bail hearings, defense lawyers can work out alternatives to pretrial detention and show how defendants' strong community ties make them unlikely to flee. In plea bargaining, defense lawyers can ensure that clients understand the various collateral consequences of convictions and persuade prosecutors to offer plea bargains that spare defendants deportation, loss of a job, or exile from the family home. In pretrial motions, defense lawyers can test the legal sufficiency of the police investigation and the prosecution's case. And before and at trial, defense counsel can highlight alternative culprits and weaknesses in the prosecution's case.

All of these stages are sufficiently complicated and fraught to ensure that defense lawyers can make a real difference in a substantial fraction of serious cases. That sometimes means getting a dismissal or acquittal for a client who may be innocent; more commonly, it means ensuring that a defendant's punishment is commensurate with what he deserves and what similar defendants generally receive.

Simplifying Misdemeanors and Violations

There is room to debate how many months of actual imprisonment should trigger an automatic right to appointed counsel. A weekend in jail by itself is unlikely to disrupt someone's whole life, so the current rules requiring appointed counsel for any actual imprisonment and even suspended sentences are overbroad. But a week or two in jail can cost someone his job; a month or two can cost someone his apartment and strain his family; three or six months may cost someone his house. Wherever one draws the triage line, whether at two weeks, one month, or six months' imprisonment, some cases will not make the cut. Appointing lawyers is one way to promote access to justice, but there are other, cheaper ways to do so. We should apply some of the ideas already explored for civil justice to minor criminal cases as well.

Legislatures should create lawyer-free courts for cases below the seriousness threshold. In many traffic courts, police officers handle cases rather than prosecutors. In some small-claims courts, both sides must represent themselves without lawyers so as to ensure a level playing field. Just as the increase in criminal lawyers over the nineteenth century bred complexity and made defense lawyers essential, so excluding lawyers or greatly restricting their role would help to simplify matters and reduce the need to appoint them. For some kinds of cases, the victim could appear, giving him the added benefit of having his day in court.

These courts could abolish or greatly simplify their rules of procedure and evidence. Because there is no right to a jury trial in these cases, there is much less need for rules of evidence and procedure to keep hearsay and the like out of the jury's hearing. As it is, very few minor cases currently involve motions, legal research, or fine points of law. For the most part, the issues are who did what, who saw what, and who deserves what punishment. These issues of historical fact and blameworthiness involve storytelling that does not require legal training.

When litigants struggle to address the salient issues, the judge can take the lead by asking questions to establish defenses or the elements of the crime. In every criminal court in America, there is already a licensed lawyer who is an expert in the applicable law and well versed in the elements of crimes and defenses. That person is called the judge. Instead of proceeding as a neutral arbiter between two represented parties, the judges in these new misdemeanor courts should imitate their colleagues in traffic or small-claims courts: They should explain the process briefly to the litigants, shepherd the cases to completion, and question all of the witnesses to establish guilt or innocence or applicable defenses.

To compensate for laymen's lack of experience and learning, judges could have probation officers interview and investigate the backgrounds of key witnesses, as well as collect documents and other evidence. Probation officers already do much of this before sentencing (and special masters may do something similar in civil cases); they would just have to do it sooner and more proactively. Judges could also prompt each side to think about possible witnesses and sources of evidence, such as nearby residents, security guards, surveillance cameras, and cellphone records, not to mention alibi witnesses such as defendants' bosses and coworkers. They could actively oversee plea bargaining, much as mediators do in civil cases. Judges could appoint scientific and forensic experts in the sliver of cases that call for them. And they themselves could handle much of the questioning of witnesses.

These courts should also offer extensive *pro se* assistance. Dedicated court clerks could explain how cases proceed and answer questions, instead of turning defendants or victims away. They could offer written guidance, training sessions, and webinars. Fill-in-the-blank forms and software could help litigants to tell their own stories and focus in on any key disputed facts.

In addition, these courts could abolish or greatly loosen the unauthorized-practice-of-law rules applicable in them. Defendants could bring a friend or relative to help explain their stories. Translators would be available to help defendants with limited proficiency in English. Guardians could speak for youths, and social workers or therapists could assist mentally retarded and mentally ill defendants.

Note also that one could constrict the across-the-board *right* to appointed counsel while leaving judges *discretion* to appoint counsel for exceptionally complex cases. But only a fraction of misdemeanors are likely to qualify or benefit much. Run-of-the-mill cases often have little for lawyers to do. That is why criminal justice professionals may refer to low-level violations as "disposables" and give them cookie-cutter treatment. Insisting on lawyering for every one of these cases is a mirage.

Finally, one can even envision forms of e-adjudication. One of the simplest advantages of current technology is the ability to shift information gathering across time and space. Right now, criminal courts require all the players (defendant, witnesses, police officers, prosecutors, defense lawyers, etc.) to appear at the same time and place for hearings or trials. Typically, there is more than one case per day set at that same time (and often as many as a hundred or so in a first-instance court), so all of the players in all of the cases for that day traditionally appear at the same time and then wait while the cases are handled in some order. Because everyone needs to be there at the same time, continuances are regular occurrences and witness/victim fatigue is the rule and not the exception.

In these less formal courts, we could use asynchronous eBay-style dispute resolution to work out the facts and plea bargains in most cases within a few days. Witnesses and defendants could upload statements or documents, and then a time could be set for a videoconference allowing for cross-examination. Rather than requiring misdemeanants, witnesses, victims, and the police to miss work for repeated court appearances, the players could submit evidence as they went on their own schedules. Misdemeanants could also avoid languishing in holding cells for months, awaiting appointment of lawyers or for the appearance of all the relevant parties.

FAQ pages could correct common misconceptions about supposed defenses that are legally invalid, narrowing issues down to factual ones. Results could be posted on public websites. For the fraction of cases that remain hotly disputed even after mediation, Skype video-conferencing, published on the Internet to allow public access, could further streamline matters, particularly for fine-only misdemeanors. Doing so would bring down the hassle, cost, and wasted time to the benefit of all involved.

E-adjudication carries definite tradeoffs and costs. One must be careful not to exclude the public from e-proceedings. Public oversight, through the right to a public trial, plays an important role in overseeing and checking courts and abusive police work. Proceedings need to be serious and dignified enough to give litigants their day in court. But misdemeanor courts are currently so hurried that these innovations might actually provide more of a hearing than many litigants get now. And a threshold of jail time for a live appearance in court could triage out the most minor cases, as we effectively do for traffic tickets.

Long-Term Effects

Changing the right to counsel would have static effects right now: It would immediately save money on low-level cases. But, over time, changing the rules would also have dynamic effects on the way other parts of criminal justice operate. The system's many forces interact, and caseload pressures in one place hydraulically influence how prosecutors, defense lawyers, and judges do their jobs at other stages.

For instance, many crimes can be charged either as felonies or as misdemeanors: Think of charging a moderate theft as petty larceny versus grand larceny, or a bar fight as simple assault versus aggravated assault. Even the same charge can sometimes be a misdemeanor or a felony at the prosecutor's or judge's discretion. California lawyers call such crimes "wobblers." In such borderline cases, prosecutors would have much say in whether to proceed in a traditional, adversarial criminal court or to let police officers handle them as misdemeanors in streamlined misdemeanor courts. They would thus have strong incentives to sort cases by their severity and need for additional resources.

For those cases that involve little or no imprisonment or collateral consequences, prosecutors would have strong incentives to strike quick plea bargains to lower charges. For those involving repeat criminals or aggravated harm, both sides would have lawyers and resources to prepare more carefully, to ensure that tougher penalties are warranted. That would encourage prosecutors to engage in more thoughtful triage and sorting of which wrongdoers really need substantial jail time and collateral consequences.

There would also be a whole class of offenses that prosecutors and defense lawyers never see. Like traffic courts, a whole class of low-level criminal activity would be removed from our complicated and burdensome criminal procedures. These courts would also be natural places for experimentation, like the current trend towards drug courts or courts that emphasize alternatives to incarceration.

Another benefit of these reforms would be to alleviate the high costs that our overburdened system imposes on minor cases, particularly pretrial detention. It is shocking that many misdemeanants are detained without bail for several months while awaiting appointment of a lawyer or a court date. The pretrial detention often exceeds the likely sentence, pressuring most to plead guilty in exchange for time served regardless of whether they are guilty. That detention also costs many defendants their jobs and apartments. Streamlined misdemeanor courts could adjudicate cases more quickly, often shortly after arrest, without waiting for lawyers and the delays they commonly introduce. Thus, a simpler and swifter justice system would be a fairer one too: As the venerable legal maxim puts it, justice delayed is justice denied.

Lastly, as state funds grow tighter and the public becomes more aware of America's extraordinarily high incarceration rate, particularly for young black men, there is increased public pressure to rethink American over-criminalization. There is a growing sense that prosecutors and police have too much discretion and that our laws make almost everyone a potential felon.[1] The public's revulsion at the militarization of the police also suggests that the time is ripe to rethink our approach to law and order. Our criminal system is one of those odd political areas where libertarians on the right and liberals on the left have a remarkable amount in common. The reforms suggested in this chapter could be part of a broader structural reform.

The Grand Bargain

Some caveats are in order. In our sclerotic criminal justice system, no reform is simple. This is especially true of trying to rationalize criminal-defense funding with a grand bargain, requiring many different actors to compromise. Critics will accuse us of conjuring up a pipe dream, as legislatures will be tempted to snatch the savings from misdemeanor cases rather than reallocating them to felonies. Nevertheless, it is worth exploring and working towards some sort of compromise.

If the scope of the right to appointed counsel were narrower, hopefully appellate judges would be willing to put more teeth into that right. Much of the problem with the right to counsel has been one of breadth versus depth. In steadily broadening the right to counsel's scope, we have unwittingly caused judges and legislatures to water it down so as to avert overwhelming costs. Reversing that dynamic will not be easy, but it is possible. If courts can focus on the effectiveness of felony counsel, they should be more willing to put teeth into requirements to investigate, negotiate, and litigate. They might reverse more often if their rulings did not risk disrupting as broad a swath of convictions.

Drawing a bright line between felonies and misdemeanors, and treating felonies so much more seriously and expensively, would also encourage more legislative thoughtfulness about exactly what criminal behavior should qualify as a felony. Likewise, requiring the police to carry the laboring oar in misdemeanor court would discourage over-charging, since the officers themselves would be stuck prosecuting their arrestees.

This grand bargain would, however, be substantially more feasible and appealing than the broader efforts of *Gideon* boosters. Its narrower breadth frees up the funding for its greater depth. And the grand bargain's emphasis on parity with prosecutorial pay, caseloads, and resources frames it as a matter of leveling the playing field as opposed to giving criminal defendants a handout. Finally, it is far more realistic than hoping for more from *Gideon*, because it openly allows for different levels of expense and safeguards based on the seriousness of the crime, instead of continuing to pretend that we can give everyone a Cadillac defense on a Yugo budget.

CHAPTER 12

Conclusion:
Fewer Lawyers, More Justice

The False Equation of Lawyers with Justice

Lawyers who read this book may well perceive it as pessimistic, fatalistic, or defeatist. Are we not just giving up on *Gideon*'s shining dream of increasing justice for all and instead throwing second-class sops to the poor? Are cheaper substitutes mere window-dressing, alibis for a system that does not care and cannot be bothered to afford its ideals? How can we live up to the promises of "Justice the Guardian of Liberty" and "Equal Justice Under Law," inscribed on the sides of the U.S. Supreme Court, if we content ourselves with letting the rich hire lawyers while the poor cannot? The ringing pronouncements of *Gideon* held such great promise; are we really going to abandon those promises?

The first step to recovery is to overcome denial. The suggestions in this book are not a retreat from the shining promise of *Gideon*; they are a recognition that *Gideon* has largely failed or at least fallen far, far short. If every criminal defendant had an exceptional lawyer willing and able to work hard on her case, this book would not be necessary. If the poor and the middle class could afford a civil lawyer to deal with everyday legal problems, there would be no *pro se* crisis to address. This is not where we find ourselves. At a certain point, it is no longer acceptable to pursue strategies that have failed for a half a century. We have now reached that point.

All options must be on the table, not just pushing for more money to pay more lawyers to handle more cases one on one. A lawyer is like a hammer, and to a hammer every problem looks like a nail, so we lawyers inevitably conflate lawyers with justice. Lawyers are, naturally, used to their (our) own approach to justice, where each side to a dispute or negotiation hires its own lawyer and the lawyers negotiate a deal or fight it out in litigation (with all of its complicated procedures). But this is not the *only* way to settle disputes or reach agreements. Lawyers and lawyer-driven processes are *one way* to secure justice, not justice itself.

In some kinds of cases, such as felony prosecutions, lawyers are essential to navigating complex procedures and substantive laws. But there are other avenues for providing justice, particularly when the substantive laws and procedures are or can be made simpler. And in some respects, lawyers are in tension with justice. Speed, simplicity, respect, and procedural fairness matter directly to litigants. Often, these goals are not served well by insisting on lawyers and formalities, versus other ways of achieving justice.

From Lawyer-Pessimism to Techno-Optimism

Once you abandon the presupposition that the answer to our systemic legal problems is more lawyers, a bevy of options become available and pessimism turns to optimism. Rather than bemoaning the death of the false promise of a lawyer for every problem, we can recognize that technology and new approaches to dispute resolution have led us to the threshold of a new golden age of access to justice. In this regard, we are very much techno-optimists. Technology has transformed multiple areas of our economy and government; now is the time to let it transform our approach to law.

Amazingly, it is already happening all around us. Because our statutes, regulations, and court decisions are now online, ordinary Americans have more access to the laws that govern them than ever before. When courts streamline procedures and create standardized forms for matters like divorces or legal name changes, everyone is better off (except for the lawyers who used to be able to charge for those services). When LegalZoom and Rocket Lawyer sell legal documents for a fraction of the price charged by a lawyer, we all have greater access to law and legal remedies.

Information technology brings creative destruction to a stodgy field, offering many new ways of providing legal help cheaply and quickly. Some of these innovations are evolutionary, such as cheaper legal education, better lawyer reviews, and lawyers bidding down the price of services in online auctions for unbundled legal assistance.

Other changes are more revolutionary. They offer brand-new ways of handling existing work, including online manuals, fillable forms, and webinars. We are particularly excited about online dispute resolution such as that used by eBay and Modria. These disruptive new technologies let the parties resolve most disputes themselves, reserve human intervention for a fraction of cases, and need few or no lawyers to run them. While lawyers are used to focusing on the unique complexities that require personalized tweaking, most needs and disputes fall into recurring patterns. Thus, big data as well as machine learning can automate the handling of most such problems at higher speed and lower cost. This is especially important for low-value transactions, where the transaction cost of traditional legal help would force parties to swallow their grievances and lump it.

OK, But Can It Happen and Will It Actually Work?

Can it actually happen? Yes! The changes we hope for are coming very quickly in civil cases. Computerization of drafting, legal research, and even legal advice has already radically driven down the price of legal services, and we are at the very beginnings of that process, where only the lowest-hanging fruit (like uncontested divorces) has been reached. The for-profit sector is barging into law at an accelerating pace. The free provision of legal documents and advice will also grow as access-to-justice commissions, courts, lawyers, and legal aid societies continue to standardize forms and processes for common legal problems.

In-court changes will be slower, because judges still run courts and are less tech-savvy and more tradition-bound. Consider Chief Justice John Roberts' 2014 Year-End Report on the Federal Judiciary. The Report includes a lengthy explanation of why American "courts will often choose to be late to the harvest of American ingenuity."[1] Why "choose" to move slowly on technology? Because, "like other centuries-old institutions, courts may have practices that seem archaic and inefficient—and some are. But others rest on traditions that embody intangible wisdom."[2] Roberts compares the technology race to the race between the tortoise and the hare, with the hare symbolizing advocates of new technologies and the victorious tortoise our wisely cautious judiciary. All in all, it is a pretty remarkable Report. Chief Justice Roberts is the titular head of the federal judiciary, one third of our tripartite government, and the most influential American judge. In a public report on the state of the federal judiciary, he makes an explicit and unapologetic argument *against* embracing new technologies.

Nevertheless, in civil courts, the flood of *pro se* litigants has made change a possibility and in many courts a priority. This is especially so as the *pro se* phenomenon moves up the income scale and judges see their neighbors and friends appearing without lawyers. The slowest change of all will come where change is probably needed most: in criminal court. Nevertheless, as civil courts change and become more *pro se*–friendly, criminal courts will eventually face pressure to adopt similar reforms.

So if these changes are coming, will they actually be an improvement? If you ask a typical American lawyer, she will predict that computerization and *pro se* reforms will be a disaster for everyone concerned. There are three easy responses.

First, it would be hard not to improve on the status quo. When ordinary Americans cannot afford to file for divorce or draft a will to determine who gets their homes and care of their children when they die, it is well-nigh time for market disruption.

Second, some of the suggested changes are already having a positive effect in medicine. Medical care is even more important, more technical, and more rapidly evolving than legal needs. Yet, spurred by financial pressure and vast unmet needs, the market has developed a variety of ways to meet a variety of needs at a variety of price points. Beside traditional doctors' visits and slow, costly emergency rooms, there are now midwives, nurse practitioners, physician assistants, alternative medicine, telemedicine, urgent-care centers, minute clinics, nurse helplines, medical websites, online chat rooms, and increasing over-the-counter drug options. Loosening of doctors' monopoly has made medical help cheaper, faster, and more widely available without government intervention, a new entitlement program, or new funding. The system has learned how to do triage at various points, funneling the fraction of cases that require a doctor's attention away from the high volume of simple, routine, repetitive needs that need cheaper, faster alternatives.

The increasing use of medical protocols closely parallels the idea of standardizing and structuring the provision of legal services. Medical protocols are agreed, standardized ways of performing a task. Protocols are repeatable and reproducible and created via experimentation and data collection. They reduce reliance on human discretion and ask doctors, nurses, and other medical professions to handle a task the same way, in the same order, every time.

The most famous protocol is requiring hand washing or hand sanitizing before and after every patient contact. Since the mid-nineteenth century, hand washing has been recognized as a critical tool to preventing the spread of infection across patients. In recent years, however, hospitals have made leaps forward in saving lives by adding additional sinks and hand-sanitization stations and requiring all employees to wash their hands upon entering or exiting each room or treatment area.

Not all protocols are so simple. There are protocols for emergency-room treatment of gunshot wounds and protocols for heart surgery. Some doctors have objected: The protocols strip them of autonomy, and in some cases an individualized approach may actually work better. Doctors, like lawyers, consider their work an art as much as a science, and protocols seem insulting. Rather than calling upon their individual experience and expertise, protocols require lockstep conformity. But medicine, unlike law, has been data-driven for years, and the data do not lie: Properly created protocols work better than human intuition. Are some truly exceptional doctors better than the protocols? Yes. Are there some exceptional cases where the protocols fail? Sure. But system-wide conformity brings better results.

There is an obvious parallel in law. Standardizing legal forms and court processes will eliminate discretion and may result in some square pegs in round holes. But if the process is data-driven and adjustable based upon the results, it can absolutely be cheaper, easier, and better.

Third, consider the United Kingdom and Australia. In the twentieth century, the U.K.'s system was a lot like ours. An Irish judge once quipped that English justice was open to all, just "like the Ritz Hotel."[3] But in the twenty-first century, England has radically deregulated its market for legal services, making it the freest in the developed world. In 2003, Sir David Clementi, a non-lawyer, led an independent review of the regulatory framework for legal services in England and Wales.

The report suggested a massive regulatory overhaul and a deregulation of most of the market. In 2007, the Legal Services Act became law. The Act allows non-lawyers to provide legal advice, allows lawyers to organize in alternative business structures, and creates a new, consumer-driven licensing board and complaint system.[4] Australia and New Zealand have taken a similar approach.[5]

The results have been pretty encouraging. England has seen the announcement of supermarket lawyers, literally. The Co-Operative, a member-owned company that runs grocery stores all over the U.K., has announced plans for a legal division that will offer everything from conveyancing to family law to wills at a discount and on site in some of their shops. British lawyers were not amused. In 2010, they led a protest against the commoditization of legal services, in which they dressed as grocers and gave out cans of baked beans marked: "Legal services by supermarkets is as ridiculous as lawyers selling beans."[6] And yet, the transition has been remarkably smooth so far.

We thus have a natural experiment among English-speaking common-law jurisdictions. Canada and the U.S. remain wedded to a lawyer-run regulatory scheme designed to maintain a relatively strict lawyers' monopoly on legal services. Australia, England, and Wales have a much more wide-open approach. It is still early, but there is no evidence of a collapse of the legal system in Australia or the U.K. and there is substantial evidence of increased competition, lowered prices, and, most importantly, market innovation.

If It Is That Simple, Why Do Lawyers Object?

Some, but only some, of the fault lies with lawyers' self-interest. Mandating appointed counsel creates more jobs for lawyers. Keeping the current justice system and expanding its intake helps bar associations and law schools to grow. In theory, professional licensure is supposed to ensure high quality and protect the public. But as in so many other industries, the organized bar's lobby captures efforts to regulate. It keeps barriers to entry high and rarely punishes shamefully bad lawyering, but vigorously fights upstart competitors—much as taxi drivers fight Uber or accountants and tax lawyers fight tax reform.

Of course if the problem were only self-interest, it would actually be easier to solve. Many proponents of an ever-expanding *Gideon*, and opponents of any non-lawyer-driven solutions, are sincere, well-meaning, and not consciously selfish. The broader culprit is the ideology of legalism sustained by law schools and the organized bar. The downsides of this approach are all too apparent: a slow, costly, opaque justice system that bewilders everyone except lawyers. Our high-cost, intricately filigreed model is unsustainable and out of date in the twenty-first century, especially for the repeated, common problems of ordinary Americans.

In an Internet world of online, automated dispute resolution, we are still chugging along in Latinate legalese, at great expense, even for mundane, repetitive disputes such as divorces and evictions. The whole model of legal education and service delivery is built around a bespoke, individually tailored model of paying individual lawyers to resolve disputes. Even middle-class people cannot afford this system, let alone the poor. After rent and secretarial support, not to mention student loan repayments, lawyers can barely break even at $100 or more an hour. But few people can afford even five or ten hours' help at that price, let alone the dozens required to pursue a contested lawsuit. The model does not work, except for big corporations fighting over lots of money or injured plaintiffs suing insurance companies.

The lesson of *Turner v. Rogers* is one on which all nine Justices, across the political spectrum, were able to agree: Lawyers sometimes make proceedings *less* fair, not more. And the lesson of criminal procedure is that the more lawyers enter a system, the slower and more complex they make its procedures and rules of evidence, so that non-lawyers can no longer navigate it by the end.

And yet it is very hard for lawyers to accept these criticisms. The lawyer's role in protecting liberty through zealous advocacy of individual clients is a key component of the profession's mythology. We lawyers tell ourselves a heroic story in which we are the guardians of justice and champions of liberty. And these stories are often true, as far as they go. Defense lawyers and the U.S. Supreme Court did manage to obstruct the legalized lynching in *Powell v. Alabama*, sparing the Scottsboro Boys the death penalty, although many of them were eventually convicted regardless. Civil-rights lawyers did pursue the heroic campaign that resulted in *Brown v. Board of Education* and desegregated America, combatting the legacy of Jim Crow. Defense lawyers do prevent the conviction of innocent defendants such as Clarence Earl Gideon.

But, reveling in these triumphs, lawyers too often use the extraordinary to govern the ordinary. Many see every routine case as a snowflake, unique in all its complexity. But not every loitering or eviction case is the next *Brown v. Board of Education,* and our system cannot operate on the assumption that every litigant can and should have her own lawyer-champion ready to pursue every factual and legal argument regardless of expense or time. That admission grates upon American ears, but it is a simple statement of fact: In any free-market system, different citizens will be able to afford different amounts and types of legal services. If we ignore that fact, we make the perfect the enemy of the good.

Aren't We Forgetting About Another Kind of Complexity?

Even if all of our suggestions were magically adopted, another type of complexity would remain. Throughout this book, we have been very careful to refer to "procedural complexity" in an effort to differentiate procedural law from what lawyers call substantive law. Procedural law is what it sounds like: It is all of the various rules, customs, and practices that govern how to resolve disputes in court. In courts where the majority of the cases involve one or more *pro se* litigant, procedures need to be changed to reflect that reality. Whatever benefit there is to procedural complexity in a federal antitrust case, with expert lawyers on both sides, there are almost no benefits when lawyers are not present and ordinary Americans lack access to a court system that their tax dollars pay for.

That said, procedural complexity is only part of the reason people feel compelled to hire lawyers. Substantive complexity, the intricacies of the underlying statutes, regulations, and court decisions themselves, is probably an even bigger factor. This sort of complexity is harder to spot and much harder to fix. It is also harder to quantify its costs and benefits or even its causes.

This is because much of the complexity of American law comes from immutable, structural factors. Federalism adds complexity, as citizens can find themselves governed by a mix of federal, state, and even county and city laws. The rise of the administrative state adds complexity, as regulations and administrative processes join statutes as governing law. Common-law courts and their system of precedent also add complexity. Because every past decision of a court of record potentially has some precedential value, there is another massive source of law, often written by lawyer-judges in legalese and Latin and often inaccessible to ordinary Americans.

It is much too difficult in this country to find all the relevant laws that bear on a problem and penetrate their meaning, relationship, qualifications, and exceptions, not to mention case law and commentary explicating it. It is also difficult to plan and comply with laws that are vague, ambiguous, poorly drafted, and honeycombed with exceptions. No wonder the public hates filing taxes.

Of course, America is hardly alone in seeing a rise in legal complexity. If you ask citizens of Japan, Germany, or Brazil if their laws are too complex, you will almost certainly hear a resounding "Yes!" Even China has seen an uptick in scholarly articles complaining about the growing complexity of their legal regime. Technology has made it easier to create and record new rules and regulations, and citizens also expect more from their governments than ever before.

The costs and benefits of regulatory regimes and the size of the modern state are well beyond the scope of this book. There is a particular kind of legal complexity, however—the complexity created by lawyers and judges—that bears a brief mention since it is invisible to most Americans. The problem is that, all too often, judges and lawyers focus on doing justice *ex post*; that is, looking back at the equities of particular cases. This is, in some ways, the greatest strength of common-law courts: Judges retain some flexibility to tailor the written law and precedents to a particular set of facts and to avoid results that seem unfair or at odds with the spirit, if not the letter, of the law.

But in a system where judicial decisions are written and carry precedential value, there are significant costs to this flexibility. The most obvious costs are multiple exceptions to even the clearest of rules and the creation of multifactor balancing tests to handle the most mundane of legal tasks. Exceptions and balancing tests offer judges great discretion to adjust the law to reach almost any set of facts. They also create a massive amount of uncertainty in the system. When we tweak and refine the laws too much, these subtleties may make it extremely hard to plan *ex ante*, that is, going forward, without a bevy of lawyers to prognosticate about what a court would likely say or do. This is true even after parties file lawsuits: Settling cases before or after filing is hard, in part because the parties have different predictions of what the court will rule or what discretionary exceptions exist or might be created with the right legal help.

These complexities and refinements make the law obscure. Lawyers are used to that, but ordinary citizens need to know and understand their rights and responsibilities without having to hire a lawyer every time. One of the reasons Jeremy Bentham focused obsessively on the need to codify the laws was the importance of making rules clear, understood, and open to criticism and reform. Those virtues are especially important in a democracy. Today, many citizens have the sneaking suspicion that the rich and powerful can exploit loopholes in the tax code or hire good lawyers to get around criminal laws and environmental rules. That understandable suspicion of unequal justice undercuts faith in the legal system's legitimacy. Complexity is thus at odds with equal justice under law.

As René Descartes put it, "a state is governed much better when it has only very few laws that are observed very strictly."[7] Two more recent scholars have attempted to put Descartes' wisdom into action. Richard Epstein's 1995 classic, *Simple Rules for a Complex World*,[8] is a great starting point for considering broader legal simplification. Epstein powerfully describes a problem that has only gotten worse in the last twenty years and then argues for the wisdom of tackling complicated issues with a limited number of relatively straightforward rules. Philip K. Howard has likewise made a career of arguing against legal complexity and for a return to leadership, discretion, and common-sense regulation in books like *The Rule of Nobody, Life Without Lawyers*, and *The Death of Common Sense*.[9] Both Howard and Epstein recognize the wellspring of complexity: Governments hate uncertainty and unfairness, so they try to create more detailed and more complicated laws and regulations to cover every possible exigency. When these laws fail to address the next unforeseen exigency, lawmakers add on another layer of complexity.

Simplifying the substantive laws, unfortunately, is far more easily said than done given entrenched special interests. For instance, the public loathes the IRS and the absurdly complex tax code. Yet, even though tax-simplification proposals are popular, they are almost always stalled by inertia. Bevies of special interests succeed in blocking change, not the least of which are the many accountants and tax lawyers who profit from everyone else's pain. Well-organized special interests often mobilize to block reforms that are broadly popular with the diffuse public.

That battle, however, is for another day. Even within the complex laws with which Americans are stuck, a range of reforms and looser procedures can greatly improve access to justice. Overcoming inertia and the myriad forces of resistance will not be easy, but technology and the forces of change are already well on their way to doing so.

Notes

Chapter 1

1. The facts of Adnan Syed's case and the investigation, trial, and re-investigation are taken from the various episodes of Sarah Koenig, This American Life, *Serial* (podcast series 2014), *available at* serialpodcast.org.

2. *In re Application of Maria C.*, 451 A.2d 655 (Md. 1982) (Smith, J., dissenting).

3. Sarah Koenig, *Lawyer Gutierrez Agrees to Disbarment: Missing Funds Spurred Investigation; Illness Blamed for Irregularities*, BALTIMORE SUN, June 2, 2001.

4. These statistics come from Jessica Steinberg, *Demand Side Solutions to the* Pro Se *Crisis* (2015), draft on file with authors.

5. Joseph Callanan, *Pro Se Bankruptcy Filings Growing Faster than Other Debtor Relief*, ABA Litigation News, December 29, 2011, https://perma.cc/U3XM-YGAR.

6. World Justice Project, THE WORLD JUSTICE PROJECT RULE OF LAW INDEX 26–29 (2014).

7. Derek C. Bok, *A Flawed System of Law Practice and Training*, 33 J. LEGAL EDUC. 570, 571 (1983).

Chapter 2

1. Stephen B. Bright, *Will the Death Penalty Remain Alive in the Twenty-First Century?: International Norms, Discrimination, Arbitrariness, and the Risk of Executing the Innocent*, 2001 WIS. L. REV. 1, 17–18 (2001).

2. *See* Alex Kozinski & Misha Tseytlin, *You're (Probably) a Federal Criminal, in* IN THE NAME OF JUSTICE: LEADING EXPERTS REEXAMINE THE CLASSIC ARTICLE "THE AIMS OF THE CRIMINAL LAW" 43, 43 (Timothy Lynch ed. 2009).

3. Mary Pat Flaherty, *400 Drunken-Driving Convictions in D.C. Based on Flawed Test, Official Says*, WASHINGTON POST (June 10, 2010), https://perma

.cc/DS4H-9R6P. In March 2011, the PHILADELPHIA INQUIRER discovered the same problem. See Allison Steele & Joseph A. Slobodzian, *Phila. Breath-Test Readings Off for 1,147 Cases*, PHILA. INQUIRER, Mar. 24, 2011, at A1 (finding that four Breathalyzer machines were improperly calibrated).

4. *See, e.g.*, Virginia, *Eligibility for Court-Appointed Counsel* (2016), *available at* https://perma.cc/6V3D-L8AG.

5. BUREAU OF JUSTICE STATISTICS ONLINE, SOURCEBOOK OF CRIMINAL JUSTICE STATISTICS tbl. 4.1.2010.

6. Laurence A. Benner, NAT'L LEGAL AID & DEFENDER ASS'N, THE OTHER FACE OF JUSTICE 77 (1973); Norman Lefstein, AMER. BAR ASS'N STANDING COMM. ON LEGAL AID & INDIGENT DEFENDANTS, CRIMINAL DEFENSE SERVICES FOR THE POOR 14 (1982) (emphasis omitted); Richard Klein & Robert Spangenberg, ABA SECTION OF CRIMINAL JUSTICE, THE INDIGENT DEFENSE CRISIS 25 (1993); AMER. BAR ASS'N, *GIDEON'S* BROKEN PROMISE: AMERICA'S CONTINUING QUEST FOR EQUAL JUSTICE 8 (2004); THE CONSTITUTION PROJECT, JUSTICE DENIED 6–7, 59; NAT'L ASS'N OF CRIMINAL DEFENSE LAWYERS, *GIDEON* AT 50: A THREE-PART EXAMINATION OF INDIGENT DEFENSE IN AMERICA, PART I—RATIONING JUSTICE: THE UNDERFUNDING OF ASSIGNED COUNSEL SYSTEMS 8 (2013).

7. THE CONSTITUTION PROJECT, NAT'L RIGHT TO COUNSEL COMM., JUSTICE DENIED: AMERICA'S CONTINUING NEGLECT OF OUR CONSTITUTIONAL RIGHT TO COUNSEL 52, 57, 59 (2009).

8. THE CONSTITUTION PROJECT, JUSTICE DENIED, at 57–58, 61.

9. THE CONSTITUTION PROJECT, JUSTICE DENIED 62. This disparity holds true even after one adjusts for the proportion of cases defended by lawyers other than public defenders.

10. NALP: THE ASSOCIATION FOR LEGAL CAREER PROFESSIONALS, 2012 PUBLIC SECTOR & PUBLIC INTEREST ATTORNEY SALARY REPORT 14 (2012); THE CONSTITUTION PROJECT, JUSTICE DENIED 63. The statement of the public defender is quoted in that source from Tara Cavanaugh, *Timeline of Events for the Missouri Public Defender System*, COLUMBIA MISSOURIAN, Oct. 19, 2008.

11. NAT'L ASS'N OF CRIMINAL DEFENSE LAWYERS, *GIDEON* AT 50, at 16; THE CONSTITUTION PROJECT, JUSTICE DENIED 64.

12. NAT'L ASS'N OF CRIMINAL DEFENSE LAWYERS, *GIDEON* AT 50, at 8, 12–16, 20–32; THE CONSTITUTION PROJECT, JUSTICE DENIED 64.

13. NAT'L ASS'N OF CRIMINAL DEFENSE LAWYERS, *GIDEON* AT 50, at 16–17.

14. NAT'L ASS'N OF CRIMINAL DEFENSE LAWYERS, *GIDEON* AT 50, at 17–18.

15. NAT'L ASS'N OF CRIMINAL DEFENSE LAWYERS, *GIDEON* AT 50, at 22, 27.

16. When a defendant's sanity "is seriously in question" and will be "a significant factor at trial," the Constitution guarantees him a right to a court-appointed psychiatric expert. *Ake v. Oklahoma*, 470 U.S. 68, 68, 83 (1985). Courts, however, are often reluctant to authorize such experts, and when

they do they may provide a paltry sum of several hundred dollars to pay for
the expert examination and report. THE CONSTITUTION PROJECT, JUSTICE
DENIED 93–95; AMER. BAR ASS'N, GIDEON'S BROKEN PROMISE: AMERICA'S
CONTINUING QUEST FOR EQUAL JUSTICE 10–11 (2004). The example of
Houston investigators is from THE CONSTITUTION PROJECT, JUSTICE DENIED
62. For examples of cramped, noisy, zoo-like office space with no privacy and
too few telephones (in San Francisco) and offices without desks or bookcases
(in Maryland), see Lefstein, CRIMINAL DEFENSE SERVICES FOR THE POOR
at 33–34, 49. New Orleans' public defenders, for example, had almost no
investigative support, no money for expert witnesses, and an inadequate
library. State v. Peart, 621 So. 2d 780, 784 (La. 1993). For examples of how
judges punish or remove lawyers who seek expert funding, request compensation above normal fees, or litigate zealously, see AMER. BAR ASS'N, GIDEON'S
BROKEN PROMISE 21.

17. Robert N. Boruchowitz et al., NAT'L ASS'N OF CRIMINAL DEFENSE
LAWYERS, MINOR CRIMES, MASSIVE WASTE: THE TERRIBLE TOLL OF
AMERICA'S BROKEN MISDEMEANOR COURTS 14–15 (2009) (quoting Chief
Justice Jean Hoefer Toal, Supreme Court of South Carolina, South Carolina
Bar Ass'n, 22nd Annual Criminal Law Update (Jan. 26, 2007)); NAT'L LEGAL
AID & DEFENDER ASS'N, A RACE TO THE BOTTOM: SPEED AND SAVINGS
OVER DUE PROCESS: A CONSTITUTIONAL CRISIS ii–iii (2008).

18. The caseload recommendations are from the NATIONAL ADVISORY
COMM'N ON CRIMINAL JUSTICE STANDARDS AND GOALS: COURTS Standard
13.12 (1973); ABA STANDARDS FOR CRIMINAL JUSTICE: PROVIDING DEFENSE
SERVICES Standard 5.53 & cmt. (3d ed. 1992). For figures on actual caseloads,
see THE CONSTITUTION PROJECT, JUSTICE DENIED 68–70; AMER. BAR ASS'N,
GIDEON'S BROKEN PROMISE 18; Boruchowitz et al., NAT'L ASS'N OF CRIMINAL
DEFENSE LAWYERS, MINOR CRIMES, MASSIVE WASTE 21. The trial judge's
appraisal of Rick Teissier's workload is quoted in State v. Peart, 621 So. 2d 780,
784, 789 (La. 1993).

19. NAT'L ASS'N OF CRIMINAL DEFENSE LAWYERS, GIDEON AT 50, at 16.

20. Larry S. Pozner, Life, Liberty and Low-Bid Lawyers: The Defiling of
Gideon, CHAMPION, July 1999, at 9.

21. Benner, THE OTHER FACE OF JUSTICE 29; Lefstein, CRIMINAL DEFENSE
SERVICES FOR THE POOR 56; Klein & Spangenberg, THE INDIGENT DEFENSE
CRISIS 3–4; AMER. BAR ASS'N, GIDEON'S BROKEN PROMISE 17–18; THE
CONSTITUTION PROJECT, JUSTICE DENIED 68–70.

22. An overview of "meet 'em and plead 'em lawyers," as well as the lack
of motions and trials, is in AMER. BAR ASS'N, GIDEON'S BROKEN PROMISE 16,
19. The Atlanta example is from Trisha Renaud & Ann Woolner, Meet Em and
Plead Em: Slaughterhouse Justice in Fulton's Decaying Indigent Defense System,
FULTON COUNTY DAILY REP., Oct. 8, 1990, at 1 (cited in Stephen B. Bright,
Essay, Counsel for the Poor: The Death Sentence Not for the Worst Crime but for

the Worst Lawyer, 103 YALE L.J. 1835, 1850 (1994)). The description of Teissier's guilty pleas is from *State v. Peart*, 621 So. 2d at 784. The Florida example is from Alisa Smith & Sean Maddan, NAT'L ASS'N OF CRIM. DEF. LAW., THREE-MINUTE JUSTICE: HASTE AND WASTE IN MISDEMEANOR COURTS 23 tbl. 9 (July 2011).

23. AMER. BAR ASS'N, *GIDEON'S* BROKEN PROMISE 23, 26–27; Stephanos Bibas, *Plea Bargaining Outside the Shadow of Trial*, 117 HARV. L. REV. 2463, 2491–93 (2004). The empirical study of the states and counties where defendants wait for weeks or months after a bail hearing for a lawyer is Douglas L. Colbert, *Prosecution Without Representation*, 59 BUFF. L. REV. 333, 386–412 (2011) (reporting that ten states plus the District of Columbia provide lawyers in time for bail hearings statewide, ten states do not, in twelve states a majority of counties provide lawyers by then, and in eighteen states a majority of counties do not).

24. Lisa McIntyre, THE PUBLIC DEFENDER: THE PRACTICE OF LAW IN THE SHADOWS OF REPUTE 80 (1987); Charles Ogletree, Jr., *Beyond Justifications: Seeking Motivations to Sustain Public Defenders*, 106 HARV. L. REV. 1239, 1240–41 (1993); Abbe Smith, *Too Much Heart and Not Enough Heat: The Short Life and Fractured Ego of the Empathic, Heroic Public Defender*, 37 UC DAVIS L. REV. 1203, 1210–11 (2004).

25. For examples of sleeping, drunk, drugged, alcoholic, and mentally impaired defense lawyers, see Bright, 103 YALE L.J. at 1835, 1843 & nn. 53–54, 1859; Jeffrey L. Kirchmeier, *Drink, Drugs, and Drowsiness: The Constitutional Right to Effective Assistance of Counsel and the* Strickland *Prejudice Requirement*, 75 NEB. L. REV. 425, 426–27, 455–63 (1996), *Recent Cases—Sixth Amendment—Ineffective Assistance of Counsel—Sixth Circuit Holds that Defense Counsel's Nap During the Defendant's Cross-Examination Does Not Clearly Violate the Sixth Amendment*, 125 HARV. L. REV. 1498 (2012) (criticizing Muniz v. Smith, 647 F. 3d 619 (6th Cir. 2011)). The quotation is from Hal Strauss, *Indigent Legal Defense Called "Terrible,"* ATLANTA J.-CONST., July 7, 1985, at 12A (quoted in Bright, *supra* at 1852). The facts of Judy Haney's case come from Katya Lezin, FINDING LIFE ON DEATH ROW 99–127 (1999); *Haney v. State*, 603 So. 2d 368 (Ala. Crim. App. 1991); *Ex parte* Haney, 603 So.2d 412 (Ala. 1992).

26. For these and many similar anecdotes, see Bright, 103 YALE L.J. at 1835–61 & n.51. The James Messer example is at *id.* at 1859–60 (citing *Messer v. Kemp*, 760 F.2d 1080, 1096 n.2 (11th Cir. 1985) (Johnson, J., dissenting), *cert denied*, 474 U.S. 1088, 1090 (1986) (Marshall, J., dissenting from denial of certiorari)). The examples of racial slurs are from *id.* at 1843 n.51 (citing *Goodwin v. Balkcom*, 684 F.2d 794, 805 n.13 (11th Cir. 1982); *Ex parte* Guzmon, 730 S.W. 2d 724, 736 (Tex. Crim. App. 1987); and Record Excerpts at 102, *Dungee v. Kemp*, No. 85-8202 (11th Cir.), *decided sub nom. Isaacs v. Kemp*, 778 F.2d 1482 (11th Cir.), *cert. denied*, 476 U.S. 1164 (1986)).

Chapter 3

1. These facts come from CRIMINAL PROCEDURE STORIES 1 (Carol Steiker ed. 2006); Dan T. Carter, SCOTTSBORO: A TRAGEDY OF THE AMERICAN SOUTH (rev. ed. 2007); James Goodman, STORIES OF SCOTTSBORO (1994).

2. The Supreme Court had first held that the Bill of Rights did not apply to the states in *Barron v. City of Baltimore*, 32 U.S. (7 Pet.) 243 (1833). The Court declined to read the Fourteenth Amendment's Due Process Clause as extending the Fifth Amendment's grand jury requirement to the states in *Hurtado v. California*, 110 U.S. 516, 534–35 (1884). The Court had held that the Fourteenth Amendment's Due Process Clause forbade a trial dominated by a lynch mob in *Moore v. Dempsey*, 261 U.S. 86, 90–92 (1923).

3. Our account of *Powell* draws upon Michael J. Klarman, *The Story of* Powell v. Alabama: *The Supreme Court Confronts "Legal Lynchings," in* CRIMINAL PROCEDURE STORIES 1; Dan T. Carter, SCOTTSBORO: A TRAGEDY OF THE AMERICAN SOUTH (rev. ed. 2007); and James Goodman, STORIES OF SCOTTSBORO.

4. Our account of English legal history draws heavily upon John H. Langbein, THE ORIGINS OF ADVERSARY CRIMINAL TRIAL (2003).

5. John B. Taylor, RIGHT TO COUNSEL AND PRIVILEGE AGAINST SELF-INCRIMINATION: RIGHTS AND LIBERTIES UNDER THE LAW 48, 50 (2004).

6. The New York practice is reported in Mike McConville & Chester Mirksy, *The Rise of Guilty Pleas: New York, 1800–1865*, 22 J.L. SOC'Y 443, 454–55 (1995). The California and Florida practices are found in Lawrence M. Friedman, CRIME AND PUNISHMENT IN AMERICAN HISTORY 245 (1993). The Massachusetts practice is reported in George Fisher, PLEA BARGAINING'S TRIUMPH: A HISTORY OF PLEA BARGAINING IN AMERICA 286 n.16 (2003).

7. The quotation about "quasi-judicial officers" is from Robert Ferrari, *The Public Defender: The Complement of the District Attorney*, 2 J. AM. INST. CRIM. L. & CRIMINOLOGY 704, 707 (1912). The other quotation is from Mayer C. Goldman, *The Public Defender*, 11 J. AM. INST. CRIM. L. & CRIMINOLOGY 280, 281–82 (1920); *see also* Robert Ferrari, *On the Public Defender: A Symposium*, 6 J. AM. INST. CRIM. L. & CRIMINOLOGY 370, 375 (1915).

8. *Powell v. Alabama*, 287 U.S. 45, 57, 68–69, 71 (1932).

9. *Norris v. Alabama*, 294 U.S. 587 (1935); *Patterson v. Alabama*, 294 U.S. 600 (1935).

10. *Johnson v. Zerbst*, 304 U.S. 458 (1938); *Betts v. Brady*, 316 U.S. 455, 472 (1942).

11. *Gideon v. Wainwright*, 372 U.S. 335 (1963); *id.* at 351 (Harlan, J., concurring).

12. *Argersinger v. Hamlin*, 407 U.S. 25, 33–37 (1972).

13. *Scott v. Illinois*, 440 U.S. 367, 373 (1979); *Alabama v. Shelton*, 535 U.S. 654 (2002).

14. *Strickland v. Washington*, 466 U.S. 668 (1984); *Williams v. Taylor*, 529

U.S. 362 (2000); *Wiggins v. Smith*, 539 U.S. 510 (2003); *Rompilla v. Beard*, 545 U.S. 374 (2005); *Padilla v. Kentucky*, 559 U.S. 356 (2010).

15. *Crawford v. Washington*, 541 U.S. 36, 62 (2004).

16. Stephanos Bibas, *The Psychology of Hindsight and After-the-Fact Review of Ineffective Assistance of Counsel*, 2004 UTAH L. REV. 1, 1–4.

17. *State v. Peart*, 621 So. 2d 780, 788–92 (La. 1993); *State v. Citizen*, 898 So. 2d 325, 336–39 (La. 2005); *State v. Lynch*, 796 P. 2d 1150, 1155–62 (Okla. 1990); *Hurrell-Harring v. State*, 930 N.E. 2d 217 (N.Y. 2010); Ronald F. Wright, *Parity of Resources for Defense Counsel and the Reach of Public Choice Theory*, 90 IOWA L. REV. 219, 244–51 (2004).

18. *Brown v. Allen*, 344 U.S. 453, 537 (1953) (Jackson, J., concurring in the result).

19. Bibas, *The Psychology of Hindsight*, 2004 UTAH L. REV. 1; Marc Miller, *Wise Masters*, 51 STAN. L. REV. 1751, 1786–87 (1999).

Chapter 4

1. Tennessee Supreme Court, *Court-Approved Divorce Forms*, https://perma.cc/42V2-SAQ6 (last visited Oct. 26, 2016).

2. Hadfield, *Higher Demand, Lower Supply?*, 37 FORDHAM URB. L.J. at 134–40.

3. *Id.* at 139–40 & tbl. 1.

4. WORLD JUSTICE PROJECT, THE WORLD JUSTICE PROJECT RULE OF LAW INDEX 176 (2014).

5. LEGAL SERVICES CORPORATION, DOCUMENTING THE JUSTICE GAP IN AMERICA (2009), at https://perma.cc/4C5W-V2S8.

6. Rob Paral & Assocs. & The Chi. Bar Found., LEGAL AID IN COOK COUNTY: A REPORT ON BASIC TRENDS IN NEED, SERVICE AND FUNDING 16–17 (2010), available at https://perma.cc/MA8Y-Q3E7 (stating that in 2009 eighty percent of services provided by civil legal aid programs in Chicago consisted of "brief services").

7. Texas Access to Justice Foundation, *Access to Justice Facts*, https://perma.cc/MU7G-8PM5.

8. Hadfield, *Higher Demand, Lower Supply?*, 37 FORDHAM URB. L.J. at 134–40.

9. Gillian K. Hadfield & Jamie Heine, *Life in the Law-Thick World: The Legal Resource Landscape for Ordinary Americans*, https://perma.cc/E7DF-4WWM.

10. Emily A. Spieler, *The Paradox of Access to Civil Justice: The "Glut" of New Lawyers and the Persistence of Unmet Need*, 44 U. TOL. L. REV. 365 (2013).

11. Richard Zorza, *Access to Justice: Economic Crisis Challenges, Impacts, and Responses* (2009), https://perma.cc/4MSC-PNPB.

12. The Law Offices of Scott Justice, *Tennessee Divorce FAQ's*, https://perma.cc/YV5A-Y7NF (last visited October 21, 2016).

13. *See*, e.g., Jona Goldschmidt, *The Pro Se Litigant's Struggle for Access to Justice: Meeting the Challenge of Bench and Bar Resistance*, 40 Fam. Ct. Rev. 36 (2002).

14. *Lawyer Demographics: Practice Settings*, Am. Bar Ass'n, https://perma.cc/G9F9-X3SW; Ronit Dinovitzer & Bryant Garth, *Lawyers and the Legal Profession, in* The Handbook of Law and Society 105, 111 (Austin Sarat & P. Ewick eds., 2015); Ronit Dinovitzer, *The Financial Rewards of Elite Status in the Legal Profession*. 36 Law & Soc. Inquiry 971, 985 (2011); Marc Galanter, *Mega-Law and Mega-Lawyering in the Contemporary United States, in* The Sociology of the Professions: Lawyers, Doctors and Others 152, 156 (Robert Dingwall & Philip Lewis eds., 2014); Dr. Julie Macfarlane, *The Evolution of the New Lawyer: How Lawyers Are Reshaping the Practice of Law*, 2008 J. Disp. Resol. 61, 80 (2008).

15. Tom Baker, *Blood Money, New Money, and the Moral Economy of Tort Law in Action*, 35 Law & Soc'y Rev. 275, 275, 277 (2001); Gillian K. Hadfield, *Exploring Economic and Democratic Theories of Civil Litigation: Differences Between Individual and Organizational Litigants in the Disposition of Federal Civil Cases*, 57 Stan. L. Rev. 1275, 1289–90 (2005); John T. Nockleby & Shannon Curreri, *100 Years of Conflict: The Past and Future of Tort Retrenchment*, 38 Loy. L.A. L. Rev. 1021, 1053–54 (2005).

16. Paul Campos, Don't Go to Law School (Unless) 5–6 (2013). The 2009 survey can be found here: https://perma.cc/A68L-QF4J. Results improved marginally in the 2014 survey: https://perma.cc/956R-QPAQ.

17. Deborah Rhode, *Whatever Happened to Access to Justice?*, 42 Loy. L.A. L. Rev. 869, 887 (2009).

Chapter 5

1. James Willard Hurst, The Growth of American Law: The Law Makers 282 (1950).

2. *Id.*

3. *See* Alfred Z. Reed, Training for the Public Profession of the Law 87–88 (1921).

4. *See* Pound, The Lawyer from Antiquity to Modern Times, at 227–28.

5. *See* George Fisher, Plea Bargaining's Triumph: A History of Plea Bargaining in America 123, 297 (2003) (discussing injuries, civil lawsuits, and the growth of the bar in late nineteenth-century Massachusetts).

6. The facts in this paragraph and the next come from Smith, Justice for the Poor, at 133–49.

7. *Id.* at 11.

8. Scott Cummings, *The Politics of Pro Bono*, 52 U.C.L.A. L. Rev. 1, 11–13 (2004).

9. Emery A. Brownell, Legal Aid in the United States (1951).

10. Terry Radtke, *The Last Stage in Reprofessionalizing the Bar: The Wisconsin Bar Integration Movement, 1934–1956*, 81 MARQ. L. REV. 1001, 1007 (1998); RICHARD ABEL, LAWYERS IN SOCIETY: THE COMMON LAW WORLD 199 (1988).

11. B. Peter Pashigian, *The Market for Lawyers: The Determinants of the Demand for and Supply of Lawyers*, 20 J. L. & ECON. 53, 63 (1977).

12. *See* Alan W. Houseman, *Political Lessons: Legal Services for the Poor—A Commentary*, 83 GEO. L.J. 1669, 1672–73 (1995).

13. *Id.* at 1673–74.

14. Mark Aaronson, *Representing the Poor: Legal Advocacy and Welfare Reform During Reagan's Gubernatorial Years*, 64 HASTINGS L.J. 933, 981 (2013); Houseman, *Political Lessons*, at 1681 n.59.

15. Unless otherwise noted, all of the facts in the next three paragraphs come from Alan W. Houseman & Linda E. Pearle, SECURING JUSTICE FOR ALL (2006).

16. LSC, *House-Senate Agreement Cuts LSC Funding*, https://perma.cc/2LXL-6LUS; Joe Palazzolo, *Legal Services Facing a Big Budget Cut*, WALL ST. J., November 15, 2011. Funding has bounced back, but not caught back up, in the years since. LSC, *Management's Recommendation for LSC's FY 2017 Budget Request*, https://perma.cc/RY2W-TLD9.

17. Deborah L. Rhode & Lucz Buford Ricca, *Protecting the Profession or the Public? Rethinking Unauthorized Practice Enforcement*, 82 FORD. L. REV. 2587, 2591–92 (2014); Clint Bolick, *Access to Legal Services: The Market Provides*, 49 ARIZ. ATT'Y 76 (2012).

18. David Hoffman, A COURSE OF LEGAL STUDY 760 (Arno Press, 1972) (1836); *see* Maxwell Bloomfield, *David Hoffman and the Shaping of a Republican Legal Culture*, 38 Md. L. Rev. 673, 678–83 (1979).

19. *See* George Sharswood, AN ESSAY ON PROFESSIONAL ETHICS 7–8 (4th ed., Philadelphia, T & J.W. Johnson & Co. 1884).

20. David J. Dreyer, *Culture, Structure, and Pro Bono Practice*, 33 J. LEG. PRO. 185, 193–94 (2009).

21. Scott L. Cummings & Rebecca L. Sandefur, *Beyond the Numbers: What We Know—and Should Know—About American Pro Bono*, 7 HARV. J. L. & POL. REV. 83 (2013).

22. Michael Millemann, *The State Due Process Jurisdiction for a Right to Counsel in Some Civil Cases*, 15 TEMPLE POL. & CIV. RTS. 733, 764–65 (2006).

23. *See Mallard v. Iowa*, 490 U.S. 296, 302–303 (1989).

24. Reginald Smith, JUSTICE AND THE POOR 100 (1921).

25. *Mallard v. U.S. Dist. Court for the Southern Dist. Of Iowa*, 490 U.S. 296, 303–04 (1989).

26. *Sandoval v. Rattikin*, 395 S.W. 2d 889, 893–94 (Tex. Civ. App. 1965), *cert. denied*, 385 U.S. 901 (1966).

27. Note, *The Indigent's Right to Counsel in Civil Cases*, 76 YALE L.J. 545 (1967). Other similar works include Note, *The Right to Counsel in Civil*

Litigation, 66 COLUM. L. REV. 1322 (1966); Note, *The Indigent's Right to Counsel in Civil Cases,* 43 FORDHAM L. REV. 989 (1975); Note, *The Emerging Right of Legal Assistance for the Indigent in Civil Proceedings,* 9 U. MICH. J.L. REFORM 554 (1976); Comment, *Current Prospects for an Indigent's Right to Appointed Counsel and Free Transcript in Civil Litigation,* 7 PAC. L.J. 149 (1976).

28. *In re Gault,* 387 U.S. 1, 40–41 (1967) (extending the right to counsel to juvenile proceedings if confinement is possible).

29. *Argersinger v. Hamlin,* 407 U.S. 25, 37 (1972).

30. 452 U.S. 18 (1981). All of the facts from the next three paragraphs come from this case.

31. *Id.* at 20–22.

32. *Id.* at 27 (citation and quotation marks omitted).

33. *Id.* at 25 (emphasis added).

34. *Id.* at 26–27 (emphasis added).

35. Robert W. Sweet, *Civil* Gideon *and Confidence in a Just Society,* 17 YALE L. & POL'Y REV. 503, 503 (1998). A Westlaw search in the JLR database for the term "civil Gideon" finds 140 articles, with only three mentions predating Sweet's article. In fact, from this search it appears that from *Lassiter* until 1997 only one law review article was written about civil *Gideon. See* Earl F. Johnson, Jr., *The Right to Counsel in Civil Cases: An International Perspective,* 19 LOY. L.A. L. REV. 341 (1985).

36. Maryland in particular came quite close, *see* Stephen J. Cullen & Kelly A. Powers, *The Last Huzzah for Civil* Gideon, 41 MD. B.J. 24 (2008); *Frase v. Barnhart,* 840 A. 2d 114, 131–39 (Md. 2004) (Cathell, J. concurring); *Touzeau v. Deffinbaugh,* 907 A. 2d 807 (Md. 2006).

37. *See* Jason Boblick, *A Consumer Protection Act?: Infringement of the Consumer Debtor's Due Process Rights Under the Bankruptcy Abuse Prevention and Consumer Protection Act of 2005,* 40 ARIZ. ST. L.J. 713, 735 & n. 167 (2008).

38. *Turner v. Rogers,* 131 S. Ct. 2507 (2011).

39. *Lassiter v. Dep't of Soc. Servs.,* 452 U.S. 18 (1981).

40. *Id.* at 26–27.

Chapter 6

1. James Q. Wilson, "The Politics of Regulation," in *The Politics of Regulation,* ed. James Q. Wilson (New York: Basic Books, 1980), 360.

2. All of the facts and citations for this subsection can be found in BENJAMIN H. BARTON, THE LAWYER-JUDGE BIAS IN THE AMERICAN LEGAL SYSTEM 105–59 (2011).

3. One of the earliest and best-known cases is *In re Day,* 54 N.E. 646 (Ill. 1899), glowingly discussed in Blewett Lee, *The Constitutional Power of the Courts over Admission to the Bar,* 13 HARV. L. REV. 31 (1899).

4. Charles W. Wolfram, *Lawyer Turf and Lawyer Regulation—The Role of the Inherent-Powers Doctrine,* 12 U. ARK. LITTLE ROCK L. REV. 1 (1989).

5. Benjamin H. Barton, *An Institutional Analysis of Lawyer Regulation: Who Should Control Lawyer Regulation—Courts, Legislatures, or the Market?*, 37 GA. L. REV. 1167, 1172–73 (2003).

6. *Id.* at 1209.

7. Robert R. Kuehn and Bridget M. McCormack, *Lessons from Forty Years of Interference in Law School Clinics*, 24 GEORGETOWN J. L. ETHICS 24 59 (2010).

8. Glenn Reynolds, *Ham Sandwich Nation: Due Process When Everything Is a Crime*, 113 COLUM. L. REV. SIDEBAR 102 (2013), http://www.columbialaw review.org/ham-sandwich-nation_Reynolds.

9. *See* Jeffrey T. Ulmer & Mindy S. Bradley, *Variation in Trial Offenses Among Serious Violent Felons*, 44 CRIMINOLOGY 631 (2006).

10. Stephanos Bibas, THE MACHINERY OF CRIMINAL JUSTICE (2012).

11. *Lafler v. Cooper*, 132 S. Ct. 1376 (2012); *Missouri v. Frye*, 132 S. Ct. 1399 (2012); *Padilla v. Kentucky*, 130 S. Ct. 1473 (2010).

12. *Argersinger v. Hamlin*, 407 U.S. 25, 43–44 (1972).

13. Jonathan D. Casper, AMERICAN CRIMINAL JUSTICE: THE DEFENDANT'S PERSPECTIVE 101 (1972).

14. Richard A. Posner, THE PROBLEMATICS OF MORAL AND LEGAL THEORY 163–64 (1999).

15. See Joseph H. King, *Outlaws and Outlier Doctrines: The Serious Misconduct Bar in Tort Law*, 43 WILLIAM AND MARY L. REV. 1011, 1030 (2002).

16. *See* Meredith J. Duncan, *The (So-Called) Liability of Criminal Defense Attorneys: A System in Need of Reform*, 2002 B.Y.U. L. REV. 1, 30–34 (2002).

17. Meredith J. Duncan, *Criminal Malpractice: A Lawyer's Holiday*, 37 GA. L. REV. 1251, 1270–71 (2003).

18. ABA, Total National Lawyer Counts, https://perma.cc/Q9UX-4HEW; ABA, *Lawyer Population and Agency Caseload Volume 2009*, https://perma .cc/9Z34-S8JL. Unless otherwise footnoted, the remaining data in the next two paragraphs come from these sources.

19. *See* Letter from Carl Pierce, Chairman, Tennessee Supreme Court Task Force on the Study of Self-Represented Litigant Issues in Tennessee, to Marcy Easton, President, Tennessee Bar Association (July 30, 2007), https:// perma.cc/2SQF-87JC.

Chapter 7

1. George Santayana, *Reason and Common Sense, in* 1 THE LIFE OF REASON 284 (1905).

2. This quotation is commonly misattributed to Albert Einstein, Benjamin Franklin, and Mark Twain, but there are no published sources demonstrating its use before about 1980. It appears in Rita Mae Brown's novel *Sudden Death* 68 (1983).

3. The facts and decisions discussed in this and the next several paragraphs are taken from the briefing, record, and opinion of the U.S. Supreme Court in *Turner v. Rogers*, 131 S. Ct. 2507 (2011).

4. *Id.* at 2518–20.

5. The discussion of noncompliance with the law is in Erica J. Hashimoto, *The Problem with Misdemeanor Representation*, 70 WASH. & LEE L. REV. 1019, 1023–31 (2013). The rates of denial of appointment of counsel are from NEW YORK STATE DEFENDERS ASS'N, INC., DETERMINING ELIGIBILITY FOR APPOINTED COUNSEL IN NEW YORK STATE: A REPORT FROM THE PUBLIC DEFENSE BACKUP CENTER 59–61 (1994). Unfortunately, we lack nationwide data about appointment-of-counsel denial rates, but the range of rates in New York State suggests substantial variation and substantial numbers of denials in at least some places.

6. The relative lack of evidence is discussed in *Martinez v. Court of Appeal of California*, Fourth Appellate Dist., 528 U.S. 152, 164 (2000) (Breyer, J., concurring). The empirical study of federal and state *pro se* felony defendants is in Erica J. Hashimoto, *Defending the Right of Self-Representation: An Empirical Look at the Pro Se Felony Defendant*, 85 N.C. L. REV. 423, 447–54, 460–63 (2007).

7. Erica J. Hashimoto, *The Price of Misdemeanor Representation*, 49 WM. & MARY L. REV. 461, 489 (2007).

8. The study of two juvenile courts is W. Vaughan Stapleton & Lee E. Teitelbaum, IN DEFENSE OF YOUTH: A STUDY OF THE ROLE OF COUNSEL IN AMERICAN JUVENILE COURTS 50, 66–67, 156–59 (1972). The study of unemployment-benefit appeals is D. James Greiner & Cassandra Wolos Pattanayak, *Randomized Evaluation in Legal Assistance: What Difference Does Representation (Offer and Actual Use) Make?*, 121 YALE L.J. 2118, 2143–44, 2149–53, 2174–75 (2012). The two housing-court studies that found representation effects are Carroll Seron et al., *The Impact of Legal Counsel on Outcomes for Tenants in New York City's Housing Court*, 35 LAW & SOC'Y REV. 419, 427, 429 (2001), and D. James Greiner et al., *The Limits of Unbundled Legal Assistance: A Randomized Study in a Massachusetts District Court and Prospects for the Future*, 126 HARV. L. REV. 901, 924, 926–31, 937–45 (2013). The one that did not is D. James Greiner et al., *How Effective Are Limited Legal Assistance Programs? A Randomized Experiment in a Massachusetts Housing Court* (Sept. 1, 2012) (manuscript at 38–40), *available at* http://papers.ssrn.com/sol3/papers.cfm?abstract_id=1880078.

9. Herbert Kritzer, LEGAL ADVOCACY: LAWYERS AND NONLAWYERS AT WORK (1998).

10. *Id.* at 201.

11. Henry J. Friendly, *"Some Kind of Hearing,"* 123 U. PA. L. REV. 1267, 1276 (1975).

12. *Pasqua v. Council*, 892 A.2d 663, 674 (N.J. 2006), *abrogated by Turner v Rogers*, 131 S. Ct. 2507 (2011); Br. of Senators DeMint et al. as Amici Curiae in Support of Respondents at app. 8a, *Turner*, 131 S. Ct. 2507 (No. 10-10) (reporting results of empirical survey of New Jersey's and other states' child-support enforcement authorities).

13. *Id.* at 1288; Greiner & Pattanayak, 121 YALE L.J. at 2154; Greiner et al., 126 HARV. L. REV. at 933 tbl.4.

14. *See* John H. Langbein, THE ORIGINS OF ADVERSARY CRIMINAL TRIAL 16–17 (2003); John H. Langbein, *Understanding the Short History of Plea Bargaining*, 13 LAW & SOC'Y REV. 261, 262–65 (1979); *Gideon*, 372 U.S. at 344–45 (quoting *Powell*, 287 U.S. at 69).

Chapter 8

1. COLIN RULE, ONLINE DISPUTE RESOLUTION FOR BUSINESS (2002).

2. For example, many Federal courts require in-person mediation, *see* Peter N. Thompson, *Good Faith Mediation in the Federal Courts*, 26 OHIO ST. J. ON DISP. RESOL. 363, 383–84 (2010).

3. Eric Johnson, *Modria Wants You to Settle Your Workplace Problems (and Even Patent Disputes) Online*, ALL THINGS D, November 24, 2012, https://perma.cc/86EW-5Q47.

4. Modria, *American Arbitration Association Selects Modria to Power New York No Fault Caseload*, March 5, 2014, https://perma.cc/P7EC-VSHC.

5. Nathaniel Rich, *Silicon Valley's Start-Up Machine*, N.Y. TIMES, May 2, 2013, http://www.nytimes.com/2013/05/05/magazine/y-combinator-silicon-valleys-start-up-machine.html?pagewanted=all&_r=0; *Wevorce*, https://perma.cc/B4TX-V36Q (last visited October 16, 2016).

6. Consumer Protection BC, *Resolve Your Dispute,* https://perma.cc/HMQ9-G9SG (last visited October 16, 2016).

7. There are some short videos describing the process available here: https://perma.cc/6997-RDAM (last visited October 16, 2016).

8. *See* Jill Gross, *Vikki Rogers on UNCITRAL's Working Group III on Online Dispute Resolution*, ADR PROF BLOG, July 30, 2012, *available at* https://perma.cc/M83J-2VY7.

9. Europa Press Release, *A Step Forward for EU Consumers: Questions & Answers on Alternative Dispute Resolution and Online Dispute Resolution*, March 12, 2013, https://perma.cc/BY6S-YEV8.

10. Richard Susskind, TOMORROW'S LAWYERS 13 (2013).

11. *See* Gillian K. Hadfield, *Equipping the Garage Guys in Law*, 70 MD. L. REV. 484 (2011).

12. Joshua Kubicki, *2013 Was a Big Year for Legal Startups; 2014 Could Be Bigger*, TECH COCKTAIL, February 14, 2014, https://perma.cc/42FK-2A82.

13. Daniel Fisher, *Silicon Valley Sees Gold in Internet Legal Services*, Forbes, October 5, 2011, https://perma.cc/E8DE-HSDM.

14. LII, *Wex*, https://perma.cc/35BB-NCQB (last visited October 16, 2016).

15. *See, e.g.,* Wikipedia, *Due Process, available at* https://perma.cc/5545-MGRB (last visited October 16, 2016).

16. California Courts, Online Self-Help Center, https://perma.cc/PUN6-ME4M (last visited October 16, 2016).

17. Bonnie Hough, *Self-Represented Litigants in Family Law: The Response of California's Courts*, CAL. L. REV. CIRCUIT, February 10, 2010, https://perma.cc/9MGN-ZXY8.

18. National Center for State Courts, *Self-Representation State Links*, https://perma.cc/KT3M-3SFK (last visited May 29, 2016).

19. ABA, *State Access to Justice Commissions: Lists and Links*, https://perma.cc/BK4V-KWS5 (last visited October 16, 2016).

20. Tennessee Supreme Court, *Court-Approved Divorce Forms*, https://perma.cc/XJ2Q-JYKE (last visited October 16, 2016).

21. IIT Chicago-Kent College of Law, *A2J Author*, https://perma.cc/EFR9-D7ZJ (last visited October 16, 2016).

22. The facts in the next two paragraphs come from Rochelle Klempner, *the Case for Court-Based Document Assembly Programs: A Review of the New York State Court System's "DIY" Forms*, 16 FORDHAM URB. L.J. 1189 (2014).

23. Lawhelp.org, *Find Help Near You Now*, https://perma.cc/Q28B-XFYC (last visited October 16, 2016).

24. Texaslawhelp.org, *Homepage, available at* https://perma.cc/8LSL-AQTW (last visited October 16, 2016).

25. LegalZoom, *Legal Forms*, https://perma.cc/4NYK-YL7X (last visited October 16, 2016).

26. Ingrid Lunden, *Is Rocket Lawyer Free to Use 'Free'? Court Denies Rival LegalZoom Its Motion for Summary Judgment, Orders Trial for False Ad Claims*, TECH CRUNCH, October 18, 2013, https://perma.cc/8YWN-UDRL.

27. LegalZoom, *Legal Document Review, available at* https://perma.cc/M5RH-49MN (last visited October 16, 2016).

28. LegalZoom, *Legal Forms, available at* https://perma.cc/9R2Q-FFDS (last visited October 16, 2016).

29. Eric Goldman, *Lawsuit Against Avvo for Lawyer's Profile Dismissed as SLAPP–Davis v. Avvo*, TECH. & MARKETING BLOG, March 29, 2012, https://perma.cc/4P2M-XALE.

30. MDFamilylawyer.com, *Fixed Fee Online Legal Services*, https://perma.cc/8B56-3TXM (last visited October 16, 2016).

31. *Id.*

32. National Law Foundation, *Practical Forms for Attorneys, available at* https://perma.cc/5736-2ZRB (last visited October 16, 2016).

33. John G. Locallo, *Behind the Technology Curve? The ISBA Can Help*, 100 ILL. B.J. 124 (2012).

34. LegalZoom, *LegalZoom S-1 Form*, SEC.GOV, May 10, 2012, https://perma.cc/2Y8D-ZAKR.

35. ABA Standing Committee on Ethics and Professional Responsibility, *Formal Opinion 08-451, Lawyer's Obligations When Outsourcing Legal and Nonlegal Support Services*, August 5, 2008, https://perma.cc/62D5-TS88.

36. Jordan Weisman, *iLawyer: What Happens When Computers Replace*

Attorneys?, The Atlantic, June 19, 2012, https://perma.cc/GB53-CMCG; Joe Palazzo, *Why Hire a Lawyer? Computers Are Cheaper*, Wall St. J., June 18, 2012, http://online.wsj.com/article/SB1000142405270230337920457747263 3591769336.html.

37. Joe Palazzolo, *How a Computer Did the Work of Many Lawyers*, Wall St. J., January 17, 2013, http://blogs.wsj.com/law/2013/01/17/how-a-computer-did-the-work-of-many-lawyers.

38. William T. Robinson, *Legal Help for the Poor: The View From the A.B.A.*, N.Y. Times, August 30, 2011, http://www.nytimes.com/2011/08/31/opinion/legal-help-for-the-poor-the-view-from-the-aba.html.

39. Lininger, 101 Nw. U. L. Rev. Colloquy at 158–59; Bolick, 49 Ariz. Att'y 76.

40. Michael Braunstein, *Structural Change and Inter-Professional Competitive Advantage: An Example Drawn From Residential Real Estate Conveyancing*, 62 Mo. L. Rev. 241, 257–58 (1997) has an excellent overview of these arguments.

41. ABA Comm. on Professionalism, In the Spirit of Public Service: A Blueprint for the Rekindling of Lawyer Professionalism 52 (1986).

42. NASDAQ OMX GlobeNewswire, *Legalzoom Enters into Agreement with State of Washington*, GlobeNewswire, https://perma.cc/GPY6-KKNJ.

43. Nathan Kopel, *Seller of Online Legal Forms Settles Unauthorized Practice of Law Suit*, Wall St. J., August 23, 2011, *available at* http://blogs .wsj.com/law/2011/08/23/seller-of-online-legal-forms-settles-unauthorized-practiced-of-law-suit/.

44. Fisher, *Silicon Valley Sees Gold in Internet Legal Services*, Forbes, October 5, 2011.

45. Terry Carter, *LegalZoom Business Model OK'd by South Carolina Supreme Court*, A.B.A. J., April 25, 2014, https://perma.cc/Q42A-PTXT.

46. The rest of the facts in this paragraph are drawn from Ben Barton, *LegalZoom Fought the North Carolina Bar–and LegalZoom won*, Bloomberg Law, November 13, 2015, https://perma.cc/X26J-FUE5.

47. *Unauthorized Practice of Law Comm. v. Parsons Tech. Inc.*, 179 F.3d 956, 956 (5th Cir. 1999) (vacating the District Court's injunction banning Quicken Family Lawyer after the Texas Legislature amended its 1939 unauthorized practice of law statute).

Chapter 9

1. Katherine Bladow, Using Social Media to Support Self-Represented Litigants and Increase Access to Justice (2011), https://perma.cc/GR2F-9E69.

2. Richard Zorza, The Self-Help Friendly Court: Designed from the Ground Up to Work for People Without Lawyers (2002). *See also*

Richard Zorza, *Self-Represented Litigation and the Access to Justice Revolution in the State Courts: Cross Pollinating Perspectives Towards a Dialog for Innovation in the Courts and the Administrative System*, 29 J. NAT'L ASSOC. ADMINISTRATIVE L. JUDICIARY 63 (2009).

3. Nathan Koppel, *Divorce-By-Form Riles Texas Bar*, WALL ST. J., February 24, 2012, http://online.wsj.com/news/articles/SB10001424052970204778 6045772394805507558 26?mg=reno64-wsj&url=http%3A%2F%2Fonline.wsj .com%2Farticle%2FSB10001424052970204778604577239480550755826 .html&cb=logged0.13556139869615436.

4. Bloomberg Editors, *For an Easy, Affordable, Lawyer-Free Divorce, Check 'Yes,'* BLOOMBERG NEWS, March 12, 2012, https://perma.cc/ZQT5-C9YR.

5. National Association for Court Management, *NACM Model Code of Conduct for Court Professionals*, https://perma.cc/M497-V2F8 (last visited July 18, 2016).

6. Ann Carrns, *California Pioneers the Court-Aided One-Day Divorce*, N.Y. TIMES, June 6, 2014, http://www.nytimes.com/2014/06/07/your-money/ court-aided-one-day-divorces-may-be-wave-of-the-future.html?module= Search&mabReward=relbias%3Aw&_r=1.

7. John A. Clarke & Bryan D. Borys, *Usability Is Free: Improving Efficiency by Making the Court More User Friendly*, NCSC, https://perma.cc/ UMK2-BJCB.

8. Donna Stienstra, Jared Batallion & Jason A. Cantone, ASSISTANCE TO PRO SE LITIGANTS IN U.S. DISTRICT COURTS: A REPORT ON SURVEYS OF CLERKS OF COURT AND CHIEF JUDGES (2011).

9. Cynthia Gray, REACHING OUT OR OVERREACHING: JUDICIAL ETHICS AND SELF-REPRESENTED LITIGANTS 1–2 (2005).

10. Zorza, THE SELF-HELP FRIENDLY COURT, www.zorza.net. *See also* Richard Zorza, *Self-Represented Litigation and the Access to Justice Revolution in the State Courts: Cross Pollinating Perspectives Towards a Dialog for Innovation in the Courts and the Administrative System*, 29 J. NAT'L ASSOC. ADMINISTRATIVE L. JUDICIARY 63 (2009).

11. Center on Court Access to Justice for All, Access Brief: *Judicial Engagement and Curriculum* (2014), https://perma.cc/DR9V-S79V.

12. *See* Lois Bloom & Helen Hershkoff, *Federal Courts, Magistrate Judges, and the Pro Se Plaintiff*, 16 NOTRE DAME J.L. ETHICS & PUB. POL'Y 475, 476–77 (2002) and Anita Davis, *A Pro Se Program That Is Also "Pro" Judges, Lawyers, and the Public*, 63 TEX. B.J. 896 (2000).

13. Tom Clarke, Richard Zorza & Katherine Alteneder, TRIAGE PROTOCOLS FOR LITIGANT PORTALS: A COORDINATED STRATEGY BETWEEN COURTS AND SERVICE PROVIDERS (2013), https://perma.cc/3HYT-2QH8.

14. LSC Technology Initiative Grants, *A Vision of an Integrated Service-Delivery System*, https://perma.cc/U3NP-YEEZ (last visited July 25, 2014).

15. *See* Richard Zorza, *Critically Important Speech by NY CJ Lippman on*

"The Judiciary as the Leader of the Access to Justice Revolution," ACCESS TO JUSTICE BLOG, March 12, 2014, https://perma.cc/U6MR-QVU4 and Richard Zorza, *California Chief Focuses on Self-Help Centers in State of Judiciary Speech,* ACCESS TO JUSTICE BLOG, March 21, 2014, https://perma.cc/44YP-TRXJ.

16. Greiner & Pattanayak, 121 YALE L.J. 2118.

17. Kritzer, LEGAL ADVOCACY: LAWYERS AND NONLAWYERS AT WORK.

18. All of the facts in the next few paragraphs come from John Henry Merryman & Rogelio Perez-Perdomo, THE CIVIL LAW TRADITION (3rd ed. 2007).

19. Ben Barlow, *Divorce Child Custody Mediation: In Order to Form a More Perfect Disunion?,* 52 CLEV. ST. L. REV. 499, 514 (2004–05).

20. *See, e.g.,* Andree G. Gagnon, *Ending Mandatory Divorce Mediation for Battered Women,* 15 HARVARD WOMEN'S L.J. 272 (1992).

21. *See* Connie J.A. Beck & Bruce D. Sales, FAMILY MEDIATION: FACTS, MYTHS, AND FUTURE PROSPECTS (2001).

Chapter 10

1. All of the facts to follow come from *Franklin v. Chavis,* 640 S.E. 2d 873 (S.C. 2007).

2. *Unauthorized Practice of Law Comm. v. Parsons Tech., Inc.,* No. CIV.A.3: 97CV-2859H, 1999 WL 47235, at *1 (N.D. Tex. Jan. 22, 1999), vacated by 179 F.3d 956 (5th Cir. 1999).

3. Deborah L. Rhode & Lucz Buford Ricca, PROTECTING THE PROFESSION OR THE PUBLIC? RETHINKING UNAUTHORIZED PRACTICE ENFORCEMENT, 82 FORD. L. REV. 258 (2014).

4. Unless otherwise noted, the material in this section is adapted from Chapter Eight of Benjamin H. Barton, GLASS HALF FULL: THE DEATH AND REBIRTH OF THE LEGAL PROFESSION (2015).

5. Milton Friedman, CAPITALISM AND FREEDOM 153 (1982).

6. William M. Sullivan et al., THE CARNEGIE REPORT, EDUCATING LAWYERS: PREPARATION FOR THE PROFESSION OF LAW 77 (2007); Walter Gellhorn, *The Second and Third Years of Law Study,* 17 J. LEGAL EDUC. 1, 2–6 (1964).

7. Marc Gans, *Not a New Problem: How the State of the Legal Profession Has Been Secretly in Decline for Quite Some Time, available at* https://perma.cc/LCA3-E6BE.

8. Donald Dripps, *Up from* Gideon (Mar. 30, 2012) (unpublished draft, on file with the authors).

9. Hadfield, 37 FORDHAM URB. L.J. at 134–39 & tbl. 1.

10. Washington State Bar Association, *Limited License Legal Technicians (LLLT),* https://perma.cc/PW5X-L8AG (last visited June 27, 2016).

11. D. Oakley et al., *Comparisons of Outcomes of Maternity Care by Obstetricians and Certified Nurse-Midwives,* 88 OBSTETRICS & GYNECOLOGY 823

(Nov. 1996); Tina Rosenberg, *In Delivery Rooms, Reducing Births of Convenience*, Opinionator Blog, *New York Times*, May 7, 2014, http://opinionator .blogs.nytimes.com/2014/05/07/in-delivery-rooms-reducing-births-of-convenience/. One may worry that studies could be tainted by possible selection effects, as healthy, low-risk mothers are more likely to gravitate toward midwives, but the Oakley et al. study attempted to control for selection bias.

12. Ateev Mehrotra et al., *Comparing Costs and Quality of Care at Retail Clinics with That of Other Medical Settings for 3 Common Illnesses*, 151 ANNALS OF INTERNAL MEDICINE 321 (Sept. 2009).

13. Cait Clarke, *Problem-Solving Defenders in the Community: Expanding the Conceptual and Institutional Boundaries of Providing Counsel to the Poor*, 14 GEO. J. LEGAL ETHICS 401, 448–52 (2001).

Chapter 11

1. Glenn Harlan Reynolds, *Ham Sandwich Nation: Due Process When Everything Is a Crime*, 113 COLUM. L. REV. SIDEBAR 102 (2013).

Chapter 12

1. Nancy Scola, *Courts 'Choose' to Lag Behind on Tech, Says Chief Justice Roberts*, WASH. POST, January 2, 2015, http://www.washingtonpost.com/ blogs/the-switch/wp/2015/01/02/courts-choose-to-lag-behind-on-tech-says-chief-justice-roberts/; *2014 Year-End Report on the Federal Judiciary*, https:// perma.cc/87EQ-B8HU.

2. *2014 Year-End Report on the Federal Judiciary* at 11.

3. *Justice in a Cold Climate*, ECONOMIST, Nov. 1, 2014 (quoting Sir James Mathew), http://www.economist.com/news/britain/21629527-cuts-take-effect-justice-system-struggling-adapt-justice-cold-climate.

4. Legal Services Act 2007 (U.K.).

5. NOEL SEMPLE, LEGAL SERVICES REGULATION AT THE CROSSROADS: JUSTITIA'S LEGIONS 57–60 (2015).

6. Jane Croft, Michael Peel & Martin Arnold, *The Legal Sector's Own Big Bang*, FINANCIAL TIMES (Sept. 22, 2010).

7. René Descartes, DISCOURSE ON METHOD AND RELATED WRITINGS 16 (Desmond M. Clarke trans., 1999) (1637).

8. Richard A. Epstein, SIMPLE RULES FOR A COMPLEX WORLD (1995).

9. Philip K. Howard, THE RULE OF NOBODY (2014); Philip K. Howard, LIFE WITHOUT LAWYERS (2009); Philip K. Howard, THE DEATH OF COMMON SENSE (1995).

Index

Index

Index

Index

Obama, Barack, 169
Office of Economic Opportunity
(OEO), 64–65
online dispute resolution (ODR),
110–16, 154–57

paralegals, 6, 7, 13, 96, 124, 161, 167,
171, 173–74, 187
Patterson, Haywood, 32
Patterson v. Alabama, 38
PayPal and online dispute resolution (ODR), 111–15
performance, retrospective assess-
ment of (*Strickland v. Washington*), 42–45
physician assistants, 175
plea bargaining
and contract attorney compensation and preparation, 24–25
and court reforms, 191–92
and excessive caseloads, 27–28
jury trials sidelined by, 21, 27–28
systemic reliance on, 82–88
political economy of *Gideon* and
civil *Gideon*
inability of judges to order
increased legal aid funding,
81–82
lack of legislative incentives for
systemic change, 79–81
legal regulatory structure, 77–79
public choice theory and lawyers' interests and incentives,
74–77
rejection of civil *Gideon* equivalent, 6–7, 98–103
shielding of criminal defense
lawyers from appellate review
and malpractice liability,
88–90
systemic lack of interest in *pro se*
reform, 90–93
systemic reliance on plea bargaining, 82–88

Posner, Richard, 88, 169
Powell, Lewis, 40
Powell v. Alabama, 31–35, 37–38,
41–42, 45, 200
practice of law, unauthorized
practice of law (UPL), 67, 133–35,
159–62, 172–74
prejudice, retrospective assess-
ment of (*Strickland v. Washington*), 42–45
probono.net, 120
pro bono representation
and legal aid funding, 10, 56–57,
63
and legal aid for the poor, 68–69
procedural complexity of American law, 68, 109
professionalization of civil law
(1880–1965), 59, 61–63
pro se litigation
A2J Author online platform for
interactive legal forms, 121–23
case triage and court reforms,
149–50, 188–91, 197
and courtroom processes,
145–50
inquisitorial judging, 12–13,
150–54
legal information, simplification, and standardization,
140–42
Manhattan Housing Court,
138–40
necessity of lawyers for, 104–5
and online dispute resolution
(ODR), 154–57
public choice theory and lawyers'
interests and incentives, 74–77
public defenders
decreased funding for, 81
excessive caseloads, 6–7, 21,
26–28
history of appointment of, 36
ineffectiveness of, 28–30